12⁹⁵

COINCIDANCE

A Head Test

OTHER BOOKS BY ROBERT ANTON WILSON

* Published by New Falcon Publications

COINCIDANCE

A Head Test

by
Robert Anton Wilson

1991
NEW FALCON PUBLICATIONS
SCOTTSDALE, ARIZONA U.S.A.

International Standard Book Number: 0-941404-50-1
International Standard Book Number: 1-56184-004-1

Library of Congress Catalog Card Number: 88-80256

First Edition 1988, Falcon Press
Second Printing 1991, New Falcon Publications

Cover: By D'vorah Curtis
Type: By Cate Mugasis

NEW FALCON PUBLICATIONS
7025 E. 1st Ave. Suite 5
Scottsdale, Arizona 85251 U.S.A.
(602) 246-3546

TABLE OF CONTENTS

FURTHER CONSPIRACIES !

If you would like to read further on the New Age Conspiracy to elevate Man's consciousness on this planet and elsewhere, get the following titles from your book dealer or order from New Falcon Publications directly:

Undoing Yourself With Energized Meditation
Secrets of Western Tantra
Zen Lies/Zen Truths
    All By Christopher S. Hyatt, Ph.D.
Revolution, Rebellion and Religiousness
    By Osho Rajneesh
Little Essays Toward Truth
    By Aleister Crowley
The Illuminati Conspiracy
    By Donald Holmes, M.D.
Freedom Is A Two Edged Sword
    By Jack Parsons
Info-Psychology
    By Timothy Leary, Ph.D.
Angel Tech
    By Antero Alli
Zen Without Zen Masters
A Handful of Zen
    Both By Camden Benares
What You Should Know About The Golden Dawn
Healing Energy, Prayer and Relaxation
    Both By Israel Regardie

And to get your free catalog of all of our titles, write to:

NEW FALCON PUBLICATIONS
Catalog Dept.
7025 E. 1ST. Ave. Suite 5
SCOTTSDALE, AZ. 85251 U.S.A.

I mention, as the most salient characteristics (of the collective unconscious) chaotic multiplicity and order; duality; the opposition of light and dark, upper and lower, right and left; the union of opposites in a third; the quaternity (square, cross); rotation (circle, sphere); and finally the centering process and a radical arrangement that usually followed some quaternity system . . .

C.G. Jung, *Psychology and Alchemy*

The mome rath hasn't been born that can outgrabe me.

James Thurber,
The Thurber Carnival

ACKNOWLEDGEMENTS

The Doctor With the Frightened Eyes; Thirteen Choruses for the Divine Marquis; and *the Married Catholic Priests' Convention;* were originally published in *The Realist,* and are reprinted with permission of the publisher. [Subscriptions to *The Realist* are available at $23 for 12 issues—Box 1230, Venice, CA 90294.]

The Godfathers and the Goddess and *Religion for the Hell of It* were originally published by *Hot Press,* Dublin, Ireland, and are reprinted with their permission.

We acknowledge with gratitude, the permission for reprinting additional material, whose official grants were received post-press time. These publishers will be specifically noted in subsequent printings of *Coincidance.*

FORE—WORDS

Into the Labyrinth

Like many another wild and anarchistic wanderer of our shattered times, I spend a lot of time asking myself questions that are officially classed as "nonsensical" by the Cambridge custodians of linguistic analysis. I ask, for instance, why are there 12 eggs in a grocer's box and 12 citizens in a jury box—or why Nagasaki is mentioned in conjunction with uranium in a book published in 1939—or why attitudes toward the female breast correlate closely with attitudes toward war and conquest. Naturally, as the Cambridge group warns, such nonsense questions lead to nonsense answers.

Some of the nonsense answers that have amused and delighted me are collected in this anthology. If there is a thesis hidden in these random explorations, it might be that nonsense has its own meanings and that Lewis Carroll, the fantasist, was just as wise as Charles Dodgson, the logician, who happened to inhabit the same body as Carroll. Or it might be that nonsense and poetry are inescapable parts of human experience as long as we have two hemispheres in our brains, one logical and the other intuitive. Or it might be that dialectical Marxism (Groucho variety) can answer questions that sane sober people can't even ask in the first place.

I have added a running commentary, here and there, which sets these pieces in their historical context, expands them, adds new thoughts, or just exemplifies the sad fact that, like most writers, I cannot resist any opportunity to explain my explanations.

COINCIDANCE: PART ONE

Synchronicity and Isomorphism
in *FINNEGANS WAKE*

The original version of this essay appeared in *Fortean Times* for Spring 1983. In rewriting and enlarging the piece for this book, I have expanded the thesis to make this a bridge to the later "Coincidance" essays which deal with synchronicity and isomorphism in art and science generally, with special reference to quantum mechanics and genetics.

Perhaps no novelist in history has been as concerned with synchronicity as James Joyce. As Samuel Beckett—a great fellow novelist who knew Joyce intimately—wrote, "To Joyce reality was a paradigm, an illustration of a perhaps unstatable rule . . . It is not a perception of order or of love; more humble than either of these, it is a perception of coincidence." Over a hundred synchronicities appear in Joyce's *Ulysses*, a novel describing an ordinary day in Dublin ("a day when nothing and everything is happening," as Edna O'Brien wrote recently). When Joyce feared that he might die without finishing *Finnegans Wake*, he selected James Stephens to complete it, not on any literary grounds *per se*, but because Stephens had been born on the same day as Joyce (2 February 1882) and in the same city (Dublin)—and also because Stephens had the same first name as Joyce (James) and had a last name which differed by only one letter from the first name of Stephen Dedalus, Joyce's self-caricature in *A Portrait of the Artist as a Young Man* and *Ulysses*.

Finnegans Wake is in many ways an extension and enlargement of the forbidden and "unthinkable" areas of human experience first explored in *Ulysses*. It is more "difficult" than the earlier book, much more "obscene," more experimental in styles, much funnier, and contains many, many more synchronicities.

As *Ulysses* was the anatomy of one day in Dublin, *Finnegans Wake* is the encyclopedia of one night in Dublin. Where *Ulysses* has a normal day-light protagonist, Leopold Bloom, who travels through real streets, *Finnegans Wake* has a multiple protagonist, abbreviated as ⊈ in Joyce's notebooks; not a "character" in the normal sense, this system-function, ⊈ , wanders through the labyrinths of alternative realities. In explicating this system-function, I shall try to indicate why Yositani Roshi once said, "There is nothing special about Enlightenment. You do it every night in your sleep. Zen is just a trick for doing it while awake." *Finnegans Wake* is another trick for doing it while awake.

The "paranormal" aspect of the synchronicities we shall be studying can be "explained" in various ways, including the Fundamentalist Materialist's favorite non-explanation or pseudo-explanation, "mere coincidence." My own preference, as shall become more clear as we proceed, is along the lines of Yositani's identification of dream processes with those things we call "mystical" or "occult." As the psychiatrist Jan Ehrenwald wrote in *New Dimensions of Deep Analysis*, the so-called "paranormal" is very normal:

> We have seen time and again that despite their apparently capricious, haphazard nature ("paranormal" events) are governed by the same laws which apply to the dream, to the neurotic symptom and to unconscious processes in general.

This was also the view of Freud in his famous essay "On the Uncanny" and of Jung in all his writings.

Since a dream conventionally requires a dreamer, Joyce as early as 1923 (one year into the writing of the book, which required 17 years) selected the name Earwicker for the waking ego of the protagonist. This is the point at which most *Wake* scholarship has gone wrong: since Earwicker is the waking ego, exegetes have thought Earwicker is the protagonist, but he is only one part of the protagonist. E or Ego or Earwicker is only part of the system-function ⊈ , which is the total protagonist, as we shall see. But before investigating ⊒ , let us look at E or Earwicker.

Joyce reputedly found the name "Earwicker" on a tombstone in Sidlesham,

England, while on holiday. In *Stephen Hero*, Joyce's autobiographical Stephen Daedalus (later to become modernized into Stephen Dedalus*) said that an artist could find an "epiphany" or revelation even in a clock on a storefront; in *Ulysses*, Stephen (now Dedalus) defined "God" as "a shout in the street." It was consistent for Joyce to find deep meanings in a casually encountered tombstone. He found a great deal in the name "Earwicker."

What follows is neither correct nor consistent etymology: Joyce believed the unconscious has no either/or logic and uses every possible or thinkable meaning.

Earwicker might derive from **Eire-Weiker**, dweller in Ireland. The Middle English **Weiker**, dweller, is related to the surving **wich**, dwelling place, as in Dunwich, Greenwich, Norwich, etc. and is also cognate with Latin **vicus**, a way or road. Coincidence has already appeared, because Joyce had planned from the beginning to base *Finnegans Wake* (hereafter *FW*) on the linguistic theories of Giambattista Vico, whose name also derives from **vicus**. To commemorate this first wonderful synchro-mesh, the word "vicus" appears in the first sentence of *FW*:

> riverrun, past Eve and Adam's, from swerve of shore to bend of bay, brings us by a commodius vicus of recirculation back to Howth Castle and Environs.

Earwicker sounds much like "earwigger" and Joyce's dreamer, a Protestant, seems to suspect that his Catholic neighbors maliciously pronounce it that way behind his back. The earwig is reputed in folklore to cause dreams by crawling into the sleeper's ear, so the association Earwicker-earwig is appropriate for a book of dreams. The earwig is also an insect, and *FW* is crowded with insects, including the Ondt and the Gracehoper in a celebrated passage, but also featured are fleas, lice, bedbugs, butterflies and others. As Fritz Senn has noted, "insects" is often a disguise for "incest" on the Freudian level of the dream.

Earwicker is a publican who owns an inn in Chapelizod, a West Dublin suburb fronting onto Phoenix Park. The only other wellknown novel about Chapelizod is Sheridan Lefanu's *The House by the Churchyard*, in which a character named Hyacinth O'Flaherty fights a duel in Phoenix Park because of a misunderstood conversation about **earwigs**. O'Flaherty appears to be killed in the duel, but later rises, just as Finnegan, in the bar-room ballad from which Joyce took his title, appears to die and then rises again. Thus,

---

*Daedalus in the myth was the maker of both a labyrinth and of wings; labyrinths and flight were important symbols to Joyce, the first standing for the conditioned guilty conscience of those raised Roman Catholic, and the latter for his attempts to escape this. But Daedalus in Greek also means "artist."

Lefanu's novel is coincidentally linked to Joyce's by the earwig theme, the Chapelizod-Phoenix Park locale and the resurrection motif.

Hyacinth O'Flaherty has another link with the resurrection theme; one of the hundreds of dead-and-resurrected gods discussed in Frazer's classic *Golden Bough* was named Hyacinth.

But "Hyacinth" was also the code-name for Lord Alfred Douglas in a homosexual poem by Dubliner Oscar Wilde; Earwicker's dream partially concerns repressed homosexuality. And the house by the churchyard in LeFanu's novel suggests Kierkegaard, whose name means "churchyard" in Danish. Kierkegaard was a compulsive masturbator and suffered chronic fears that this would lead to insanity. When the protagonist of *FW* is "on the edge of selfabyss" on page 40, this refers to both "self-abuse" (a nasty Victorian term for masturbation, which should more properly be called self-enjoyment) and Kirkegaard's favorite metaphor of the Abyss. But **biss** in German is to bite, and this brings us back to "agenbite of inwit," the medieval term for bad conscience which Stephen Dedalus uses to describe his own Catholic super-ego in *Ulysses*.

Earwicker (whose full name is Humphrey Chimpden Earwicker, and whose initials appeared in Howth Castle and Environs, by the way) is not only a Dubliner but etymologically-punningly linked to the earliest Gaelic name of Dublin, **Baile atha Cliath**, which means town of the hurdles. Hurdles are **wicker** bridges. But the early Celts practised human sacrifice by burning prisoners of war in large **wicker** structures and, by a commodius vicus of recirculation, we seem to be close to the roots of Anglo-Saxon **wicce**, which means turning (like one of Vico's historical cycles) or dancing, and thus we also approach **wicca-craft** or witchcraft.

In the course of the dream, H.C. Earwicker is repeatedly attacked by neighbors intent on lynching him for his (real or fantasized) sexual "sins." These nightmarish sequences always refer, through puns, to the ancient Celtic rituals of human sacrifice in **wicker** baskets. Thus, on the level of the Freudian unconscious (one meaning of Joyce's **ɯ**), these sequences reflect personal sexual guilt, while on the level of the Jungian collective unconscious (Joyce's **ɯ**), these are genetic memories of ancient Celtic religion. That **wicker** is etymologically related to **manger** (see your etymological dictionary) links Earwicker to Christ, who "died for our sins"—the best known scapegoat-god in our Western civilization. It is moderately curious that the anthropological link between Christ and the ancient Celtic human sacrifice is the theme of a film, made nearly 30 years after *Finnegans Wake* was published, called *The Wicker Man*.

Earwig in French is **perse-orielle**. Joyce sometimes calls Earwicker Pearse O'Reilly, punning on this, but **Pearse** and **O'Reilly** were two of the Irishmen shot by the English for instigating the Easter Uprising in Dublin, 1916. Easter Uprising, of course, brings us back to the Resurrection theme.

In fact, Padraic Pearse, the principle architect of the 1916 Uprising scheduled it for 23 April 1916, which was both Easter (and thus a symbol of Resurrection) and also the anniversary of Brian Boru's defeat of the Vikings at the battle of Clontarf (23 April 1014) and thus a symbol of Irishmen casting out foreign invaders. The guns for the Uprising were slow in arriving (Sir Roger Casement was caught smuggling some of them in, and hanged for it) so the "Easter" Uprising occurred on Monday 24 April 1916; but Joyce knew Pearse personally, and once walked out of a Gaelic class Pearse was teaching because Pearse said the ancient Irish bards were better poets than Shakespeare. Joyce could never stand that kind of chauvinism. Pearse is commemorated many times in FW, as part of Pearse O'Reilly (earwig) and by the many patrick-peatrick puns. (Patrick is Ireland's patron saint and a peat rick is the stack of peat with which the poor in Ireland heat their homes.)

thuartpeatrick (FW-3)

thus refers to Padraic Pearse, the peat rick in a poor Irishman's back yard, the cathedral of St. Patrick in Dublin (of which, more later), and the pun on which the Catholic Church alleges to be founded—**Tu est Petrus**, in Latin, or "Thou art Peter," in English. It is also the pea-trick by which language in FW says more than Logical Positivists think language can ever say.

The title of FW comes from an old bar-room ballad, in which, as we have already mentioned, Tim Finnegan, a hod carrier, has too much to drink, falls from his ladder, is pronounced dead, and is taken home for a Wake. In typical Irish fashion, the mourners get roaring drunk, start to fight, and heave whiskey bottles at each other; one whiskey bottle hits the coffin, and the "corpse" sits up crying, "Bad luck to your souls, did you think me dead?" This is an Irish folk-equivalent of the myths of Osiris, Dionysus, Attis, Adonis, Jesus, etc.—all of the dead and resurrected gods (including Hyacinth) in Frazer's *Golden Bough*. To make the implicate explicate, Pearse and O'Reilly refer to both Earwicker, because their names mean earwig in French, and to Resurrection, since they were part of the Easter Uprising.

Earwicker's name also contains an **ear**, and it has been commonplace in Joyce criticism for 60 years to note that Joyce was the most aural of modern writers, and the most musical. (In 1904, he came in second to the great John MacCormack in a singing contest, and would have come first, the judges said, if he had not refused the sight-reading test.) As Joyce's eye-sight failed, his prose became even more ear-oriented, and Brancusi portrayed him in 1932 as a spiral, symbolizing the inner ear; Joyce's father, seeing this sketch reproduced in a Dublin newspaper, said drily, "Jim has changed a great deal since moving to Paris." The threat of blindness became more and more real as the writing of *FW* went on—"it darkles (tinct! tinct!) all this our funnanimal world." The type of man that young girls should be leery of, we are told in Shaun the Postman's sermon in Book Three, is "about 50," like Joyce in the middle of the writing and has "scummy eyes" about which he makes "certain references to the deity."

Blindness as an alleged result of masturbation, and as the punishment of Peeping Tom in the Lady Godiva legend, were much on Joyce's mind in those years, one gathers. Tim Finnegan in the ballad and Peeping Tom easily blend in dream-logic (Tim = Tom) and both get merged with Atum, the Egyptian god who created the universe by masturbating. Tom Sawyer and Doubting Thomas are also linked with Tim-Tom-Atum in some of Joyce's puns: Tom Sawyer because he associated with Huck Finn (who is Finn, again—see?) and Doubting Thomas because Joyce, an Agnostic, found him the most appealing of the apostles.

There seem to be only two *incidents* in *FW*, although they go through so many variations and permutations that they eventually link to all the major themes of art, science and philosophy.

The first incident, which probably occurred at 11:32 in the morning of the day before the dream—or that's my guess as to why the number 1132 keeps recurring throughout the book, something no Joyce scholar has yet satisfactorily explained—happened when Humphrey C. Earwicker, while crossing Phoenix Park, felt the need to retire to the bushes to answer a call of nature. After taking his pants down, the misfortunate man suddenly noticed two young girls (aspects of the ⊣⊢ duality in Joyce's notebook, about which more later) who had retired to the bushes with similar needs. Maybe something else happened; maybe it didn't. We never know. Whirling around, Earwicker saw three British soldiers (aspects of the ∧⊏⋏ trinity we will come to know well) who were watching whatever the devil did happen. (This detail, the British soldiers, dates the otherwise timeless dream as sometime before 1922, when the British withdrew their troops from Ireland—although they remained, and still remain, in Northern Ireland.) Joyce describes Dublin as a "gossipocracy"—a description I believe after five years in the place—and the dream has the neighbors, told of the incident by the soldiers, accusing Earwicker of every possible "moral" offense, and some impossible ones, starting with voyeurism and exhibitionism and proceeding with nightmare logic through masturbation, making homosexual overtures to the soldiers, murdering the soldiers, cannibalistically eating them, and so on, up to and including plotting to murder the king, or the pope, or both. As in that other archetypical 20th Century masterpiece, Kafka's *The Trial*, it is absolutely impossible for the reader to decide what, if any, of all this guilt has a basis in fact and what is just Freudian fear and fantasy.

In the second incident, which certainly happened exactly at noon—"high twelve" to Freemasons—Earwicker, still in Phoenix Park, but obsessed with anxiety, encountered either a tramp who asked the time, in one version, or a gunman who tried to rob him, in another version; but in any case, instead of giving the time or his wallet, Earwicker—at least in the dream memory of the encounter—launches into a passionate defense of his sexual orthodoxy, denying vehemently that he had homosexual impulses or has committed incest with his teenage daughter (an aspect of Joyce's I function, which reconciles ⊣ and ⊢). In both versions—the tramp or the gunman—the clock strikes noon just then, symbolizing the death of the Widow's Son in Freemasonry. (FW has many hints that Earwicker is a Freemason. Friends in Ireland assure me that it was impossible to be a publican in Dublin in Joyce's time without being a Freemason, since the brewers and their salesmen were all Freemasons and so were the cops, usually. Dublin was Protestant-dominated until the coming of the Free State in 1922.) The death of the Widow's Son, of course, points forward to his resurrection when a new Freemason is "raised" at High Twelve (midnight).

The girls in the bushes appear to have been urinating; by Freudian displacement, this becomes Noah's flood (the pee is also present in "thuartpeatrick," by the way). The three soldiers then become another of Joyce's ∧⊏⋏ functions, namely Noah's three sons—Shem, Ham and Japhet, who saw Noah naked after he got drunk, as the three soldiers probably saw Earwicker with his pants down. Of these three, Noah cursed only Ham, because the other two averted their eyes.

Ham (the meat) derives from the pig; and the pig appeared on the Irish ha'penny, a coin which crossed the bar in Earwicker's pub continually. (It was the price of a half pint of porter, the cheapest kind of beer, before World War I.) The male pig, or boar, was "sacred to Adonis" in Greece—which probably means, as Robert Graves has noted, that the Stone Age boar-god got incorporated into the composite figure which became Adonis. Curiously, Shakespeare, who wrote *Venus and Adonis*, had a boar's head on his Coat of Arms (but we will come to that). Ham also suggests Hamlet, and Shakespeare also wrote a play about that melancholy Dane, but Earwicker's full name is (remember?) Humphrey Chimpden Earwicker, and Humphrey, believe it or not, derives from Hamlet. (See Brendar O'Heir's *Gaelic Lexicon to Finnegan's Wake*.) According to one version of the Hamlet legend, Hamlet did not die when he killed his uncle (father substitute) but left Denmark and became a governor of Dublin during the Danish occupation.

Some eccentrics believe Bacon wrote the plays attributed to Shakespeare. Be that as it may, the linkage from Ham to Hamlet to Bacon to the boar's head on Shakespeare's Coat of Arms to the boar who killed Adonis to the dead-and-resurrected god is perfectly clear in dream-logic, however perplexing to the Rationalist. Joyce plays endlessly with these linguistic coincidences; for instance when an American hog-caller denounces Earwicker as "York's Porker" in Chapter Three, this refers to Shakespeare's Coat of Arms with its boar's head, to Bacon (who lived at York House), to the boar-god who became Adonis, etc. and eventually links into the whole theme of Ham, Noah's flood, urination, Noah drinking and the drinking at Finnegan's Wake. (The ballad is called Finnegan's Wake; Joyce's book is called *Finnegans Wake*. The missing apostrophe creates another pun, which Joyce explained to friends as a warning to the ruling classes: the oppressed rise, eventually, in every historical cycle.)

But Joyce's symbol for the composit protagonist of *FW* was **E꜀ꟽ** remember? If **E** is the unconscious Ego or Earwicker, **m** appears to be the Freudian unconscious, **w** is the Jungian "collective" unconscious (or Sheldrake's "morphogenetic field") and **ꟽ** is, then, the non-local consciousness which Buddhists call "Buddha mind," Taoists call "no-mind," and Occidental psychology has not yet recognized, except in Timothy Leary's writings on the non-local or quantum circuit of the nervous system. We will enlarge on these brief descriptions as we proceed, but for now it is interesting, or alarming, to note that Earwicker's "sin" in Phoenix Park is associated by Joyce with the infamous Phoenix Park murders of 1882 (the year Joyce was born, coincidentally).

These murders (of British officials) were committed by the Invincibles, an Irish revolutionary group headed by one Joe Brady, but Charles Stewart Parnell, leader of the Irish Home Rule Party, was implicated in them by letters produced by the journalist, Richard Pigott. The first of these incriminating letters began,

   My dear E,
      Let there be no more hecitancy.

Because of these letters, Parnell was eventually brought to trial, but was acquitted when his counsel asked Pigott to spell the word "hesitancy." When Pigott misspelled the word as "hecitancy," and it was pointed out that the word was misspelled that way in the letters, Pigott fell into confusion and incoherence, becoming totally unconvincing to the jury, and the letters have ever since been considered forgeries. It is curious that, wherever Joyce began in constructing the synchronicity labyrinth of *FW*, the misspelled word "hecitancy" has the initials of his dreamer, HCE, and Pigott links in with the pig-Ham-Hamlet-Bacon motif, while the salutation "My dear E," connects to Joyce's symbols for the four major levels of the psyche: **E꜀ꟽ** . Even odder, Richard Pigott committed suicide after being reputidated by the court, and his son was, at the time, a classmate of Joyce's at Conglowes Wood, a Jesuit "college" (grammar school, in American terms) near Parnell's home. Joyce doesn't do much with "Conglowes" in *FW*, but "Wood" links to the theme of Swift's *Drapier Letters*, often mentioned; these letters denounced the debased coinage issued in Ireland by a royal charter given to William Wood on 16 June 1723. Curiously, 16 June was the day in 1904 immortalized in Joyce's *Ulysses*; Joyceans celebrate 16 June every year as "Bloomsday." On 16 June 1804, Parliament ordered the building of the Martello Towers in Ireland, in one of which the first chapter of *Ulysses* begins, and on 16 June 1955, Joyce's brother, Stanislaus, died.

One of the many references to the Phoenix-Park-Pigott-Parnell scandal in *FW* occurs on page 16:

You spigotty anglease? . . . Has? Has at? Hasatency?

But, since the Pigott-Pig-Ham-Bacon-Hamlet theme is interlinked with Shakespeare, it is interesting that Shakespeare's parents were named John and Mary, as were Joyce's. "Sure, there's only that Shakespeare fellow left to beat," Nora, Joyce's wife said, explaining her understanding of what Jim was doing after *Ulysses*.

Shakespeare is considered homosexual or bisexual by many commentors; Earwicker worries that the British soldiers think he was making sexual overtures by lowering his trousers. But Earwicker's disgrace occurred, remember, in Phoenix Park (like the 1882 murders); Joyce identifies the exact spot: "By the magazine wall. Where the maggies seen all." The magazine, partially destroyed by the I.R.A. in 1922 but subsequently rebuilt, was earlier the subject of the very last poem Jonathan Swift ever wrote:

> *Behold this proof of Irish sense,*
> *Here Irish wit is seen:*
> *Where there's nothing left that's worth defense*
> *They build a magazine!*

Swift was the Dean of Saint Patrick's (thuartpeatrick) and is traditionally called "The Dean" in Dublin folklore. Due to the Dublin brogue, this is pronounced "the Dane," so we are back to Hamlet, the Melancholy Dane and the Ham-Pig theme, alas; but Swift had very ambiguous romantic involvements with two ladies who were, coincidentally, both named Esther and who are thus another of Joyce's ⊣⊢ polarities—Esther van Homerigh and Esther Johnson. Swift's desire for privacy, or his morbid secrecy—take your pick—was so great that all the scholars who have written on his life have failed to determine the exact nature of his relationship with either of these ladies. (Some think both relationships were Platonic, some that one was but the other wasn't, some that both were sexual, etc.) Since Joyce believed (as he wrote in a letter) that Ireland, like Sicily, is ruled by **omerta** (silence), Swift is a fit symbol of the Irish people's (or any colonial people's) obsession with hiding what they are doing.

At this point, the equation seems to be: Swift = ∃ = the guilty man in the Freudian bushes; the two Esthers = ⊣ ⊢ = the two girls in the bushes; and, remarkably, the three soldiers = ∧⊏∧ = Peter, Jack and Martin in Swift's *Tale of a Tub*. But Peter, Jack and Martin, in Swift, symbolize respectively the Roman Catholic, Calvinist and Lutheran religions (Peter = thuartpeatrick, Jack = John Calvin, Martin = Martin Luther) and Christianity has become three forms of evasion of Freudian guilt, which may or may not be what Swift had in mind.

Contemporary with Swift and also Irish was Lawrence Sterne, author of *Tristram Shandy*. Joyce commented in a letter to Harriet Weaver that Swift and Sterne should have changed names, because Swift's writings were stern and Sterne's writings were swift. Swift and Sterne are thus versions of Joyce's Cain/Abel dualism, or ⊏∧, the male or yang equivalent of the female or yin⊣ ⊢ polarity. The Swift-Sterne oxymoron appears dozens of times in *FW*) e.g., "he sternly struck his tete in a tub . . . (and) swiftly took it out again," "the siamixed twoatalk used twixt stern swift and jolly roger," etc. Joyce may or may not have known the coincidence that Swift's predecessor as Dean or Saint Patrick's in Dublin was also named Stern; but Joyce was aware, and commented in another letter to Ms. Weaver, that **die Sterne** in German not only means "the star" but also glaucoma—the eye disease from which he himself was suffering while writing *FW*.

Joyce, in fact, first played with this English-German pun (**Sterne**/star/ glaucoma) as far back as 1918 when he wrote "Bahnhofstrasse," a poem describing his first hideously painful glaucoma attack on Bahnhofstrasse in Zurich:

>   *Ah, star of evil! star of pain!*
>   *Highhearted youth comes not again*

Glaucoma comes from the Greek, **glaucis**, shining, and is an epithet Homer habitually applies to the eyes of Athene, who was originally an owl goddess and is usually shown with an owl in Greek statuary. Athene was the goddess of juries, and we will come to know the twelve jurors (O) in *FW* intimately before the end of this book; for now it is enough to note that when they first appear, as mourners at Finnegan's wake in chapter one, they utter "a plethora of ululation." To ululate etymologically means to moan like an owl—a typical example of the **psycho-archeology** of Joyce's style, in which the Stone Age totem broods over the modern 12 jurors. (We will later ask why eggs are sold by the dozen and the Zodiac also has twelve "houses" . . .)

But Lawrence Sterne, the other half of the Swift-Sterne polarity, has many synchronistic links to *FW*, all exploited hilariously and mind-blowingly by Joyce. **Lawrence** Sterne, as we mentioned, wrote *Tristram Shandy;* Howth Castle in Dublin, an important symbol in *FW*, was built by Sir **Tristram** Armoricus St. **Lawrence**. There is a Lawrence Avenue in Howth, and another in Chapelizod where Earwicker has his pub. The patron saint of Dublin is St. Lawrence O'Toole. There is another Dublin in Lawrence County, Georgia; its motto, "Doublin' all the time" is a Joycean pun and appears on the first page of *FW*; it was founded by Peter Sawyer (thuartpeatrick) who gets mixed up with Tom Sawyer by Joyce and thus leads us back to Finn, again—Huck Finn, that is. But we will come to that.

Among the books Joyce owned in 1920 (now in the possession of Cornell University) was Plutarch's *On the E at Delphi*. Delphi, of course, was the place where an oracle, intoxicated on wine and strange drugs, descended through the various levels that Joyce symbolizes as **ᗰᗯ** and **Ǝ** ; Plutarch argues that the sign over the door of the Delphic temple, **ᗰ** really meant E, which in Greek had the meaning "I am." This, of course, is coincidentally the name God gave Moses in Exodus. Joyce's version is on the first page of *FW*:

> **nor avoice from afire bellowsed mishe mishe to tauftauf thuartpeatrick**

Ignoring for the moment that Joyce's mistress, Nora Barnacle, seems to have gotten into the text (nora voice), **mishe mishe** puns on the voice from the burning bush (from afire) calling the prophet in Hebrew: **Moishe, Moishe** (Moses, Moses in English). But in Gaelic **mishe mishe** means "I am, I am" and this is what the voice called itself when Moses intelligently wanted to know to whom he was speaking. ("Mishmosh" was Lewis Carroll's original title for "Jabberwocky" and that brings us to Humpty Dumpty, who shall play a large role in these notes shortly.) It is just another coincidence that Padraic Pearse, author of the Irish Declaration of Independence, whom we have already encountered a few times, wrote a poem beginning **Mishe Eire** (I am Ireland) which is now engraved on the entrance to Dublin Castle.

We seem to have entered a Strange Loop. If Joyce began constructing this synchro-mesh with Plutarch's ideas about the **E** at Delphi, the eventual link to the 1882 Phoenix Park murders and the Pigott forgeries (beginning "My dear E") is remarkable; if Joyce started with Pigott's forgeries, the link to Delphi is remarkable; but he seems to have started with the tombstone saying "Earwicker" in Sidles**ham**. (How did **Ham** get in again?) Several times in *FW* a speaker clears his throat by saying "Aham"—which is Sanskrit for "I am" and brings us back to both Moses and Delphi, but "A ham," one of Joyce's alternative spellings, also links back to the Ham-Bacon-Shakespeare concidences.

However, we were talking about Lawrence Sterne and *Tristram Shandy* a while back (and Tristram St. Lawrence who built Howth Castle). Tristram is the Gaelic form of Tristan. In the legend of Tristan and Isolde, there are two Isoldes (⊣⊢)—Isolde the Fair and Isolde of the White Hands. This makes a nice isomorphism with Swift and his two Esthers, and also with the two Alices of Lewis Carroll, as we shall see later. Meanwhile, Isolde the Fair was a native of Chapelizod, where *FW* is set; Chapelizod is corrupt Anglo-Gaelic for Chapel of Isolde. When Joyce writes

Sir Tristram . . . rearrived from North Armorica . . .

he includes both Tristan and Isolde of the White Hands, who lived in Armorica (northern France) and part of the name of the builder of Howth Castle (Sir Tristram Armoricus de Saint Lawrence). Immediately following is "laurens county's gorgios" which gives us the rest of the builder's name (laurens, lawrence) and locates the other Dublin, which is in Lawrence County, Georgia. If there are two Isoldes, two Esthers, two Dublins, we will soon encounter other twins (Cain and Abel, Jacob and Esau, Caster and Pollux); on the Freudian (m) level this refers to the two girls in the bushes of Phoenix Park; on the Jungian level (ш) it refers to a basic polarity which (we shall soon see) creates an isomorphism between *FW* and such diverse systems as Cabala, *I Ching* and quantum physics.

But Swift, incidentally, had a pet name for Esther Johnson. He called her Stella, which in Italian means "star" and links back to the **Sterne** (German, star/glaucoma) symbolism, Joyce's eye problems and Tristram Shandy . . .

Shakespeare, Swift and Sterne, already in synchronistic mesh with *FW*, all have **S** as the first letter of their names. Joyce named his autobiographical hero Stephen Dedalus, which begins and ends with **S**. *Ulysses* begins with an **S** ("Stately, plump Buck Mulligan . . .) and ends with an **S** ("yes I said yes I will Yes") The letter **S** in Joyce's notes for *FW* symbolizes the serpent in Eden but also stands for a mysterious figure, usually called Sanderson or Sigurson but sometimes varying to Mahan and Behan and even to Pore Old Joe in the Black Spiritual, who is both an aggressor (the Norse invaders of Ireland) and a victim (the servants and slaves of all history). Only God and James Joyce understand this mysterious **S** business, and Joyce is dead and God isn't telling.

Both incidents in Earwicker's nightmare—the one involving the 2 girls and 3 soldiers, and the one involving the beggarman or thief—took place in Phoenix Park, remember. Joyce is careful to establish that the beggar-or-thief is brunette and that Earwicker is blonde, which eventually links in with the story of Brian Boru, Ireland's medieval liberator, who was blonde and was murdered (on 23 April, 1014, remember) by a brunette Viking named Brodar. The pun brodar-brother further links this to Cain and Abel, as we shall see.

Meanwhile, the "cad"—Joyce's usual name for the threatening figure in the park, which leaves ambiguous whether he was beggar or thief—addresses Earwicker as "ouzel fin," which is corrupt Gaelic for "my blonde gentleman." Phoenix Park itself is an Anglicization of the original name, **finnischce pairc** ("field of bright waters"). The **finn** in finnischce means bright, or shining, or blonde, or fair, depending on context. We are back to Finn, again—not just Huck Finn but Finn Mac Cool, the ancient Irish hero, whose name means "blonde son of the servant woman." Finnegan in the resurrection ballad is, by this dream-logic of puns, Finn Again or the ancient hero returned: "Hohohoho, Mister Finn, you're going to be Finn again" is on page 7. Did Joyce begin with Finn Mac Cool and work his way to the link with finnischce pairc or start with the park and work his way to the hero? It fits together wonderfully in either case, especially since "cad" suggests Cadenus, in Swift's *Cadenus and Vanessa*, a poem written for Esther von Homerigh (Vanessa)—which suggests Venus in Shakespeare's *Venus and Adonis* and brings us back to the boar-god and Ham-Bacon-Hamlet.

Finn Mac Cool's wife, Graunia, eloped with a handsome young warrior named Dermot. The aged Finn pursued them from Ulster all the way to the hill of Howth on Dublin Bay. Thus we come back again to Howth Castle and Environs, the de Lawrence family who have dwelt there since 1170, Sir Tristram de Lawrence who built the castle, and Lawrence Sterne and Tristram Shandy. Here synchronicity merges with isomorphism, for the legend of Tristan-Isolde-King Mark is so similar to the triangle of Dermot-Graunia-Finn that some scholars think that Finn cycle was the model for the later and more famous Romance.

Joyce, in fact, has filled *FW* with isomorphs of this Eternal Triangle, which in the symbolism of his notes books is ш △ ⊣. Here are a few of the actors who repeat this structure, which Bucky Fuller would call a "knot" or "coherent synergy":

ш	△	⊣
Finn	Graunia	Dermot
King Mark	Isolde	Tristan
King Arthur	Guinevere	Lancelot
Hamlet Sr.	Gertrude	Claudius

Finn is coincidentally-linguistically tied to Finnegan, Phoenix Park, Huck Finn and the cad's greeting to Earwicker, "ouzel fin." Tristan is coincidentally-linguistically tied to Sir Tristram, Howth Castle and the tree-stone combination we shall soon encounter. King Arthur, whose name means "bear" is tied to the ancient Celtic bear-god we will meet often, and to Arthur Wellesley, Duke of Wellington, and Sir Arthur Guiness, the brewer, who plays a large role in FW. Hamlet brings us back to the Ham-Bacon-pig cycle.

In the "Tavern" chapter, almost the geometrical center of FW, this Ш Δ ⋌struggle becomes identified with the ancient rituals of bride-capture, in which the husband (⋌) seizes the bride (Δ) and is pursued by her father (Ш) until captured, whereupon he pays the bride-fee and the union is blessed; see Frazer's *Golden Bough* again. Gershon Legman, curiously, has found this pattern surviving in the risque jokes about the honeymoon couple (Δ⋌) whose love-making is interrupted by the rude man in the lower berth (Ш); see his amazing and hilarious *Anatomy of the Dirty Joke*. Before the end of the "Tavern" chapter, Joyce links the peril involved in the Ш Δ ⋌ relationship with the ancient rituals (see Frazer again) in which a handsome stranger (⋌) is invited to copulate with a temple priestess (Δ) and is then killed, his body being scattered over the fields to make the crops fertile. In this "knot," then, we have both Hierogamy (sex magick or the alchemical marriage) and Human Sacrifice, on the Jungian level (Ш) of psycho-archeology, while on the Freudian level (m) Earwicker is again suffering symbolic punishment for his real or fantasized sexual "sins."

But Finn Mac Cool's last name sounds like **cul**, which is French (and Latin) for ass-hole, the part of Earwicker evidently most visible to the three soldiers in the Phoenix Park incident. When Joyce writes "how culious an epiphany," he puns on **cul** and **cool**, caricatures his own doctrine that anything can be an ephiphany or revelation to the artistic mind, includes again the initials, HCE, of the dreamer and has a buried hint of the misspelled "hecitancy" in the Pigott forgeries.

Cul is also part of **O felix culpa**, a phrase from the Mass for Holy Saturday, meaning "Oh happy sin." This refers to the Fall of Adam and Eve, which is paradoxically happy because it provoked the Incarnation and Redemption. Thus, fall and resurrection (a la Tim Finnegan) is again invoked: Holy Saturday preceeds the Easter Uprising.

When Joyce addresses Earwicker as "foenix culprit" on page 23, we have the sin in Phoenix Park, the Invincibles killing English officials in the same park, the sin of Adam and Eve (**felix culpa**) and the cul-cool semantic system. When Earwicker addresses the jury later as "fellows culpows," he is implying that all men are sinners or fellow culprits (as in the hymn, "In Adam's fall /

We sinned all"); he is also making a Freudian slip and admitting he enjoyed what happened ("**happy** sin"); and the cul-cool pun is still there. In the children's games of Chapter Nine, primitive fertility rites are re-enacted— this was Norman Douglas's interpretation of children's games, by the way—and the chant "May he colp her, may he colp her, may he mixandmas colp her" is eminently suitable for a pagan sex ritual. Unfortunately, that is genetic memory only (Ш) and on the Freudian level (ℼ) Irish Catholic guilt has gotten in again: the chant contains the Catholic prayer "**Mea culpa, mea culpa, mea maxima culpa**" (my sin, my sin, my most grievous sin). Cul and cool are still there.

When the multiple Eꟺ becomes "Old Fing Cole," he combines Fin Mac Cool with Old King Cole, who called for his fiddlers three, as Earwicker's exposure of his private assets summoned guilt in the form of the three soldiers, ∧ ⊏ ⋌ .

Returning to the Phoenix Park murders of 1882, although Charles Stewart Parnell escaped conviction in that case when Pigott's letters were discredited, Parnell fell (and fell hard) a few years later, when he was named as co-respondent in a divorce suit by a Captain O'Shea. Parnell and Mrs. Kitty O'Shea had, in fact, been lovers for many years, without any objections from the Captain, who had romantic interests of his own, and most historians believe O'Shea decided to sue for divorce only when persuaded by Parnell's political enemies in the English Establishment. Be that as it may, part of the evidence against Parnell was documentation that he and Mrs. O'Shea had shared a hotel room under the names "Mr. and Mrs. Fox." Thus the fox-hunt, another paleolithic blood sacrifice, recurs again and again in *FW*, always linked to puns on Parnell or O'Shea, and often to the rhythm of the fox-hunting ballad, "John Peel" (which also contains a pun on nudity if you think about it). The fox-hunt theme, however, is also linked with Oscar Wilde, who was disgraced and destroyed when his homosexuality was revealed only a few years after Parnell was destroyed for adultery. Wilde links to the fox-hunt theme, of course, because he once described that barbaric passtime as "the uneatable pursued by the unspeak-able." Joyce has about a hundred versions of this in *FW*, of which my favorite is "The Turk, ungreekable in pursuit of armenable," which combines Wilde's joke with the Turkish-Greek-Armenian wars of the 1920s, and reflects the fact that most Europeans think Greeks are especially prone to homosexuality, whereas Greeks claim the Turks are worse **cul**prits.

The synchro-mesh here is that Parnell and Wilde were both Irish, both were hugely popular until they were in the forties, both were disgraced and destroyed for their sexual irregularities, both are linked to the fox—and, curiously, both lived at one time or another on Stephen's Green in Dublin;

we have seen that Stephen was a magic name to Joyce. St. Stephen is called Stephen Protomartyr because he was the first Christian martyr; his feast day is December 26 (the day after Christmas) and in Ireland and England, rural folk still celebrate the day curiously, by capturing a wren and carrying it through town singing, "The wren, the wren, the king of all birds / St. Stephen's day was caught in a furze." The wren is nowadays kept in a cage and released after the festivity; as recently as the first edition of the *Golden Bough*, Frazer reported that the Stone Age custom of killing the wren still prevailed. When all Dublin turns out to sing a song denouncing Earwicker in Chapter Two, it is called "the rann, the rann, the king of all verse," with a pun on the wren sacrifice. (A rann is an ancient Celtic verse-form.)

In Joyce's early short story "Ivy Day in the Committee Room," one of the characters compares Parnell to the Phoenix, the Egyptian bird of resurrection, which is said to rise reborn from its own ashes. The equation has become Phoenix Park = phoenix as symbol of resurrection = Parnell as Crucified Saviour. What rose from Parnell's martyrdom was the bloody holocaust of Easter Week 1916, as Irish nationalism reasserted itself more violently than was the case with Parnell's passive resistance tactics three decades before.

Earwicker was seen by three British soldiers, who are popularly called "Tommy Atkinses." (This links back to the Tim-Tom-Atum system, of course.) One of the witnesses against Wilde was a male prostitute named Fred Atkins. Naturally, *FW* combines both Tommy and Fred into a composite Atkins who accuses everybody, and merges with the threatening figure of the brunette cad, or tramp, or thief, in Phoenix Park. That sinister composite figure also includes the ancient Celtic bear-god. "What a quhare soort of a mahan," Earwicker mutters at one point; **mahon** is Gaelic for bear. Sometimes this figure becomes Norse playwright Bjorn Bjornssen (whose works Joyce admired) because Bjorn Bjornssen means "bear bear-son." Puns on the Latin **ursa**, bear, also abound, and Glasheen in her *Third Census to Finnegans Wake* concludes that the bear-god is one of the major figures in *FW*.

Weston Lebarre, the anthropologist, in his classic *The Ghost Dance: Origins of Religion* (published over 20 years after *FW*) describes the bear-god as one of the earliest human divinities and says that if you draw a swath a thousand miles wide, starting from the Cro-Magnon caves in Southern France and running up over the North Pole and down through North and South America, you will find traces of the bear-god cult, at various levels of persistence, within that whole area. Many of the Eskimo and Amerindian tribes still celebrate this divinity in ritual, as the Cro-Magnon paintings suggest our ancestors did; throughout modern Europe remnants of the cult are found in folk-lore—the talking bears of Norse legend, Goldilocks and the Three Bears, the children's Teddy Bear totem, etc. The reader will begin to understand what I mean when I refer to the **Ш** aspect of *FW* as "psycho-archeology."

This bear-god conflates with Giordano Bruno, a philosopher who fascinated Joyce (and more recently has fascinated Wilhelm Reich and Timothy Leary) and of course Bruno suggests **bruin**. A hermetiist and conspirator whose biographer Francis Yates thinks may have invented both Freemasonry and Rosicrucianism, Bruno was burned at the stake in Rome in 1600 for magick, heresy, plotting against the Papacy and teaching the Copernican theory of astronomy. He is another phoenix, because what rose from his ashes was the classic scientific age of Galileo and Newton.

As a philosopher, Bruno advocated a pantheistic evolutionary dualism which strangely anticipates both Darwin and modern quantum mechanics. Central to Bruno's dialectical dualism is the rather Taoist idea that everything contains and eventually becomes its own opposite (as Phoenix Park contains fire and water, if one combines its English form with its Gaelic original: the Phoenix rises from **flame** and "finnische" means clear **water**). "In filth, sublimity; in sublimity, filth" was one of Bruno's favorite paradoxes and could almost be the motto of *FW*.

Bruno signed his works "Bruno of Nola," commemorating his birthplace (a suburb of Naples). Coincidentally, Dublin in Joyce's day had a bookstore called Brown and Nolan. The warring opposites (Λ Ⴐ) who struggle all through *FW* go by many names—Cain and Abel, Jacob and Esau, Shem and Shaun, Earwicker and the Cad, Mick and Nick (St. Michael and Satan), Mutt and Jute, Mercius and Justius, Glugg and Chuff, Butt and Taff, Muta and Juva (these last five are all variations on Mutt and Jeff from the comics), the Ondt and the Gracehoper, the Mookse and the Gripes, tree and stone, etc.—but recurrently they are Brown and Nolan, who eventually combine to become Bruno of Nola (⋏⋌) as tree and stone (life and death) combine to become Tristan (⋏⋌). In this dialectic, Bruno has been taken apart and put back together again in strict isomorphism to his own philosophy.

Bruno's first name was Giordano. In English, this is Jordan, which is delightful for Joyce. Jordan is the river in which Jesus was baptized, and the river as female symbol is paramount in *FW* (as we shall see); but in Cockney and Dublin slang, a **jordan** is a chamber pot, bringing us back to the urination theme.

Bruno also suggests Latin **bronn**, thunder, and Greek **Zeus bronnton**, Zeus the thunderer. **Zeus bronnton** may be totally onamatopoetic, since it suggests the sounds of both rain and thunder. This brings us back to Vico, who believed religion was born of the fear of thunder. It is curious, however, that the cycle Giordano-Jordan-baptism (of Jesus) also brings us back to Vico, whose first name, Giambattista, means John the Baptist. (It is also curious that Vico was contemporary with Swift, and William Butler Yeats believed Swift invented the same historical theory as Vico independently.) The "tauftauf" in "tauftauf thuartpeatrick" also links to Vico as John the Baptist (Giambattista) because "taufen" in German means to baptize, while the stuttering effect of "tau ... tau ... thua" suggests both Parnell and Lewis Carroll, who were both stutterers. Similar stuttering runs through the book, always linked with masturbation anxiety, as is explicit in the "Stuttering Hand" on page 4.

Vico believed that language, along with religion, was inspired by thunder, the first "words" being attempts to "talk" to the terrifying Thing in the sky that he claims frightened primitive humanity into forming magical circles and tribes.

Thunder strikes ten times during FW. The linkage here is thunder-Vico-vicus-Eirweiker-Earwicker.

Like Joyce himself, Vico had a morbid fear of thunder, induced by some childhood trauma. Vico's trauma is unknown; Joyce's was a governess who told him thunder was the sign God was about to strike a sinner with lightning. (When asked once how a man of such moral courage could be afraid of thunder, Joyce replied drily, "You were not raised an Irish Catholic." Vico was raised, like Bruno, a Neapolitan Catholic.)

Like Finnegan in the ballad, Vico once fell off a ladder, was pronounced dead, and startled his mourners by sitting up in his coffin. Even more like Finnegan, when he finally did die, Vico had a funeral service of appalling violence, as his admirers and detractors got into a brawl which turned into a riot. (They were disputing whether he was a heretic and should or should not be buried in a sanctified Catholic cemetery.)

Like Joyce, Vico believed that poetry arose out of creative etymology ("incorrect etymology," in Academese). Like Joyce—and also like Whorf and Korzybski—Vico believed a radical change in language could alter our perceived reality-tunnels. (Is that happening yet, dear reader?)

All through the long night of FW, the 50ish Earwicker struggles against the young Cad, King Mark battles to get Isolde back from the young Tristan, Finn Mac Cool pursues his bride Graunia and her young lover Dermot, and Ibsen's Master Builder (sometimes almost a masturbator in Joyce's "siamixed twoatalk") struggles against the younger architects who are replacing him. Vico, who had a long legal battle with his own son, said before Freud that revolutions were rebellions of sons against fathers, and his historical dialectic influenced Hegel and Marx.

Nineteen years before beginning FW, Joyce taught school in Dalkey, County Dublin, which has a Vico Road. Seventeen years before FW, Joyce taught in Trieste, which has a Via Giambattista Vico.

Vico said that every verbal coincidence was a poem showing a new reality. Joyce, who derived his name from Latin and French roots for "joy," liked to remind friends that Freud in German also derives from **freude**, joy. The phrase, "his pseudojocax axplanation," in Chapter Four, reminds us that our word for joke also comes from the Latin root for joy, which might have interested the author of *Wit and its Relation to the Unconscious*. (The double ax in jocax-ax suggests Minos, which had the double ax as its symbol and where Daedalus, Joyce's prototype, built the labyrinth.)

Let us consider this entire synchronicity network in relation to one of the minor characters in *FW*, General Pierre Cambronne (1770-1842). All that most people know about Cambronne, and all that concerns dreaming Earwicker, is that, when asked to surrender at Waterloo, Cambronne replied with wonderful brevity, "**Merde**." This is enough to make him a powerful symbol.

The first time the thunder strikes (on page 3) it includes the letters "—konnbronn—" which contains Latin **bronn**, thunder, and sounds like Cambronne. The thunder's crash is then dream-distorted into Finnegan falling from the ladder, Humpty Dumpty falling from the wall, the fall of the Wall Street stock market in 1929 and an ambiguous "great fall of the offwall," which includes all these (and the walls of Jericho?) and suggests defecation (offall). This quickly becomes the battle of Clontarf, in which the Irish, led by Brian Boru, defeated the Vikings, led by King Sitric.

Both "Brian" and "Boru" sound enough like **bruin** to recur often in connection with the bear-god and Bruno. The battle of Contarf, I hope you remember by now, occurred 23 April, 1014, and the 2 girls and 3 soldiers are there, hiding, in the date. More wonderfully, Brian was blonde, like Earwicker and Finn, and Brian was killed by a Viking named Broder, who was brunette, like the Cad in the park who afflicts our misfortunate hero all night long. Brodar and killing, of course, suggest brother-murder and bring us back to Cain and Abel (⌈∧) . . .

A tour guide takes us around Clontarf (on the north side of Dublin Bay), blending Brian Boru's death with the fall of Humpty Dumpty and Earwicker's defecation in the park: "He was poached on that eggtentical spot . . . Load Allmarshy . . . Onheard of and umscene . . . erde from erde." The last phrase is mingled English/German for "earth from earth" but it contains an elided **merde** that brings us back to General Cambronne again; the Freudian concept of war as anal sadism is strongly implied, as are recent ethological discoveries about excretion as a territorial marker.

Cambronne continues to appear in various guises throughout: "Brum! Brum! Cumbrum!" cry the cannons at Waterlook page 9. "Cumbrum, cumbrum," they repeat on page 134. On page 421 we find: "Sept out of Hall of that, Ereweaker with the Bloody Big Bristol. Bung. Stop. Bung. Stop. Cumm Bumm. Stop. Come Baked to Auld Aireen." Here General Cambronne mingles with Earwicker's territorial mark in Phoenix Park, the possible etymology of Earwicker from Eire-weiker with its link to vicus and Vico, and the strains of "Come Back to Erin," a meaningfl song to the exiled Irish writer of all this. A Bristol, of course, is Cockney slang for a pistol, which dream-fashion has been taken from the Cad in the park and transferred to the victim; but a pistol is an obvious symbol to Freudians. General Cambronne's defiant cry of "**merde**" at Waterloo fits neatly into all this because, among other things, Phoenix Park has a Wellington Monument, dedicated to the victor of that battle, and water-loo ties in with the river-urination theme, loo being Cockney and Dublin slang for the toilet. (The reason there is so much Cockney slang in Dublin is that so many Cockney soldiers were stationed there for so many centuries.)

The anal General Cambronne theme gradually merges with the case of an anonymous Russian General about whom Joyce heard from his father, John Stanislaus Joyce. (In the unconscious one General = another General.) It seems that John Joyce knew a certain Buckley, who served with the Royal Fusiliers in the Crimean War, and was involved peripherally with the Charge of the Light Brigade, that epiphany of military heroism and stupidity. On another occasion in the same war, Buckley caught sight of a Russian General in a field and was about to shoot him when the General lowered his pants to take a crap. It made the man look so "human." Buckley said, that he couldn't shoot. When the General finished and pulled his trousers up, however, he became an Enemy Officer again and Buckley shot the poor bastard dead.

In Joyce's version, Buckley shoots the Russian General for the crime of "homosodalism," an ambiguous phrase to say the least of it. Various Atkinses are involved, invoking Tommy Atkins and the three soldiers in Phoenix Park and also Fred Atkins, the male prostitute in the Wilde case. Also involved are Brown and Nolan, who were actually two officers at the Charge of the Light Brigade; conveniently for Joyce, this brings us back to Brown and Nolan's bookstore in Dublin and the dialectic of Bruno of Nola. Buckley's gun fires twice: "Cabrone! Combrune!" We are back at Waterloo with General Cambronne, but the **brun**ette Cad in the park is back, too, and with him echoes of the bruin or bear-god, and the brunette Brodar who killed Brian Boru. Since Buckley is from the Galic root for youth and Joyce emphasizes the General's old age, we are also back in the tangles of the Oedipus complex again.

Joyce tells the story in a parody of the style of Synge's black comedy, *The Playboy of the Western World.* That is coincidentally appropriate because the

Synge play deals with a man who claims to have killed his father, and that man happens to be named Christy Mahon; Christy suggests the dying-rising god again, and Mahon, remember, is Gaelic for bear. When the Russian General becomes a "Brewinbaroon," we are back to Brian Boru at Clontarf, but also encountering another repeating figure in *FW*, Sir Arthur Guiness, the brewing baron (brewin baroon) whose first name, Arthur, brings us back to the bear-god since **arth** is an old root in Indo-European tongues meaning bear, and links into Artemis, whose name means bear and who was both a bear goddess and a bare goddess (in the Acteaon legend). Arthur also ties Arthur Guiness in neatly with Arthur Wellesley, Duke of Wellington, bringing us back to Waterloo, and King Arthur, bringing us back to the isomorphism of Arthur/Finn/King Mark as Ш figure, Guinevere/Graunia/Isolde as Δ and Launcelot/Dermot/Tristan as ⋌. Sir Arthur Guiness also had two "warring" sons (∧ ⊏) who got into a feud over ownership of the brewery, linking him to Adam with his feuding sons by isomorphism; and the name Guiness, the invaluable O'Hehir tells us, is an Anglicization of Gaelic **Mac Angus**, which means son of Angus and coincidentally links to Isolde the Fair, who was the daughter of Angus.

When Jute tries to pass one of Wood's debased coins to Mutt in Chapter One, the latter says he would prefer real money, just as Swift did in *The Drapier Letters*, and Jute claims "Ghinees hies good for you," which implies that English coins (guineas) are good for Ireland. By Chapter Seventeen this has become "Ghenghis is ghoon for you," with an invocation of the Mongol warrior. Behind both phrases is the advertising slogan seen everywhere is Ireland, "Guiness is good for you."

The Russian general's death is part of a cycle which Joyce calls "eggburst, eggblend, eggburial and hatch-as-hatch can." This includes Vico's historical cycle and its Hegelian/Marxian derivatives, Humpty Dumpty again, the Orphic egg of creation, Darwinism and the permutated initials of Humphrey Chimpden Earwicker (who perhaps suspects his Catholic neighbors of distorting his first name to Humpty as he evidently suspects them of twisting his latter name to earwigger. It is a bitter burden to be a Protestant in Holy Catholic Ireland.)

If the all-inclusive ᛝ is simultaneously man (Earwicker/Adam/Finn etc.), mountain (Howth Hill, Ш) insect (earwig) and egg (Humpty Dumpty), he is a walking text of evolution. His story includes "weatherings and marryings and buryings and natural selections," which combines Darwin with Vico's cycles again. When Isobel, his pubescent daughter, tries to justify her dawning sexuality, she evokes "the law of the jungerl" and calls on the great evolutionist in the tones of a popular Irish song: "Charley, you're my darwing." (*Charley, you're my darling*, still popular in Ireland today, hymns Bonnie Prince Charley and the tragic, gallant, foolish Jacobite crusade; but Charley the Chimp was a popular attraction in Phoenix Park zoo in Joyce's day. Perhaps HCE's middle name is Chimpden to remind us of his, and our, evolutionary forebears.) The patriarchal ego of Earwicker or **E** tries to restore Irish Puritan values, urging the young lady to improve her mind with decent literature, such as *The Old Curiosity Shape* and *Doveyed Covetfilles*, two Freudian slips that, alas, only reveal his own guilt. When the Ondt (the earwig having split in two as the warring Ondt and Gracehoper) asks a bee to "commence insects" with him, more of the truth seems to be leaking out. Fortunately, being also a flower **Ǝ** is a Hyacinth, remember, and can therefore find relief—is it not perfectly natural for a hyacinth to be seen "pollen himself" in the Spring?

One of the more mysterious characters in *FW* is a shadowy Eugenius. He seems to contain Eugene Aram, the man who first proved Gaelic is an Indo-European language and who also had an unfaithful wife, like King Arthur, Finn and King Mark—and Bloom in Joyce's *Ulysses*. Eugenius, however, also contains Eugene Schaumann, a Finn (ouch!) who happens to have shot another Russian General, Ivan Bobrikoff, on 16 June 1904. Since Schaumann was an anarchist and Joyce's alter ego, Stephen Dedalus, was also an anarchist, Stephen is humorously accused of the assassination in the Cave of Winds chapter of *Ulysses*, which takes place on 16 June 1904.

The reason Joyce picked that date to immortalize in *Ulysses* long puzzled critics and commentators; we know now, due to Joyce's letters, that it was the day on which he and Nora Barnacle first had sex, of a sort. (He wanted to have intercourse. Nora, a 20-year-old virgin from Galway, compromised by masturbating him.) There are Bloomsday celebrations in Dublin every year on 16 June and, as Stan Gebler Davies has remarked, it is mind-boggling to think how the 95% Catholic population would react if they ever understood fully what they are commemorating.

Curiously enough, Joyce first met Nora in front of Oscar Wilde's old house on Merrion Square. Wilde brings in the homosexual theme again and Merrion suggest Marion (Bloom's wife) and Marian, a Catholic adjective to describe shrines or churches sacred to the BVM or Blessed Virgin Mary. All of this gets tangled beautifully in *Ulysses*. In Chapter Three, walking toward the Pigeon House on Sandymount Strand, near the place where Nora masturbated our Immortal Author, Stephen Dedalus thinks of a blasphemous joke about the Virgin Mary trying to explain to Joseph that she was not unfaithful with another man but only with a pigeon. In Chapter Thirteen, Bloom masturbates on the same spot, while a teen-age virgin, Gerty McDowell is flirting with him, and Joyce intercuts their antiseptic sex (exhibitionism and voyeurism) with a ritual to the Virgin in the nearby Church.

Somehow the Holy Ghost, the symbolism of the dove or pigeon, and the Pigeon House have become emblems of Irish sexual frustration and Bloom's masturbation a parody of Immaculate Conception. ("Timid onanism they call purity," Joyce wrote of his countrymen in a letter. Nietzsche's *The Antichrist*, quoted in Chapter one of *Ulysses*, contains the memorable aphorism, "The Immaculate Conception maculates conception.")

Oscar Wilde, who keeps popping up in all these synchronicity clusters, was the first proponent of the theory that Shakespeare was homosexual. Wilde was also called "a great white caterpillar" by Lady Colin Campbell, and Wilde as caterpillar often gets blended with Earwicker as earwig in Joyce's "mooxed metaphors."

Brian Boru died on 23 April, 1014, and Shakespeare died on 23 April, 1616. Shakespeare was also born on 23 April, 1565, a meta-synchronicity that will concern us later in this chrestomathy.

A mysterious voice cries "More pork" several times in *FW*. This is probably, on the **E** level, a memory of a customer in Earwicker's pub the evening before the dream, but it links to the Ham-Bacon-Shakerspeare theme, and Moore Park was the place where Swift first met "Stella" (Esther Johnson). In Gaelic **Padraic mor**, pronounced p'ork moor, is Saint Patrick, but can also refer to Padraic Pearse, the author of "**Mishe Eire**," the Irish Declaration of Independence, and the Easter Uprising.

Nora Barnacle's voice appears on the first page of *FW* linked with Padraic Pearse, St. Peter, Moses at the burning bush and the pun on which the Catholic Church alleges to be founded:

> **nor avoice from afire bellowsed mishe mishe to tauftauf thuartpeatrick**

The place where Nora was working as a chambermaid when Joyce met her, Finn's Hotel, appears on the last page:

> **There's where . . . First . . . Finn, again!**

The week that *FW* was published, the Russo-Finish War of 1939 broke out. Joyce wrote to his friend Frank Budgeon, "The prophet is vindicated! The Finn again wakes and Buckleys are coming from all directions to shoot at that Russian general."

All these coincidences mesh into one another in an endless Strange Loop that makes *FW* a model of the interconnectedness of all things asserted by Bell's Theorem in quantum mechanics, 26 years after *FW* was published. (We will return to that eerie subject.) Thus, Richard Pigott is linked to Shakespeare, not only by the Ham-Hamlet-Bacon puns, but by the fact that

Shakespeare had a boar's head on his Coat of Arms. The 2 girls (⊣ ⊢) and 3 soldiers (∧ ⊏ ⅄) in the park are isomorphic to Dublin's own Coat of Arms which has 2 dancing girls and 3 castles (military symbols). 2 and 3 suggest the death dates (23 April) of Brian Boru and Shakespeare. Ireland is a living synchronicity, having 4 provinces divided into 32 counties and also having been converted to Christianity by St. Patrick in 432 A.D. If Ǝ is both Hamlet and Humpty Dumpty, he easily becomes a "homlette" and the association ham and egg points forward to breakfast when the dreamer finally wakes. When Joyce wants to link cuckolded King Mark with Mark Twain, he not only has the link Mark-Mark but also the Finn-Mark isomorphism (both were cuckolds) and the fact that Twain sounds like twin bringing us back to the twins Cain and Abel (⊏∧) who become unified ⅄ who is also Tristan.

And so on, **ad infinitum**? It already seems so, and we will find more evidence of infinite regress later in these pages.

Werewolf Bridge

The earliest version of this poem was written in Yellow Springs, Ohio, in 1962. This version was composed in Dublin, Ireland, in 1987. "A work of art is never finished, only abandoned," as Paul Valery said.

Werewolf Bridge

At midnight, as I rise from my coffin, I ask:
Am I Christ or Mehmet Ali Agca?
Am I Count Dracula or just another Hiroshima Werewolf
Howling for human flesh?

In my mad and werewolf heart
I have howled half a century away
In despair and rage:
The bread and wine of werewolf Mass

Every God-damned, man-damned morning, I ask:
Is this the beginning of another cardboard day
Or is it the first day of the rest of the universe?
Will nothing happen or will everything happen?

In my green and bleeding soul
I have sung half a century away
In laughter and in scorn
The flesh and blood of werewolf Time

Every twilight as the shadows fall, I ask:
How many missiles are aimed at Moscow?
At New York and London? At Paris and Rome?
At the naked skin of God?

In my high and mountain skull
I have mocked half a century away
In measure and in fact:
The line and square of werewolf Space

One dizzy moment above the Liffey I forget, I ask:
Is this O'Connell Bridge or Butt Bridge?
Am I on the Ha'penny Bridge perhaps?
Is this another endless werewolf bridge?

Until defiance builds of its own ruin
A truth more brave than the truth of death
My werewolf heart shall rage against
Both werewolf God and werewolf Man

Until terror builds of its own heat
A myth more green than the myth of life—
But my werewolf heart is pierced at last
By the silver bullet of the Lady's gaze

My werewolf self is atom-bombed
By the golden sunrise of the Lady's smile:
I am the Beast the Lady rides,
I am the stars within Her hair.

The Motherfucker
Mystique

My first article was published in 1959 and by 1972 I had sold over 2000 articles, stories and poems but had not yet managed to persuade anybody to publish me in book form. Then I got baptized and was reborn and learned what publishing is all about.

My first book published—which was not my first book written—was called *PLAYBOY's Book of Forbidden Words* and was a discursive dictionary of obscenity and invective. It was written while Dell was meditating over my actual first book, *Illuminatus!* (composed in collaboration with Robert Shea). Dell's meditations were prolonged and profound, to say the least of it—only after five years did they decide to publish the monstro-novel, and then they insisted that it should be cut by 500 pages and divided into three volumes. After five years of struggle, Shea and I capitulated.

Meanwhile, to try to get a book into print while Dell was still in the middle of its five-year meditations on *Illuminatus!*, I agreed to write *PLAYBOY's Book of Forbidden Words*, which turned into another disaster and again proved my naivete about the publishing industry. The book was not my idea, but that of an editor at Playboy Press, who asked me if I could write a history of foul language. I said, sure, I could, since I knew a lot about linguistic history and also knew how to do research; we signed a contract, and I went ahead—quickly producing a book of high erudition and (I think) some wit. It turned out that this was not what was wanted. The erudition and the linguistic history were exised, along with much of the wit, and in his hurry to turn my work into a more commercial production, the editor in many sections replaced correct grammar and syntax with the kind of pidgin English generally encountered only in TV advertisements.

I was horrified, but I was also flat broke at the time, and Dell still had not decided whether or not to publish *Illuminatus!* Motivated entirely by cowardice and panic, I allowed *Forbidden Words* to go out, under my name, even though it was mostly at that point the editor's text, or the text he thought a moron audience could understand. The book failed miserably, and went out of print quickly. I have never mourned it, and I dread the day when scholars rediscover it and begin blaming me for all that is wrong with it.

Meanwhile, somewhat reconstructed, here is a sample of what my very first book contained. I have selected for republication my comments on the most controversial endearment in the English language.

MOTHERFUCKER

Literally, a motherfucker is one who copulates with his mother, of course; but the word is seldom intended literally. Being the most insulting obscenity in American English, **motherfucker** has given birth to various timid, euphemistic or quasi-humorous variations, such as **motherjumper, mother-ferrier, mo'fo', mammyjammer, futhermucker,** the truncated adjective **mothering** (as in "Where the hell is that mothering wrench?") and the deaconic **mother** that has lately invaded middle-class speech—as when, in the Billy Wilder film, *The Apartment,* Jack Lemmon says to the bartender, referring to a martini, "Give me another of those little mothers."

Motherfucker is usually thought to be of black origin, but some linguists claim it appeared first among poor whites. It is used quite prominently in many classic pieces of black folklore—for instance, the ballad of Stackerlee or Stagolee, which has numerous variations and is known in almost every black community. This epic contains the unforgettable boast:

> *I've got a tombstone disposition and a graveyard mind*
> *I'm a bad motherfucker and I don't mind dyin'*

This is in the tradition of the boasts of the Homeric heroes, the Irish orations of Finn Mac Cool, and the brags of Davy Crockett (who once claimed to be "half horse and half alligator.") Stackerlee's second line above should be pronounced "baaaaaaad" with some glee in the voice; to be a **baaaaaaad motherfucker**, in ghetto speech, is not to be despised. The term is almost complimentary, and certainly respectful: it signifies the virtue which Mexicans call **cojones** (testicles and/or courage) or **machismo** (super-masculinity). A **baaaaaaad motherfucker** might be unethical by ordinary standards, but you would rather have him on your side than against you: he is hard as a Fundamentalist's skull and would rather die than crawl. Bobby Seale, Chairman of the Black Panther Party, named his son Malik Nkrumah Stagolee Seale. In his introduction to *Seize the Time*, Seale explains "One of my son's names derives from the lumpen proletariat politically unaware brothers in the streets. Stagolee fought his brothers and sisters, and he shouldn't have. The Stagolee of today should take on the messages of Malcolm X, as Huey Newton did, to oppose the racist, capitalist oppression our people and other people are subjected to."

Another black epic gives further dimension to the motherfucker mystique. Shine, the cook on the Titanic, leaps overboard after the collision with the iceberg and starts swimming. The captain's daughter comes up on deck and pleads with him to save her. His answer is unsympathetic—

> *There's pussy on the land and pussy on the sea,*
> *But the pussy on the land is the pussy for me*

—and he swims on. A shark attempts to devour him, but Shine again refuses to be deflected from his purpose, saying:

> *You're the king of the ocean, the king of the sea,*
> *But you gotta be a swimmin' motherfucker to outswim me*

Shine is standing on a corner in Harlem two hours before the news of the sinking of the Titanic reaches New York.

(Curiously, James Joyce heard this ballad in Paris in the 1920s and was fascinated by it. It may account, in part, for the fact that the Titanic plays a large role in *Finnigans Wake*.)

Shine may not be a baaaaaaad motherfucker in the full meaning of that title, but he is in the vicinity. He has the will power to postpone sexual gratification, can outswim a shark, and beats the wireless telegraph across the Atlantic. However, there is another kind of motherfucker who is distinctly less admirable (in the Latin meaning of that word), and he is usually known as a **signifying motherfucker**. Such a person has all the surface attributes of a baaaaaaad motherfucker, but caves in under attack: he is mostly bluff. (In black speech, **signifying** means using words without the will or intent to back them; most U.S. government promises are regarded as **signifying** in the ghetto.) The classic example is the Signifying Monkey in a legend so old that some folklorists think it goes all the way back to Africa, as the cast of characters suggests. It is worth recounting at length, I think.

> *Deep down in the jungle, near a dried-up creek,*
> *The signifying monkey hadn't slept for a week.*
> *Every night when he was ready for a piece*
> *Brother Lion came by a-roaring like po-lice.*

The monkey decided to down the lion, but being only a signifier he does not attempt a frontal assault; instead, he uses the old let's-you-and-him-fight gambit, telling Lion that Brother Elephant has been "calling him out of his name," to wit:

> *He says he fucked your mammy, and your auntie, too,*
> *And if you ain't careful, he's gonna fuck you*

This puts Brother Lion in a proper rage and he charges off to face the elephant down:

> *He ran through water, he ran through mud,*
> *He came to a bar called the Bucket of Blood.*
> *There sat Elephant, two whores upon his knee,*
> *He was drinking boiler-makers and smoking tea.*
> *Lion walk up and spit right in his eye,*
> *Say, "Rise, motherfucker, you're gonna die!"*

Elephant majestically delivers one powerful kick and Lion crawls away "more dead than alive." As he staggers weakly toward his den, he passes the signifying monkey who laughs and brutally tells him:

> *"The sky is blue and the grass is green,*
> *And you're the dumbest motherfucker this jungle's ever seen!"*

Alas, the monkey laughs too loud and loses his balance. Lion is on him with all four feet as soon as he hits the ground. This is where the monkey's real signifying comes into play. With "tears in his eyes" and great sincerity, he offers an apology and a ringing declaration that he will reform and mend his ways. The gullible lion spares him—whereat the signifying little bastard scrambles up the tree again and, laughing, declaims:

"The sky is still blue, and the grass is still green,
And you're still the dumbest motherfucker this jungle's ever seen!"

The monkey laughs so loud at this point that he again falls out of the tree. The legend ends as grimly as some of Aesop's fables:

Deep down in the jungle near a dried-up creek,
Nobody seen that monkey for more than a week,
But there's a new tombstone and here's what it say:
"Here's where a signifying motherfucker lay."

The black meaning of motherfucker, then, is far from simple, and a baaaaaaad motherfucker is admirable or at least awe-inspiring whereas a signifying motherfucker is merely contemptible.

When motherfucker journeyed down town and entered white speech, it lost this ambiguity and became merely the roughest insult around. At one time it was a sport in the armed forces to use it on new recruits from middle-class backgrounds and then duck: they almost always started throwing punches. As the word became better established, it gradually became less shocking and now is often used as casually and cordially as **son of a bitch**. In fact, like "son of a bitch," motherfucker can be recognized as cordial if it is proceeded by "old"—even over the phone where you can't see the friendly smile: "Is it you, Joe, you old motherfucker?" It can still get a rise out of those who have led sheltered lives, apparently including some policemen. In New Jersey a few years ago, a Black Panther organizer was arrested for saying to a white traffic cop, "Just a minute, motherfucker." The attorney for the defense argued, as I have here, that **motherfucker** is not always an insult or provocation in black speech, and may even be a compliment, but the judge decided it was unlikely to be friendly when coming from a Panther to a policeman. The accused was fined.

Inherent in the term motherfucker is the charge of mother-son incest, a taboo that is close to being universal, anthropologists say, and which, unlike other sexual restrictions, is almost universally obeyed, too. Kinsey and his associates found that father-daughter incest was much more common than anybody had thought before they did their surveys, but they never found a single real case of mother-son incest. The word **motherfucker** may have forced its way into our consciousness, but the deed itself is still unthinkable.

Mammary Metaphysics

The next essay comes from another potboiler I did for Playboy Press, called *The Book of the Breast*.* As usual, my philosophical and sociological speculations got in the way of lubricity which the editor really wanted, but he got fired along about then and a new editor, Martin Ebon, liked this book so much it was printed just as I wrote it. Curiously, it was the only one of my books for Playboy Press that sold well enough to earn regular royalties for me over a period of several years.

Ezra Pound noted in *Make It New* that if a book has a form, you had better tell the reader, instead of assuming that he or she will notice the logical structure for themselves. I prefer to just drop a vague hint here and there. Those who are hip to Cabala might realize that it is no accident that this essay immediately follows the dissertation on baaaaaaad motherfuckers and signifying motherfuckers.

* Now published by Falcon Press, entitled *The Goddess Obsession*

TO: JEHOVAH YAHWEH
CARE: CELESTIAL HOTEL (SUITE #666)
PRESIDENTIAL TIER, PARADISE

DEAR GOD:
THIS IS TO INFORM YOU THAT YOUR CURRENT
POSITION AS DEITY IS HEREWITH TERMINATED
DUE TO GROSS INCOMPETENCE STOP YOUR CHECK
WILL BE MAILED STOP PLEASE DO NOT USE ME AS A
REFERENCE RESPECTFULLY,
                          MALACLYPSE THE YOUNGER
              —Malaclypse the Younger, *Principia Discordia, or*
      How I Found Goddess and What I Did to Her When I Found Her.

It has often been observed that there is marked similarity between the words for *matter* in Indo-European languages (Latin *materium*, French *matiere*, etc.) and the words for measurement (French *metre*, English *measure*, etc.). More interestingly, both groups seem to relate to the words for *mother* (Latin *mater*, German *mutter*, French *mere*). The earliest calendar, or device for measuring time, dated at around 30,000 B.C. has a distinctly female figure marking every 28th day. This figure has not yet been explained—a Cro-Magnon woman's attempt to figure out her menstrual cycle? A schedule for the rituals of the moon goddess? In either event, it seems that the starry cosmos, in those days, was conceived as a great mother who had given birth to the life of the earth. Wise old women (the *wiccas*, wise ones, from whom we get the word *witches*) were thought to have a special affinity with her. Above all, this goddess was not a metaphor or an idea; she was a living presence, just as the American Indians to this day refer to the earth as a living mother and still fondly expect that eventually she will throw off the maniacal whites whose technology seems to be largely an attack on her. Quite similarly, the early Romans conceived the thickest band of stars in the sky as the *Via Galactica*, the Way of Milk, from which we get our familiar expression the Milky Way. To them and to the Greeks this was literally a mist of milk across the heavens, spurted upward from the breasts of the earth-goddess, Hera.

Goethe's *Faust* provides a classic example of the same breast quest conveyed in a different symbolism:

FAUST:
A lovely dream once came to me;
I then beheld an apple tree,
And there two fairest apples shone.
They lured me so I climbed thereon.

YOUNG WITCH:
Apples have been desired by you
Since first in Paradise they grew;
And I am moved with joy to know
That such within my garden grow.

Freud commented tersely on this exchange: "There is not the slightest doubt what is meant by the apple-tree and the apples." In fact, *a nice apple-dumpling shop* is Cockney slang for a pair of firmly rounded breasts.

Some readers will be thinking of the Garden of Eden at this point, and they are probably right. It has long puzzled and provoked scholars that both Eve in that story, and the Goddess Eris in Greek mythology, are associated with *apples* and that the apples in both cases made a great deal of trouble. In the Hebrew story, Eve insists on eating a certain apple (actually, Genesis only says *fruit*, but tradition has always identified it with the apple), and Yahweh, the local volcano-god, is thrown into a fury and curses her and all mankind, for reasons that are far from perfectly clear. In the Greek story, Zeus slights Eris by not inviting her to a banquet on Olympus and she gets her revenge by manufacturing a golden apple inscribed KALLISTI ("To the prettiest one") and rolling it into the banquet hall. Immediately all the goddesses begin squabbling, each claiming to be the prettiest one and entitled to the apple; this quarrel worsens until men as well as gods are drawn into it and eventually the Trojan War results. Eris became known as the goddess of chaos and the golden apple is called the apple of discord.

The similarities here—the role of the female, the presence of the apple, the sequence of supernatural calamaties—suggest that there might be a common origin to these myths. Such is indeed the case, according to Joseph Campbell's monumental four-volume study, *The Masks of God*. The Genesis text is very late and has altered the original myth to fit the patriarchal context of the religion of Yahweh. Originally, Eve was not Adam's wife, but his mother; she was not a human, but a goddess; and the outcome was not tragic, but triumphant—after the magic fruit was eaten, Adam himself became a god. (There is still a hint of this in the Genesis version, in which Yahweh says nervously, "Behold, the man has become as one of us [the gods], to know good and evil.") What was originally involved was probably a psychedelic sacrament, like the Eleusinian festival in Athens, in which the worshipers ate certain (hallucinogenic) foods and became one with the Mother Goddess Demeter. Eve and Eris, in short, are negative patriarchal versions of the *bona dea* (good goddess) of Rome, the earth-mother whose milk covers the sky at night, the Isis of Egypt, Ishtar of Babylon, the all-protective figure who has descended directly from the huge-breasted Venus of Willendorf—that numinous deity who is just an extension on the cosmic scale of the vision of the infant at the breast.

Nor is she entirely dead yet. Robert Graves in *The White Goddess* insists that all true poets have a vision of her at some time or another, at the very least in their dreams. Contemporary witch covens still worship her and I have personally attended a quite beautiful ceremony—in Minneapolis, Minnesota, no less—in which she was invoked and spoke through the witch queen to declare:

> You shall be free, and as a sign that you be really so, be naked in your rites, dance, sing, feast, make music and love. All in my praise, for I am a gracious goddess, who gives joy upon earth; certainty, not faith, while in life; and upon death peace unutterable, rest and the ecstasy of the goddess. Nor do I demand aught in sacrifice, for behold, I am the mother of all living, and my love is poured out upon the earth.

This is quite lovely, I think; and it is also, beyond debate, a purely oral religion. The goddess is an extension of the infant's picture of the breast, if the breast could speak. Thus, Wolfgang Lederer, M.D., describes the great mother goddess as virtually an extension in space-time of the breasts themselves:

> Her breasts, for instance, for the sake of which the Babylonians called her "The Mother with the fruitful breasts," she whose breasts never failed, never went dry—they were occasionally . . . reduced to stylized rings or spirals, but they were more often lustily stressed, and most impressively so by multiplication. The great Diana of Ephesus is usually represented with numerous breasts—I count up to 16—and the Mexican Goddess of the Agave, Mayauel, has 400. Their function is obvious enough, and some of the most beautiful and touching icons of the goddess show her with the infant at her breast, whether she be the Egyptian Isis with the child Horus or her equivalent in Asia Minor, Ur, prehistoric Sardinia, Mexico and Peru or contemporary Africa, or of course one of the innumerable virgins with child of Christian art: these, especially during the later middle ages, accomplish such tenderness and intimacy of expression, such union of animal warmth and purest spirituality, that one is easily long lost in contemplation. . . .
>
> Moreover, the Goddess we describe is no mere human mother, giving human milk to the child of her flesh and blood, nor yet simply a divine mother, with a child human or divine: for from her nipples may flow, not milk, but honey—as in Palestine, which was the land of milk and honey on her behalf, or at Delphi, where her priestesses were called *Melissai*—"bees"— and her shrine was likened to a beehive. Or, wonderful to behold, all kinds of fishes may drop from her nipples, as among the Eskimo. Indeed, she not only gives birth to all manner of animals, she also feeds them, giving each what it needs, and "Alma Mater" that she is, she may—wonder of wonders— give such to bearded men, to scholars, feeding them wisdom. She is, in short, the source of all food, material or spiritual.

No wonder she is proud of her breasts. And, hence, quite naturally, she holds them, either to show them off, or to offer more conveniently their fullness . . . *

Statues of the goddess, holding her breasts in this "offering" position, have been found all over prehistoric Europe and Asia. They must have been, at one time, as common as the more familiar mother-with-child later adopted by Roman Christianity.

In contrast, and despite the orality of Jesus himself, the Judeo-Christian faiths are strongly anal† and their stern Father God demands endless sacrifices, offers no joy on earth but only duty blindly obeyed, and threatens sadistic tortures (for an infinite number of years, according to some theologians) to anyone who crosses him. It almost seems as if history, at least in the Occident, repeats the pattern Freud found in the nursery, from oral bliss to anal anxiety.

This was the opinion, in the last century, of the German folklorist J. Bachofen, of the American anthropoligist Lewis Morgan, and of Karl Marx's financial supporter and collaborator, Friedrich Engels. Their hypothesis of a single historical pattern, in which all societies evolve from matriarchal communism to patriarchal capitalism (and then back to communism, according to Engels), was widely accepted for about 50 years, but then evidence that conflicted with it began accumulating. Some societies were never matriarchal; some alleged matriarchies were actually only matrilineal—that is, descent and property were passed through the female line, but men still held the chieftainships or governorships; and, if some of Bachofen's inspired guesses about prehistorical Europe were startlingly right, others were glaringly wrong. The theory of primordial matriarchy was rejected by anthropologists as thoroughly as the luminiferous ether was rejected by physicists. Only in the last few years has it had some revival, under the impact of new data collected and polemically proclaimed by female scholars more or less allied with the Women's Liberation Movement.

Meanwhile, Leo Frobenius in Germany, G. Rattray Taylor in England and Joseph Campbell in our country have all collected and published voluminous data showing that if the primitive matriarchy did not exist as universally as the 19th-Century theorists imagined, something much like it existed just before the dawn of recorded history in the West and Near East

---

*Wolfgang Lederer, M.D., *The Fear of Women* (New York: Grune and Stratten, 1958)

†Martin Luther, for instance, had his peak religious experience in the privy. Later Lutheran theologians have tried to hide this fact, speaking of the room as the "tower," but Luther's own words are unambiguous; see Norman O. Brown's *Life Against Death*.

and coexisted with the first patriarchal civilizations for a while. The oral and
gentle mother goddesses are a survival of that period, and there have been
various attempts to revive its values in historical times. G. Rattray Taylor
even provides a table* showing the differences between the two kinds of
cultures, which he calls patrist and matrist. In strict Freudian terms they are,
of course, respectively, anal and oral:

Patrist (anal)	Matrist (oral)
1. Restrictive attitude toward sex	1. Permissive attitude toward sex
2. Limitation of freedom for women	2. Freedom for women
3. Women seen as inferior, sinful	3. Women accorded high status
4. Chastity more valued than welfare	4. Welfare more valued than chastity
5. Politically authoritarian	5. Politically democratic
6. Conservative: against innovation	6. Progressive: revolutionary
7. Distrust of research, inquiry	7. No distrust of research
8. Inhibition, fear of spontaneity	8. Spontaneity: exhibition
9. Deep fear of homosexuality	9. Deep fear of incest
10. Sex differences maximized (dress)	10. Sex differences minimized (dress)
11. Asceticism, fear of pleasure	11. Hedonism, pleasure welcomed
12. Father-religion	12. Mother-religion

The much-debated thesis of Charles Reich in *The Greening of America* held
that our country is passing from what he called Consciousness II to Consciousness III. It is obvious that Consciousness II is largely patrist (and anal),
while Consciousness III is largely matrist (and oral). It is not surprising to a
Freudian, then, that there was a progression from the fad of big-breasted
movie stars in the 1940s (the thin edge of the matrist wedge) to the
breakthrough of *Playboy's* barebreasted pinups in the 1950s and 1960s, to
hippiedom and women's lib in the 1960s and 1970s. It is also quite natural
that each new wave has regarded the previous wave as a sick and
compromised part of the old patrist regime.

It is curious, in passing, that the Women's Liberation Movement, the
latest and most revolutionary of these waves, is paradoxically more patrist
than much of what preceded it chronologically. This is noteworthy in regard
to Taylor's points 1, 4, 5, 7, 8 and 11—permissiveness versus restriction,
welfare versus chastity, authoritarianism versus democracy, attitude
toward research, inhibition versus spontaneity and ascetisicm versus
hedonism. On all of these issues the liberationists are distinctly moving
backward toward anal-patrist orientation rather than forward toward oral-

---

*G. Rattray Taylor, *Sex in History* (New York: Vanguard, 1955) matrist "Consciousness III." They not only incline toward Victorian prudery, but have revived the old Victorian delight in sexual slander and blackmail. Just as the great Irish rebel, Charles Stewart Parnell, fell into disgrace and was ruined when his adultery with Kitty O'Shea was discovered and denounced by the Catholic clergy, many radical heroes have been cast down from their previous eminence when these ladies published sexual exposes of them (with names omitted, but all other details immediately recognizable) in their magazines. (Sometimes the names are included, as recently happened to a gentle Black pacifist, who was not even accused of unethical acts but just of having the wrong ideas, but who nonetheless suffered the humiliation of having his mind, soul, body and his "golden penis," no less, roundly condemned in several issues of a radical journal.) Not only are their dogmas sacrosanct, democratic discussion scorned and scientific research rejected (as "male"), but many of them have announced that reason itself is deeply suspect and now frankly embrace the *"credo quia absurdum"* ("I believe because it is absurd") of the church fathers.

Rejection of science and free discussion are, of course, characteristic of all totalitarian movements; thus, nonbiblical astronomy was heretical to the Inquisition, unpalatable anthropology was "Jewish" to the Nazis, unsatisfactory biology was banned as "bourgeois" in Stalin's Russia and irritating ethology is "sexist" (and unpleasant psychology is "chauvinist") to these ladies. Like all other totalitarian fiats, this is intellectually protected by concentric circles of similar rhetoric. Thus, to question the concept of witchcraft or heresy in the days of the Inquisition automatically meant that one was a witch or a heretic. To say that science is neither Jewish nor gentile, socialist nor bourgeois, but merely the activity of independent minds attempting to be objective, opened one to suspicion of being "Jewish" in Germany or "bourgeois" in Russia. To say that behavioral sciences cannot be dismissed with epithets like "sexist" and "chauvinist" is to convince these ladies that the speaker is "sexist" and "chauvinist." To push the argument one step further and say that such protective rationalization prevents objective inquiry is to encounter the same rhetoric in a third concentric armor and again to be charged with heresy, Jewishness, bourgeois tendencies or sexism, etc. At the furthest extreme, where communication has been reduced to the mere stubborn hope of trying to communicate, is the *"credo quia absurdum"* or, in its modern form, "You're just being rational—can't you *feel* the truth?" At this point reason retires from the field, defeated as usual by the will to believe.

One is reminded of a story about Mark Twain and his very fashionable and respectable New England wife, who once tried to cure him of his salty riverboat speech. Mrs. Twain noted every cuss word he used all week long and then woke him Sunday morning and read it all back to him. Twain listened calmly and commented, "You have the words, my dear, but you haven't got the music yet."

Women's liberationists have the words of freedom, equality, human dignity, etc., but they haven't got the music at all. Perhaps this is due to the strongly anal and Germanic influence exerted by Karl Marx. But a young friend of mine, more ingeniously, explains it as the desiderata of the large number of ex-nuns in the women's lib camp who have brought with them the pontifical attitudes of the Roman patriarchy. Nonetheless, the movement is the latest wave of an obvious matrist floodtide and as such destined to play a large role in the next few decades. Let us hope that their shell of dogma will be softened by the noisy splashing of all the other odd and colorful fish swimming about in the free waters of Consciousness III.

Meanwhile, their many books proving that everything worthwhile was invented by women (like the equally excellent tomes by Black liberationists proving that all culture is of Negro origin) at least have the virtue of reminding us of the bias that makes most history texts sound as if all progress is owing to White males. It is now fairly evident that the earliest civilizations around the fertile crescent including the Nile and Euphrates were quite matrist in orientation; some may have been, as Bachofen thought, actually matriarchal, or very close to it. In Babylon, Minoan Crete, early Egypt and Etruscan Italy it appears that the chief deity was the great mother, whose statues, showing her with bared breasts, look remarkably alike whether her local name be Astarte, Ishtar, Isis or Ashtoreth. Women served as judges, priestesses, and, it appears, sometimes as governors. They had all the rights of men, could buy and sell property, engage in business, sign contracts, obtain easy divorce and they were widely considered to have a capacity superior to males in understanding what the goddess wanted and expected of her human children. From all one can gather, they had none of the misanthropy of current women's lib types or of the 19th-Century suffragettes. But why should they have hated men? At that stage, men had apparently never oppressed them.

"History begins with the emergence of men from female rule," Robert Graves has written, with slight exaggeration, in *Mammon and the Black Goddess.* Other historians, without any obvious promale or antifemale bias, still dissent from this broad view and suggest that female rule (in the manner of the male rule we are familiar with in later times) was comparatively rare and that somethihg more like that elusive ideal *sexual equality* seemed to prevail in these early city-states. More remarkable yet, the absence of defenses or other signs of embattlement around these sites has convinced many archeologists that there was no organized warfare, either, and it even seems that slavery itself did not emerge until much later. Will Durant, in *The Story of*

Civilization, quoting a wide sampling of the best archeological evidence, argues persuasively that slavery was created *after* the subjugation of women *and was probably inspired by it*.

In China, curiously, a very similar pattern has been discerned by contemporary scholarship. As Joseph Needham demonstrates in a remarkable six-volume study, *Science and Civilization in China*, the matrist and matriarchal values were preserved in that remarkable text, the *Tao Te Ching*, which praises a figure quite cognate with the great goddess of the Mediterranean area:

> *The Valley Spirit never dies*
> *She is called the Eternal Woman*

and urges all the usual matrist qualities already listed in the table from G. Rattray Taylor. Needham concludes that Chinese culture, before the Chou dynasty, was probably matrilineal and vaguely along the lines of Bachofen's classic matriarchies.

Even after the rise of the patriarchal governing class, women retained most of their traditional rights in Sparta until well within historical times. (Plato, whose *Republic* is considered pro-Spartan propaganda by some historians, included equality for women in his ideal nation, along with such other Spartan institutions as state socialism and lamentable Stalinist censorship of the arts.) Even in Athens, where the wives were reduced to a condition only slightly above that of the slaves, the courtesan class had most of the freedom enjoyed by nonslave males. The Athenians seem to have made the great divorce between sexual love and sexual reproduction that characterizes so many later societies. Their lyric poems are almost always written to courtesans or to young boys; they never seem to have felt romantic about the women who mothered their children.

Throughout these first pagan patriarchies, however, love and sex were still enjoyed and praised as great ornaments of life and inextricably connected with the religious life. The Old Testament, like the popular marriage manuals circa 1920-1960, glorifies sex in marriage as the highest of human joys—and does not neglect the breasts. ("Rejoice with the wife of thy youth . . . Let her breasts satisfy thee at all times," Proverbs 5:18-19.) The Song of Solomon even seems to the literal-minded reader, to be praising fornication—but subtle rabbis and Christian theologians have repeatedly argued that it means quite the opposite of what it appears to say. (Actually, as Robert Graves has noted, the Song looks very much like the chants which accompanied rites of fertility-magic in the old matriarchal religion or in the still-surviving witch cult.)

Early Egyptian religion, it might be noted, was largely sexual in basis and totally concerned with the great mother goddess, variously known as Nuit, Isis, Nu-Isis, etc. Set, the snake god, representing the phallus, was the only male god in those days to achieve a rank roughly equal to the goddess, and only because he was necessary to her divine function as mother of all. (The phallic snake god, which the Egyptians acquired from the Congo region, still survives as an important figure in African and Haitian voodoo. Some cults derived therefrom survive in New Orleans and other parts of the American South.) The Nuit-Isis cults summarized their teaching in the aphorism, revived in our time by Aleister Crowley, "The Khabs is in the Khu." (*Khabs* is the divine or eternal part of humanity; *Khu* is the female genital, origin of our word *cunt*.) It is not "licentiousness" or lack of religion, but the *sexual* basis of their religion, that led the Egyptians to portray their gods in manners shocking to Christian observers: Atum depicted as masturbating, Isis as performing fellatio on her brother-husband Osiris, etc. Another biological depiction of Egyptian origin, Isis nursing the infant Horus, was, however, acceptable to the Christians and some of these statues later found their way into Christian temples, with Isis renamed Mary and Horus changed to Jesus. But by then the meaning had been lost and, as Kenneth Grant says in *The Revival of Magic*, the physical basis of Egyptian religion had become the metaphysics of the Christian and Hellenistic philosophers. That is, insofar as sex was admitted into religion at all, a la the Song of Solomon, it was interpreted as a symbol of spiritual relationship.

Homer's favorite adjective for well-stacked females was *bathykolpos*, which means having ample breasts. Considering that the poet was, according to all ancient sources, blind, he must have learned to appreciate this feature by the braille system, and he evidently enjoyed the experience. Interestingly enough, Homer's values are largely matrist. Some have even suggested that Homeric works are older than usually assumed and actually trace back to a quasi or totally matriarchal period; Samuel Butler, Robert Graves and Elizabeth Gould Davis have all argued that Homer *was* a woman. Certainly, he regarded Achilles and the other military heroes in his poems as somewhat crazy and saved his real affection for Odysseus, who started out as a draft-dodger, went to the war reluctantly and always exercised his celebrated craftiness in trying to find a way to get home to his beloved wife and away from all that pointless bloodshed. It has also been observed that Homer has a special fondness for the old goddesses and tends to treat Zeus as something of a comic character, much like the old crank of later farcical writers. Nevertheless, one modern women's lib writer, Nancy R. McWilliams, has denounced Homer as male chauvinist because Odysseus had all the fun of the Trojan War to himself and didn't invite Penelope to come along and share the butchery.

Whether Homer was a feminist, a male chauvinist or a woman himself (herself?), he (she?) has all the qualities found in recent male poets, who are notoriously antigovernment, antiwar, antiauthority and fond of women, children, nature and sexuality. Obviously, he was in Freudian terms an oral personality. In any case, his values (and those of later poets like Euripides, Sophocles, the anonymous authors of the *Greek Anthology*, etc.) were always compatible with sexual love, however much the relationship between men and women had been rendered problematical by the patriarchal system, which had reduced women to second-class citizens.

With the coming of Christianity, this last vestige of the old matrist system crumbled. Women became less than second-class citizens: They became outcasts, pariahs, tools of Satan to be feared and distrusted. Their breasts became, not a proof that the high gods loved the world and deliberately graced it with beauty, but a sly trap designed by Satan to lure men into fleshly sin. Women were "sacks of dung," according to Origen: they deserved to be treated like untrustworthy slaves, Augustine reasoned, because it was a woman, Eve, who had brought evil into the world; they were inclined to fornicate with devils, according to Sprenger the Inquisitor, because their lusts were too extreme to be satisfied by mortal men. If they were not all witches, the Fathers agreed solemnly, they certainly needed a lot of careful watching.

Considering that the current women's lib writers largely share the antisexual bias of the church fathers, it is curious that they haven't yet revived Augustine's celebrated argument that sexual *feeling* is itself a curse imposed upon us as punishment for the sin of Adam and Eve. According to the bishop's curious reasoning, Adam and Eve, before the Fall, had no sexual feelings at all, and this is the way God intended us to be. To the question, how did they manage to reproduce without sensation, Augustine gave an answer that is worthy of the consideration of ladies like Ti-Grace Atkinson: The organs of generation, he says, moved by "Will Power." His defense of this assertion, probably the most influential flight of reasoning in the whole history of Christian theology, is worth reproducing:

> There are persons who can move their ears, either one at a time, or both together. There are some who, without moving the head, can bring the hair down upon their forehead, and move the whole scalp backwards and forewards at pleasure. Some, by lightly pressing their stomach, bring up an incredible quantity and variety of things they have swallowed, and produce whatever they please, quite whole, as if out of a bag. Some so accurately mimic the voices of birds and beasts and other men that, unless they are seen, the differences canot be told. Some have such command of their bowels that they can break wind continuously at pleasure, so as to produce the effect of singing.*

---

*St. Augustine, *The City of God* (New York: Modern Library, 1950)

All such powers, Augustine claims, are remnants of the capacity of Adam's will to control his entire body; it was with such a mind-over-matter attitude that he and Eve approached sex, and not by the matter-over-mind compulsion that now acts upon us. This charming picture of the sexual, and other, acrobatics in the Garden of Eden was literally believed and any trace of the oral "oceanic feeling" (or any other kind of feeling) in the sex act was a sure sign of sin. Women, who provoked such streamings of energy in males by merely walking on the street, were obviously an extremely dangerous lot and the church took good care to see that any remaining rights they still possessed were quickly and thoroughly removed. In Catholic teaching, a woman was not allowed to divorce a man for beating her regularly, for catching V.D. and transmitting it to her, for bringing his girlfriends to the house and copulating before her eyes, for murder, for insanity, for torturing dogs in front of their children, or for any similar peccadillos. However, if he refused to produce new Catholics in her womb, and did not inform her before they were married that he had no intention of ever having children she could obtain an annulment of the marriage. (Recently the church liberalized the grounds for annulment but only after the Italian government passed its first civil-divorce law over strenuous church opposition.)

To climax the degradation of women, the church has also ruled that in any difficult obstetric situation, where a choice between the life of the mother and the life of the child seems necessary, the doctor must strive to save the unborn. At one time, this teaching extended to those abnormal pregnancies in which the fetus attached to the tube and could not possibly be born alive; even here, the doctor was supposed to try to save it, although it was known that this would cost the life of the mother. (This ruling was only changed in the 1930s.)

In all this, of course, we see Freud's famous "anal personality" carried to its logical extreme. Although oral persons tend to be more "reasonable" in the venacular sense of that word, anal persons worship reason and follow it with remorseless tenacity wherever it leads, although often having an equal capacity to ignore facts, which are after all on the sensory or sensuous level and therefore somewhat suspect. Augustine "proved" that unbaptized infants are unfit for heaven; and, since purgatory and limbo hadn't been invented yet, there was only one place left for them, hell. This is shocking to modern sensibilities, but logic had led Augustine to it and he was not a man to back down from a logical position just because it seemed revolting to normal human feelings. (Feelings, after all, were quite suspect: Adam and Even didn't have any, remember?) Less appalling, but more amusing, Aquinas reasoned that female vultures are fertilized by the wind, not by male vultures. A little observation, of the sort any empiricist would have undertaken before publishing on the subject of vultures, could have prevented such a blunder; but the Fathers were interested in logic, pure logic, and facts were notoriously as illogical as feelings.

Of course, all this was a big pretense. Mr. Murdstone told David Copperfield's mother that her loving kindness was less "rational" than his sadism, and perhaps even believed it himself, but any psychologist will realize that Murdstone happened to enjoy caning little boys on the buttocks, just as many Englishmen (for reasons peculiar to that culture) still do. So, too, it is hard to escape the conclusion that the church fathers enjoyed bullying, torturing and especially *frightening* others, just as the members of the Gestapo did. De Sade in his marvelously frank way analyzed the joy in frightening people as a refined form of the sadistic compulsions that drove him, and many psychoanalysts have noted the same connection. Sermons on hell, to hysterical and fainting congregations, are the psychological equivalent of the racks, whips, iron boots and other overtly sadistic implements of the Holy Inquisition.

The exact number of people killed in the various witch-hunts, crusades, inquisitions, religious wars, etc., is not recorded anywhere, but the total must run into the tens of millions; Homer Smith, an atheist, arrives at a figure of 60,000,000 in his *Man and His Gods*, but he is exaggerating (I hope). One Roman pagan skeptically remarked in the 4th Century A.D., that "there is no wild beast more blood-thirsty than an angry theologian." He had only seen the beginning of the feuds between various sects of Christians; the fury rolled on for another 13 centuries before it began to abate. Of course, Homer Smith's estimate of 60,000,000 victims is obtained by including all the Moslems killed in the several Crusades, and the non-Whites in Africa that the Americans and Oceana wiped out in the process of Christianizing the world. For Europe itself the very careful G. Rattray Taylor arrives at conclusions that make Hitler seem like a piker compared to the churchmen:

> In Spain, Torquemada personally sent 10,220 persons to the stake. . . . Counting those killed for other heresies, the persecutions were responsible for reducing the population of Spain from twenty million to six million in two hundred years. . . . While the well-known estimate of the total death-toll, from Roman times onward, of nine million is probably somewhat too high, it can safely be said that more persons were put to death than were killed in all the European wars fought up to 1914.*

Let us all piously hope that the current mood of tolerance among Christian clergymen is not just a passing fad but that it represents a real break with their tradition

---

*Taylor, *op. cit.*, p. 127

The whole story of the Christian fury and its bloody career is the most distressing tale in history, especially when one remembers that it was all started by a gentle Jewish philosopher who preached love and forgiveness. For our purposes here, the saga of Christian rage illustrates what happens when the repression of the breast and of all oral values is carried to an extreme, and when humorless men reason logically from supernatural and unproven premises to their inevitable conclusions. It was permissible to torture the accused during the witch-hunt mania because in no other way could confessions be obtained in great numbers, though everybody knew that there *must be* great numbers of witches. It was permissible to promise mercy in order to get a confession and then to break the promise by burning the accused at the stake—this was technically no lie because it was truer than ordinary truth. They were being saved from hell, dig, and so they did obtain mercy after all. The earth was the center of the universe because the Bible says so—if telescopes led to different conclusions, they were instruments of the devil. Children of witches should be compelled to watch their mothers burn at the stake—this was the only way to undo the wrong teachings they must have acquired from her.

Does all this sound absurd and hideous to you? In Freudian terms, that is because a great many oral and female values have crept back into our society in the last few centuries. None of this sounded absurd or hideous to the totally anal personalities of men like Augustine and Aquinas and Luther. They were not mad, but coldly logical: They never believed anything that they could not prove in neat, technically precise syllogisms. In the last century, the great mathematician George Boole even proved that the whole methodology of theological logic could be converted into mathematical equations, and every bit of it was sound, internally consistent and valid— once the original assumptions were granted. There was nothing wrong with the brains of the theologians. It was simply that their feelings had atrophied. Later, when we examine Jungian psychology and the Hindu *chakras*, we will see that banishing the goddess archetype had impoverished their sensibility and deadened certain emotional centers which we now assume are innate in all human beings. They are not; all emotions must be exercised and nourished, just like muscles, or they atrophy. The church fathers had entirely disposed of all oral components. The fact that the female breast was banished from European art for several centuries means much more than appears at first glance. That denial of one part of the human body did not "cause" all the other strange behaviors we have chronicled, but it was certainly related to them. When the breast began to stage a comeback, oral values in general began to reappear in European culture.

The first early waves of the new paganism appeared in southern France in the 11th and 12th centuries. Ideas from the Sufis and other Arabian mystics began to find an audience. The sexual doctrines of the Sufis, involving semiritualized intercourse with a beloved female as a specifically religious act, found a particularly enthusiastic support in certain circles—and have gone on to influence the vocabulary of our poets ever since, as Ezra Pound first demonstrated in his *Spirit of Romance* and as Denis de Rougemont has shown at even greater length in *Love in the Western World*.

Overtly, the new spirit began with Eleanor of Aquitaine, whose reputed bare-breasted ride through Jerusalem may or may not have actually happened, but has been widely believed for centuries. This was in many ways a historical turning point, and obviously much more was involved than a mere prank. At the very least, she showed a great sense of appropriate symbolism. Eleanor seems to have cherished both her beauty and her intellect and could not be persuaded by any male priesthood of a male god that she should hide either. (There were no Marxian feminists around to tell her she was making herself a "sex object.") She also seems to have convinced a large segment of the French nobility that love is a greater sport than war and that a man who wrote love poems was more virile than a conqueror of cities. This led to the outbreak of Provencal "troubadour" poetry and the similar verse of minnessingers in South Germany, along with the famous "Courts of Love" in which subtle points of sexual etiquette and romantic decorum were taught. The cynical remark that "love was invented in the 11th Century" is not true, but it is emphatically true that most of our modern ideas about love were invented then, largely due to Eleanor's influence. A song about her—

> *I would give the whole world*
> *From the Red Sea to the Rhine*
> *If the Queen of England tonight*
> *In my bed were mine*

—has survived eight centuries and was recently set to modern music by Carl Orff as part of his popular "Carmina Burana" suite. Actually, after becoming Queen of England Eleanor had a rather wretched old age. Her husband, Henry II, a jealous type, put her under house arrest in a rather lonely castle and firmly ended her personal involvement with the cultural revolution she had instigated.

The revolution, however, continued. The troubadour cult of love became a powerful rival to the church's cult of asceticism and the feudal lords' cult of war; the role of women was steadily elevated—and, as Ernest Jones pointed out in his psychoanalytical history of chess, the role of the queen on the chessboard changed from the weakest to the strongest piece. Strange and radical doctrines were preached by groups like the Cathari, who seem to have practiced the same kind of sexual occultism that Aleister Crowley revived in our own century; the Beguines, independent women who established their own religious order outside the Catholic hierarchy; the Knights Templar, who combined Christianity with Sufi sex-mysticism learned in Jerusalem; and the Brethren of the Common Purse, who practiced voluntary communism. Eventually, the church itself was infected with the new spirit, and the Mother of Jesus, a shadowy and insignificant figure previously, advanced, like the queen in chess, to a dominant position which she still holds in orthodox Catholic countries. As a sort of climax, the greatest of all Catholic poets, Dante, made his childhood sweetheart, Beatrice Portinari, so important in his *Divine Comedy* that she inadvertently overshadows Jesus, God the Father and even the Virgin Mary herself, making this orthodox Christian poem a more exalted personal love-lyric than the deliberately heretical poems in which the French troubadours had blasphemously raised their mistresses and girl friends above the saints. Pierre Vidal was knowingly and flagrantly toying with Sufi heresy when he wrote, "I think I see God when I look upon my lady nude," but Dante got the same effect without realizing quite what he was doing.

Vidal, in fact, can be considered in some ways the model of the new love-oriented man that Eleanor had set up as a contrasting ideal to the warrior or the saint. Half-mad or totally mad, Vidal was nonetheless a master craftsman of rhyme whose verse is still praised for its technical perfection and exuberance. The victim or hero of his own infatuations and the constant scrapes they landed him in, he even on one occasion convinced a whole town that he was a werewolf in order to impress a lady who had turned him down. He not only convinced her and the town, but did such a good job that a panic started and he had to flee. He was hunted with dogs through the hills around Arles (where Van Gogh also went mad and saw cosmic visions seven centuries later—locals attribute such brain fevers to the mistral or "that damned wind" as they call it). Vidal finally was brought to trial for witchcraft and barely escaped being burned at the stake.

Somewhat similar, although less bizarre, was the case of Sordello (hero of a very inaccurate poem by Browning), who persuaded a married lady, Cunniza da Romano, to elope with him. In a Europe still totally Catholic, there was no way of legalizing such a relationship, but Sordello and Cunniza evidently trusted the heretical "Courts of Love" more than the dusty tomes of the church fathers. (Dante, curiously, did not put either of them in his Hell. Sordello is in Purgatory, and, odder yet, Cunniza is in Paradise— because she freed her slaves. A number of scholars have questioned Dante's

orthodoxy.) For Cunniza, Sordello wrote what Ezra Pound among others
has praised as the noblest hyperbole in the history of love poetry:

> *If I see you not, lady with whom I am entranced,*
> *No sight I see is worth the beauty of my thought.*

This kind of thing evidently became commonplace: The troubadour
Cabestan was murdered by a jealous husband who then (possibly
considering himself a figure in Greek tragedy) cut out poor Cabestan's heart
and served it at dinner to his faithless wife, telling her it was a deer's. When
she had enjoyed it, the scoundrel told her what it had actually been, and she
threw herself from a balcony and died on the rocks below. This near-
incredible but true story is dramatized in Pound's *Canto 4* and Richard
Aldington's "The Eaten Heart"; I cannot imagine why Puccini did not make
an opera of it.

Eventually, the Knights Templar were suppressed by the Inquisition (123
of them were burned at the stake after being tortured into confessing a long
string of abominations which most historians regard as fictitious) and the
Albigensian Crusade was launched—ostensibly against the sexually permissive
Cathari sect, but once rolling, decimating the population of southern France
in what Kenneth Rexroth has bitterly called "the worst actrocity in history,
before the invention of Progress." The Templars did not revive until the
18th Century and the Cathari only came back in the 1920s. The values of
papist patriarchy reconquered all Europe until the Protestant schism and
retains Southern Europe to this day.

Romantic poetry with its matrist and oral values survived and actually
prevailed. Geoffrey Chaucer imported the ideology to England with his
Knight's Tale and some of his shorter rondels; by Elizabethan times this had
virtually become the *whole* of poetry. Thus, Shakespeare could write about
anything that struck his imagination when he was writing for the stage, but
as soon as he started writing poetry for the printed page, he fell inevitably
into the language, the themes, the traditional conceits and the entire
apparatus of troubadour love-mysticism. So great was Shakespeare's
influence, in turn, that when modern poets finally began writing about
other subjects around 1910, established opinion was shocked and it was said
that such material was "unpoetic"—as if Homer's battles, Ovid's mysticism,
Juvenal's indignation, Villon's earthiness, Lucretius's rationalism, the *Greek
Anthology*'s cynicism, Piers Plowman's social protest, etc., had never existed
and *only* the troubadour love-mystique had ever been poetry.

Considering how anal our culture had largely been, except for the matrist
interlude of Eleanor and her circle, it is astonishing to realize that (just like

our religious progenitor, Jesus) our most influential poet-dramatist, Shakespeare, was a distinctly oral type. A fairly consistent imagery of interrelated themes of sucking and chewing runs through all the plays and sonnets and has helped scholars determine that contrary to more romantic theories they are all the work of one person. (Examples: "Sucking the honey of his vows"—*Hamlet*; "If music be the food of love, play on"—*Twelfth Night*; "Where the bee sucks, there suck I"—*The Tempest*; "What a candy deal of courtesy . . . "—*Henry IV, Part One*.) Oscar Wilde's theory that the bard was homosexual, or bisexual, is not as well-established as gay liberation writers like to think—Shakespeare's actual imagery is virtually always heterosexual, as Eric Partridge demonstrates in *Shakespeare's Bawdy* by simply listing all the sexual references in the complete works. But, like Jesus, he had so strong a tender ("feminine") component that people who identify masculinity with brutality are naturally inclined to think he was queer. The nicknames recorded by his contemporaries—"Sweet Will" and "Gentle Will"—indicate rather clearly that this bearded, bald-headed, chronically impoverished, socially unacceptable and runt-sized son of a small-town butcher was much closer, in type, to Allen Ginsberg than to Ernest Hemingway. Nevertheless, he adored the ladies—literally—and it seems more than a few of them adored him in return. It is apt that Venus is the aggressive seducer of Adonis in his long poem on that legend; men of this type very often "play the waiting game" (as Kurt Weill called it in *September Song*) and allow the woman to make the advances. (If they are chess players, they will favor the "soft" Reti or Alekhine openings instead of the aggressive center games.) James Joyce even argued, on the basis of the sexual imagery in the plays, that Anne Hathaway had seduced Shakespeare; certainly, theirs was a slightly forced wedding, the first child being born six months after the marriage ceremony.

The bard's romanticism, which no English or American poet has ever managed to escape catching to some degree, comes right out of Eleanor's and Pierre Vidal's Sufi-influenced sexual mysticism, as we have seen. Another influence, as Francis Yates has argued plausibly in *Giordano Bruno and the Hermetic Tradition*, was the arch-heretic Bruno of Nola, burned at the stake in Rome in 1600. Bruno seems to have been the model for Berowne in Shakespeare's *Love's Labour's Lost*. He was in England around 1583-85 and his sonnet sequence, *De gli eroici furori*, published at Oxford in 1585, is a celebration of sexual love with interspersed prose passages relating these poems to the mystic quest for Unity (Freud's "oceanic experience"). Berowne's great speech in *Love's Labour's Lost*—

> For valour is not Love a Hercules
> Still climbing trees in the Hesperides?
> Subtle as Sphinx, as sweet and musical

As bright Apollo's lute, strung with his hair;
And when Love speaks, the voice of all the gods
Make heaven drowsy with the harmony

—is not mere pretty language, as such things usually are in Shakespeare's countless imitators. It is a heretical statement, following Bruno's sonnets and the tradition of Eleanor of Aquitaine, boldly declaring the path of the lover superior to that of the soldier or the ascetic. As Francis Yates suggests, it is even possible that Prospero the Magician in *The Tempest* is also modeled on Bruno's magico-Hermetic practices, which involved quite a bit of the old Cathari-Templar-troubadour tradition of sexual occultism.

Ezra Pound, the modern poet who has given the most careful attention to historical research on the evolution of these notions, explains in somewhat guarded language (he was writing for the prudish English public in 1933):

> They [the troubadours] are opposed to a form of stupidity not limited to Europe, that is, idiotic asceticism and a belief that the body is evil. . . .
> The senses at first seem to project a few yards beyond the body . . . [in] a decent climate where a man leaves his nerve-set open, or allows it to tune in to its ambience, rather than struggling, as a northern race has to for self-preservation, to guard the body from assaults of weather. . . .
> He declines, after a time, to limit reception to his solar plexus. The whole thing has nothing to do with taboos and bigotries. It is more than the simple athleticism of *mens sana in corpore sano*. The concept of the body as perfect instrument of the increasing intelligence pervades. . . .
> We appear to have lost the radiant world where one thought cuts through another with clean edge, a world of moving energies . . . *magnetisisms that take form, that are seen, or that border the visible*, the matter of Dante's paradiso, the glass under water, the form that seems a form seen in a mirror, those realities perceptible to the sense . . . untouched by the two maladies, the Hebrew disease, the Hindoo disease, fanaticisms and excess that produce Savonarola. . . . *

John Donne, who may have influenced English romantic poetry almost as much as Shakespeare, attended Oxford while Bruno was lecturing there and seems to have picked up some of the Nolan's doctrines. The fact that Donne's poems often have double and triple meanings, concealed jokes and hidden symbolism is a critical commonplace, but this has not usually been

---

Literary Essays of Ezra Pound (New York: New Directions, n.d.) In *The Spirit of Romance*, with more clarity but equal caution, Pound grants that what was involved was a yoga utilizing "the opposite polarities of male and female." De Rougemont in *Love in the Western World* leaves no doubt that it was classic Tantric yoga, prolonging the sex act into a trance in which the "souls" or "magnetisms" are, to some degree, visible.

related to the use of similar red herrings by the "Hermeticists" like Bruno who always sought to conceal their sexual teachings from the Holy Inquisition by such devices. In this connection, Donne's *The Ecstasy* is notable as a poem that has almost always been misunderstood by scholarly commentators. Here are the key stanzas, with emphasis added by me in the form of italics:

> Where, like a pillow on a bed,
>   A pregnant bank swell'd up to rest
> The violet's reclining head,
>   *Sat we two*, one another's best.
> So t' intergraft our hands, as yet
>   Was all the means to make us one,
> *And pictures on our eyes to get*
>   *Was all our propagation.*
>
> As 'twixt two equal armies fate
>   Suspends uncertain victory,
> Our souls, which to advance their state
>   Were gone out, hung 'twixt her and me.
>
> And whilst our souls negotiate there
>   We *like sepulchral statues* lay;
> *Allday the same our postures were*
>   And we said nothing all the day.

This is generally described as an exemplar of "Platonic love," but it is almost certainly nothing of the kind. Readers unaware of the Tantric-Sufi tradition in Tibet, India and the Near East and its transmission through the Templar-troubadour cult and the various "alchemists" and Illuminati assume that if Donne and his lady *"sat"* together they must have been without sexual contact. Actually—see any Tibetan painting of the *yabyum* position, as it is called—sitting in each other's laps in the double-lotus position is basic to all sexual yoga. According to some writers there are neurological reasons for this—it allegedly diverts the sexual energy or bioelectricity from the central nervous system and sends it into the autonomic (involuntary) system—but, from a Freudian point of view, it restores the male to the *purely passive* role of the infant at the breast and thus represents the oralization of the genital embrace. Not unexpectedly, the purpose of this is to recapture Freud's "oceanic experience" or the "trance of Unity" as mystics call it. In some traditions, influenced by Gnostic magic ideas, the couple stares into each other's eyes; cf. Donne's "and pictures in our eyes to get / Was all our propagation." This method is also a form of birth control, since it allows the male to experience orgasm without ejaculation.

It was used for contraception in the anarcho-communist "free love" commune of the Bible Perfectionists of the famous Oneida Colony in upstate New York, circa 1840-1870. Contemporary Tantric teachers tell pupils to imitate the famous statues of the Black Temple near Benares—the one with the erotic carvings—and seek a similar immobility; cf. Donne's "We like sepulchral statues lay." This position can be continued far longer than any other sexual pastime, and Baba Ram Dass may have been using it on the famous occasion when, under LSD, he remained in sexual ecstasy for hours and hours; cf. Donne's "All day the same our postures were."

As for Donne's claim about the souls leaving the bodies—well, ask anyone who has mastered this art. You will hear even more astonishing claims. Dr. Bergler's notion that the infant thinks the mother's breast is part of his own body may not be so fanciful, after all.*

It is remarkable that this poem has been mistaken for some ethereal or Platonic idealism. Donne's other poetry of that period is explicitly bawdy† and even here, in *The Ecstasy* itself, he ends by explicitly rejecting traditional spiritualization of the love relationship, saying:

> Love's mysteries in souls do grow,
> *But yet the body is his book.*
>   [Italics mine]

Some readers, acknowledging that there is abundant evidence of a secret sexual-occult tradition in Europe from the Templars onward, will yet question that the Tibetan double-lotus sitting position was part of this. If Donne is not explicit enough, here is his contemporary, the "alchemist" Thomas Vaughan, hinting at the same secret teaching in his *Coelum Terrae* (1650) under the guise of discussing the "First Matter" or "Philosopher's Stone":

---

*See the accounts of people who under the influence of marijuana could not tell what was their own body and what was their lover's, in my *Sex and Drugs* (Falcon Press, 1987)

†Here are a few tender verses from his *To His Mistress Going To Bed*:

Your gown's going off, such beauteous state reveals
As when as when from flow'ry meads the hill's shadow steals.
Off with your wiry coronet and show
The hairy diadem which on you doth grow.

License my roving hands and let them go
Behind, before, above, between, below.

To teach thee, I am naked first. Why then
What need'st thou have more covering than a man?

The true furnace [where the "Matter" is "bathed"—R.A.W.] is a little simple shell; thou mayest easily carry it in one of thy hands. . . . As for the work itself, it is in no way troublesome; a lady may . . . attend this philosophy without disturbing her fancy. For my part, I think women are fitter for it than men, for in such things they are more neat and patient, being used to the small chemistry of sack-possets and other finical sugar-sops. . . .

But I had almost forgot to tell thee that which is all in all, and it is the greatest difficulty in all the art—namely, the fire. . . . The proportion and regimen of it is very scrupulous, but the best rule to know it by is that of the Synod: "Let not the bird fly before the fowler." *Make it sit while you give fire*, and then you are sure of your prey. For a close I must tell thee that the philosophers call this fire their bath, but it is a bath of Nature, not an artificial one; for it is not of any kind of water. . . . In a word, without this bath nothing in the world is generated. . . . Our Matter is a most delicate substance and tender, like the animal sperm, for it is almost a living thing. Nay, in very truth, it hath some small portion of life. . . .

"Let him who is not familiar with Proteus have recourse to Pan."*

This is intended to baffle the ordinary reader, and it certainly succeeds. The "bird" is the sperm, which, when this method is successful, is deflected into the bladder rather than ejaculated (although Vaughan, like Bruno and the Oriental Tantrists, probably believed that it went up the spinal cord to the brain). The "work" is copulation without motion, in the sitting position. The confusing "fire" which is also a "bath" is the trance which results. The "matter" is again the sperm—note how neatly Vaughan conceals and reveals this. The reference to Proteus, god of transformations, and Pan, god of sexuality, is another hint. If the reader has not identified the "true furnace," let him consult Donne's *Love's Alchemy*, where he will find:

> And as no chemic yet th'elixir got
> But glorifies his pregnant pot.

With this much background, the reader should now be able to grasp that the "extravagant metaphors" in love poets like Vidal, Sordello, Chaucer, Shakespeare, Donne, etc., are often not a matter of flattering the lady but serious statements of a philosophy which runs directly counter to the basic assumptions of our anal-patriarchal culture. Specifically, the repeated, perfectly clear identifications of the poet's mistress with a goddess are part of the mental set, or ritual, connected with this cult. Tibetan teachers train disciples of Tantra to think of the female partner as being literally, not metaphorically, the goddess Shakti, divine partner of Shiva. The Sufis,

---

*A.E. Waite, ed., *The Works of Thomas Vaughan, Mystic and Alchemist* (New Hyde Park: University Books, 1968)

working within the monotheistic patriarchy of Islam, could not emulate this, but made her an angel communicating between Allah and man. The witch covens made her the great mother goddess. Aleister Crowley's secret teachings, in our own century, instructed his pupils to envision her as the Egyptian star-goddess, Nuit.

When anthropologist Weston La Barre says, "Mothers make magicians; fathers, gods," he means that the magic or shamanistic trance is a return to the bliss at the breast of the all-giving mother, while religion is an anal propitiation of a fearful god who is an enlarged portrait of the punishing father. These distinctions do not always remain sharp—Tantra managed to get incorporated into the patrist framework of Hinduism, and Sufi sex-magic into the equally patrist Moslem faith of Allah. In the West, however, patriarchy became extreme; Jehovah would bode no rivals, least of all a goddess equal to himself, and the magic-matriarchal-oral cults were driven underground, masqueraded as pseudo-sciences like alchemy, or came forth only in the form of poetry. Even so, patriarchy is so nervous of rivals in the West that the poet has come under considerable suspicion at many times, is often thought to be "queer" in one sense or another and, in the most anal cultures, often seems to be deliberately ignored or starved into submission. (If he is kind enough to die young, he is then forgiven and becomes a kind of secular Christ or martyr, as in the Dylan Thomas cult.) In England, the prejudice is so bad, Robert Graves notes in *The White Goddess*, that poets, when forced to identify themselves—on government forms or in courtrooms, say—will almost always use such terms as "teacher," "novelist," "historian" or whatever else they happen to be besides poets.

In *Mammon and the Black Goddess*, Graves nicely summarizes the relationship between poetry and the old oral cults of magic and matriarchy:

> The poet is, on the whole, anti-authoritarian, agoraphobic and intuitive rather than intellectual; but his judgments are coherent. Symptoms of the trance in which poetic composition occurs differ greatly from those of an induced mediumistic trance; though both seem directed by an external power. In a poetic trance, which happens no more predictably than a migraine or an epileptic fit, this power is traditionally identified with the ancient Muse-goddess. . . .
>
> Almost every poet has a personal Muse, a relationship first introduced into Europe from Sufi sources in Persia and Arabia during the early Middle Ages.

Poetry and magic, then, are based on a belief that thought can create its own reality—which Sir James Frazer in *The Golden Bough* called the theory of "the omnipotence of thought" and which Freud, in his comment on Frazer's anthropological investigations in *Totem and Taboo*, traced back to the child's power, with an outcry of desire, to make the missing mother mysteriously appear again and offer the all-providing breast. It is no accident, then, that so many poems, from the *Odyssey* right up to Joyce's great prose-poem, *Finnegans Wake*, contain magical "invocations" summoning the goddess to appear at once.

We can now see that there might have been more than a joke in the famous exploit of Eleanor's father, Guillaume of Aquitaine, who built a private brothel or harem on his land in the exact architectural style of contemporary convents. The "convents" of the old matriarchal religions, of course, had been devoted to what is alternately called hierogamy or sacred prostitution or sex magic; perhaps Guillaume had been consciously trying to revive that. And when Eleanor herself rode through Jerusalem with bared breasts, she also may have been prompted by more than high spirits. It is traditional in many schools of initiation to require some such public act, which is thought to have magical significance and also separates one sharply from the obedient servants of the existing establishment. parading those emblems of matriarchal fertility-worship through the Holy Land of the world's three strongest patriarchal religions—Judaism, Christianity and Islam—may have been an act of fealty to the old mother goddess and an invocation attempting to restore her worship.

If so, it has only been partially successful . . . thus far.

The taboo on showing the breast is certainly odd if one considers it in relation to the attractive features of other animals. One does not read of peacocks who are ashamed of their gorgeous tail-feathers, of goldfish hiding their lovely fiery-yellow markings, of lionesses having squeamish feelings about their brutal beauty. Yet a woman of today (unless she is a professional topless dancer) might still go through the processes which the psychologist Flugel described in 1930:

> A woman may, for example, refrain from going to a dance in a very *decollete* dress: (a) Because, although she thinks it becomes her and she experiences a real gratification at the sight and feeling of her bare upper body, she yet experiences a sense of shame and embarrassment at the mere fact that she should do so. The modest impulse is here directed against desire. . . . (b) Because, although she experiences none of the scruples just mentioned and freely enjoys the sight of herself in her mirror, she yet fears that she may unduly stimulate sexual desire in per prospective partners; in this case the modesty is still directed against desire, but now refers to feelings in others rather than to feelings in the self. (c) Because, on putting on the dress, she is immediately overcome by a feeling of revulsion at her own image. . . . Modesty here works against disgust aroused in her own mind. . . . (d) Because, although she may be pleased at the effect of the low-cut dress, she thinks of the shock that her appearance in it will cause to certain puritanically minded friends. . . . In this case, modesty is directed against disgust . . . in others rather than feelings in herself.*

---

*J.C. Flugel, *The Psychology of Clothes* (New York: International Universities Press, 1930)

Against this is the primordial desire to appear beautiful and fashionable.

Worse yet, the picture grows still more complex if the lady is married, for now she will consider her husband's wishes in the matter, as Flugel goes on to point out. The husband may wish her to dress daringly if he is relatively free of neurotic jealously and/or enjoys Veblen's "conspicuous consumption." Flaunting her breasts, then, is *his* way of showing other men what a prize he has captured. On the other hand, he may fear this as leading to dangerous competition. Judging by the way Arab women have traditionally been forced to dress, Arab men are particularly paranoid about such possibilities. In addition to these possible reactions, there is the complexity of "moral" squeamishness or its absence, this time in *his* head. Finally, there is the question of whether the lady is in a mood this particular night to please her husband or to annoy him. . . .

And to cap off this pyramid of absurdities, the lady also has to stop and read the latest Supreme Court ruling before finally deciding. Nine old men she's never met personally will sit in solemn conclave and announce how many inches of her are decent this year and how many inches are diabolic and obscene. We can only conclude, as Flugel did, that attitudes toward clothing and the body are entirely dominated by irrationality.

Or as Mark Twain said: "Man is a fool, and woman, for tolerating him, is a damned fool."

JAZZ HAIKU

John Coltrane

In the enormous complexity
  of his mind
he seeks the simplicity of a soul

MJQ

Milt Jackson's vibes like a waterfall.
Rain suddenly splashes my window.

Satchmo

Surrounded by love
this black man
ain't go no real friend but his music

HOW TO READ /
HOW TO THINK

The literary reader will recognize a certain influence of Ezra Pound's *How to Read* and *ABC of Reading* on the following Socratic (and sardonic) set or rhetorical questions. There is also, less obviously, a strong influence of Korzybski's *Science and Sanity* and my first 125 acid trips.

I have added a postscript in which a few new insults are added to the injury already inflicted on the literal-minded reader.

"The fear of the word is the beginning of reading."
—Hugh Kenner, *Joyce's Voices*

Some say that reading consists in such elementary tasks as assembling the letters "c" "a" and "t" and forming the image of a certain furry quadruped that says "meow." Similarly, some imagine that thinking consists of observing an event, pinning a label on it ("communism," "sexism," "good honest Americanism" or whatever) and then reacting to the event as if it were the label.

To say that these mechanical processes do not contain true reading or true thinking will be found profoundly insulting to those people who do not know any other modes of thinking or reading.

Since I do not wish to insult anybody, and since simple-minded people are easily insulted, I will try to avoid flat statements in this epistle, and will merely ask some provocative questions.

Henry James's *The Turn of the Screw* appears, to those who regard reading as defined above, to "be" an ordinary, if somewhat nasty, ghost-story. It "is" about a governess who discovers that the two children in her care are being haunted and vexed by ghosts who are not only vicious but perverse (probably child molesters).

To those who think reading/thinking requires *action* or *work*, a second story appears: the novel then concerns a hysterical governess, sexually repressed, who projects her own illusions outward and manages, without intending it, to frighten one of the children to death. The "ghosts" are "in" her head.

If reading does not require thought and work, the second interpretation "is" just pretentious nonsense invented by critics after James published his book. If reading/thinking does require work, how do we decide which interpretation is correct? And what does "correct" mean in this context?

Could James have intended both possible meanings?

Yeats's great poem on the 1916 Irish rebellion contains the line, "A terrible beauty is born." Stress "terrible" when reading it aloud; then stress "beauty." Which meaning did Yeats intend? Or did he intend both?

Blake wrote, "May God us keep / From single vision & Newton's sleep." Leaving aside for the moment his animus against Newtonian mechanics, could "single vision" refer to what I have been calling mechanical reading and mechanical thinking?

What the hell did Gurdjieff mean by his remarkable statement, "Life is real then only when I am"? Is there any sense left if one modifies it to, "A book is alive then only when the reader is"?

Husserl disagreed with traditional philosophy (and anticipated modern neurology) in denying that we passively "receive" impressions. He insisted on an intentionality of consciousness, in which we vary from intense alertness, to moderate alertness, to weak alertness, to the total passivity that Occidental philosophers regard as normal.

Do we "see" more in life when we are intensely alert? Do we see more in books and art when we are intensely alert? Is normal mechanical reading a species of what mystics call dreaming or sleep-walking?

□ □ □

"To ascribe predicates to a people is always dangerous."
—Nietzsche, unpublished note, 1873

Racism, sexism and stupid prejudice in general consist, in logical terms, of ascribing predicates to groups. This takes the form, *All k are x*. **K** represents a class or set or group and **x** is the predicate quality (e.g., "crooked," "stupid," "great sense of rhythm," "wise," "honest" or whatever).

According to Korzybski (*Science and Sanity*) there is one field, and one field only, in which it is legitimate to ascribe predicates to groups—namely, in pure mathematics. This is legitimate because the groups or sets of pure math are purely abstract and created by definition. *All k are x*, in a mathematical context, because **k** and **x** are defined that way, and because they do not exist outside of pure thought.

Once one leaves pure mathematics, the ascription of predicates to groups always introduces fallacy. Remarks about "all Jews," "all Blacks," "all women," "all men," "all plumbers," etc. are fallacies because the world consists of a phalanx of individuals. In Korzybski's handy notation, we never meet the groups; what we encounter are

woman$_1$ woman$_2$ woman$_3$ etc.

plumber$_1$ plumber$_2$ plumber$_3$ etc.

When "mystics" etc. talk about ordinary consciousness as "sleep," "dream," "illusion," etc., are they talking about something very esoteric that only other mystics can understand? Or are they talking about the extent to which normal consciousness ("mechanical consciousness" in my sense) relates to fictitious predicates attached to groups and ignores (does not perceive) person$_1$ person$_2$, etc.?

Is there some connection between "waking up" in the mystic sense, and learning to read (or to see paintings, say) in an alert, non-mechanical way?

One Zen master, when asked what Zen "is," always replied with the single word, "Attention." What the hell did he mean?

Scrutinize the following propositions:

"Usury is a crime committed against all Aryans by all Jews." —A. Hitler.

"[Rape] is nothing more or less than a conscious process of intimidation by which *all men* keep *all women* in a state of fear." —S. Brownmiller. [Italics in the original.]

To what extent do these propositions ascribe predicates to groups? To what extent do they represent "sleep," which ignores (does not perceive) e.g. the existential differences between Jew$_1$ Jew$_2$, etc. man$_1$ man$_2$, etc.?

In San Francisco I read a review of John Huston's recent movie, *Victory*, which described it as "exciting." In the *Irish Tribune* yesterday I read another review which described it as "dull." Is the excitement or dullness "in" the movie, or was it in the nervous systems of the reviewers?

Colin Wilson argues that when we say, "Life is boring and meaningless," it means that we are boring and meaningless. Can there be any truth in this?

□ □ □

"Swift disoriented his readers by confusing the genre signals: critical tradition has taught us to call Gulliver's Travels *and* A Modest Proposal *'satires,' but new readers were led to think the former a travel-book, the latter a projector's pamphlet, and were increasingly vexed as they turned the pages and found these conventions less and less helpful, which was part of what Swift intended."*

—Hugh Kenner, *A Colder Eye*

The Turn of the Screw was not the first book in which the narrator's "honesty" is problematical. There were earlier examples—most blatantly Poe's story "The Tell-Tale Heart," in which the narrator insists repeatedly that he is not mad, but the story makes most sense if we assume he "is" mad. How far "is" it permissible to carry this device? If it requires work and re-reading etc. before the reader finds the clues that reveal the narrator is (consciously or unconsciously) deceptive, is that "unfair" to the reader? Is it unfair to try to provoke the reader to work and thought? Should all books be for the lazy?

("You damned sadist: you're trying to force your readers to think." —e.e. cummings to Ezra Pound.)

When a critic says a book, or a film, or any art work "is" dull, what does this "is" mean? Does it mean—

(a) "is" in the critic's nervous system. (A relative and neurologically accurate statement, leaving open the possibility that it "is" something else in another nervous system.)

(b) "is" in the Mind of God, and therefore absolutely true.

(c) "is" in the Platonic world of Ideas?

Since critics appear notoriously dogmatic and pugnacious, it *seems* that meaning (a)—admitting relativity—is not what the mean. Is criticism then a form of theology (the only other field that claims access to "the mind of God"?) Or are we to take it that they "are" all Platonists?

If the "is" in criticism is only a convention, a short-hand, why do critics act as if they mean is-in-the-mind-of-God when challenged?

Consider:

I. It smells bad.

II. It smells bad *to me*.

Which of those appears more in accord with modern science? Which appears more in accord with medieval metaphysics (Aristotelian-Platonic ideas)?

Would you regard it as a monstrous satirical exaggeration on my part, or a mere statement of anthropological fact, if I assert that art criticism is the only place in the modern world, outside the Vatican, where medieval metaphysics (the Aristotelian absolute "is") still flourishes?

All recent psychotherapy places great emphasis on "taking responsibility." Can this be done, at all, if meanings are "outside" and have absolute is-ness?

Is "responsibility" possible at all, before one realizes that meaning is not in events but in the evaluations of the nervous system?

Van Gogh could see 28 shades of black. Why?

□ □ □

"The greatest progress that human race has made lies in learning how to make correct inferences."

—Nietzsche, *Human, All-Too-Human*

I used to own what was called The Uncritical Inference Test; I used it in all my seminars. Somewhere I lost it, and I don't know where to buy another one.

In this test, you see one inference at a time, and cannot go back and correct the early ones. It always astounds me how many uncritical or incorrect inferences are made by even allegedly educated people.

Adapting from memory, here is part of one section of that Test: A doctor's car is parked in front of 2 Elm Street. Which of the following inferences are correct?

1) Somebody is ill in 2 Elm Street. 2) The doctor lives at 2 Elm Street. 3) The doctor parked there before he could find a better parking place. 4) The doctor, whoever he or she is, is somewhere in the neighborhood. 5) Somebody stole the doctor's car and dumped it there.

It is amazing how many people will check all of these, even though they wish they could go back and uncheck the earlier ones. Of course, all the inferences are uncritical; one cannot be sure of anything, except that the car is parked there.

In *As I Lay Dying* (Faulkner) black people are always referred to as "niggers." A) This proves Faulkner was a racist. B) This proves Faulkner was being accurate in representing the language of his narrators (Mississippi poor whites). In *The Town* (Faulkner) both "nigger" and "Negro" appear. A) Faulkner was recovering from his racism. B) Faulkner was indicating different speech patterns of different classes in Mississippi. (Are these alternative inferences certain or only more-or-less probable?) (Both books were written before "Black" became fashionable.)

It is a well-known idea, not just among "mystics," but among modern psychologists, that the sad person lives in a sad world, the angry person in an angry world, etc. Then the sad person reads sad books and the angry person reads angry books? Even if those books seem funny and optimistic, say, to other readers?

"This book is a mirror. When a monkey looks in, no philosopher looks out." —Lichtenstein. Does that refer to one book only, or to all books?

To quote Gurdjieff again, "Life is real then only when I am." If normal (mechanical) consciousness consists largely of uncritical inferences, projections, glandular-emotional reactions etc. then what it perceives, in art or in life, will have many traits of dream, will it not? If consciousness is intentional (Husserl), then *making an effort to perceive* will make both oneself and the surround more vivid, more meaningful, more "real," perhaps?

"Who is the Master who makes the grass green?" (Zen *koan*)

If you look at your watch, realize you still don't know the time, and look again, were you strictly speaking *awake* the first time you looked?

Ezra Pound in one of the later Cantos writes:

> awareness restful & fake is fatiguing

What the devil does that mean? Does it connect with my topic here?

□ □ □

" . . . *to be truly human demands a real effort of will rather than our usual vague assumption of 'mutual concern.'* "

—Colin Wilson, Criminal History of Mankind

Everybody who has taken a modern literature course, even if they've never read Joyce, knows that the last word of *Ulysses* is "yes" and that the whole book leads up to that affirmation. The first word of *Ulysses* happens to be "stately," which contains "yes" backwards (StatElY). Is this an accident? If not an accident, why did Joyce do it?

Hamlet's first three speeches (short ones, by the way) each contain a pun. Was Shakespeare just feeling whimsical when he wrote that, or is it a clue to Hamlet's problems and the problem of the play itself?

St. John's *Revelations*, St. Augustine's *City of God*, Crowley's *Magick in Theory and Practise*, among others, all have 22 chapters. Is this an accident? If not an accident, what does it indicate? (Why does the first sentence of *Ulysses* have 22 words, beginning with "stately" and ending with "crossed"?)

Krishnamurti distinguishes between *thinking*, an active process, and *thought*, the result of past thinking filed away in the memory of the brain, or in a library or computer, etc. *Thought* contains all the wisdom, and much of the folly, of the past; it's a great labor-saving device. Why does Krishnamurti regard *thought* as profoundly dangerous and the enemy of *thinking*?

If a writer tries to provoke *thinking*, is this only because of "damned sadism" (cummings' joke) or is it an attempt to liberate readers from the mechanical repetition of dead thoughts?

"Is" this an essay on literature and semantics, or "is" it an essay on the most common fallacies of political thought?

Consider the following sets of statements:

Column I	Column II
He is an anti-semite.	He seems like an anti-semite to me.
She is a sexist.	She seems like a sexist to me.
They are fanatics.	They seem like fanatics to me.

Which column implies the medieval Aristotelian metaphysics (the "essence" theory) and which implies modern neurology and psychology (perception as the judgmental ACT of a perceiver)?

HOW TO READ / HOW TO THINK

(Afterwords)

This rather acerbic essay was originally written for Bob Shea's little magazine, *No Governor*. It is so short because *No Governor* is a very tiny magazine and cannot print long pieces; it is so mordant because I wrote it at a time when I was beginning to suspect that the younger generation of Americans are so ill-educated that one virtually has to write in baby-talk before they can understand anything one is saying. Despite the brevity and acidity (or perhaps because of them?) I rather like this piece. It seems to say exactly what I wanted to say in a marvelously terse manner. Perhaps I would write better if I was always compelled to be brief and always mildly annoyed and distracted by the suspicion that a large percentage of potential readers badly need a basic literacy course.

One of the irritations that provoked this piece in the first place was certain neo-pagans in California who regularly speak about Christians in the way that Hitler used to speak about Jews. When I tried to explain to some of them that hating Christians as an undifferentiated mass was as illogical as hating Jews as an undifferentiated mass, they couldn't understand me. They knew that anti-semitism was unfashionable, but anti-Christianity is not unfashionable yet (being comparatively rare) and that is about as deep as their understanding goes. They never harbor unfashionable prejudices, but they also never suspect that prejudices *per se* might be rather stupid.

Of course, this essay produced no "miracle cures." It was reprinted in another little magazine called *Golden APA* and my polemic against the Aristotelian "is" of identity went entirely over the head of one contributor to that journal, who wrote a few issues later that the Irish "are" a disgusting people. That seemed amusing to me, in a way; or, at least, I preferred to be amused rather than becoming irritated again. As John Adams said somewhere, in considering the extent of human stupidity, one must either laugh or cry, and it is more salubrious to laugh.

SHRAPNEL

James Joyce died on 13 January 1941 and was buried in the section of Flutern cemetery that borders the lion house in the adjoining *Tiergarten* [zoo]. Nora said later that he loved to listen to the lions roar when alive and she hoped he could still hear them.

the lion in the teargarten remembers . . .
FW, page 75

For the Cherrub Cat is a term in the
Angel Tiger
Christopher Smart, *Jubilate Agno*

Schroedinger's Cat is dead and alive at the same time, just like Tim Finnegan.

Brother Lion in the ballad of the Signifying Monkey receives what are the ultimate insults and threats in Macho society: "He says he fucked your mammy and your auntie, too / And if you ain't careful, he's gonna fuck you."

In *FW*, the ambiguous Marcus Lyons combines the evangelist Mark, the lion in Ezekial's vision, the element of fire, King Mark who is cuckolded by Tristan, and Mark Twain who wrote of Finn, again. Four seagulls torment poor Mark with reports on his wife's infidelities in chapter four of book two, and these seagulls utter "three quarks" which later found their way into quantum mechanics.

Leopold Bloom in *Ulysses* also seems to have a lion in his name (Leo) and Joyce was born in a house called Leoville, which had two lions on the gatepost.

Although Joyce could not have foreseen it, a recent biographical novel about Brian Boru is called *LION OF IRELAND*.

Neither Bloom nor Earwicker own dogs, but they each own a cat.

Henry James, who started writing relativistic novels even before Joyce (and even before Einstein!) seems to be mentioned in *FW* a few times—but everybody with a "James" in his name was considered worthy of mention by Joyce. ("I don't know if he was in love with me or my name," James Stephens remarked once.) "Enwreak us wrecks" on *FW* page 546 seems to combine Henry James, Henry II, and Oedipu Rex. Henry II or in the Latin of his own day *Enricus Rex* authorized the first British invation of Ireland on 23 August 1170, which makes another interesting coincidence: foreign dominion of Ireland (by the Danes) ended on 23 April 1014 with Brian Boru's victory at Clontarf and foreign dominion of Ireland (by the British) began again on 23 August 1170.

Henry II was the husband of Eleanor of Acquitaine, whose contributions to European paganism and occultism are a major theme in Pound's *Cantos*. Pound was a friend of both Henry James and James Joyce.

Because of Pound's help in getting *Ulysses* published, Joyce decided there was profound occult meaning in the fact that Pound's father was named Homer.

It is only a coincidence, of course, that there is a celebrated film about the troubled marriage of Henry II and Eleanor, and that this movie is called *The Lion in Winter*.

It is also only a coincidence, of course, of course, that their most famous son was Richard the Lion-Hearted.

Why do you live in Ireland, Dr. Wilson?

Romantic Ireland's dead and gone,
It's with O'Leary in his grave

W.B. Yeats

Romantic Ireland is not dead:
It whispers legends in my head.
Pearse's Ireland, born in pain,
Lives in Ballinspittle, and Sinn Fein;
Swift "served human liberty"   5
With the sword of mockery
And in an ecstasy of rage
Wrote many an amusing page
Until his art, his great heart, broke
In one final mordant joke: 10
Looking at the Magazine
He saw what Buddha would have seen;
Fanatic Ireland, in spite of Joyce,
Speaks in every Ulster voice.
Yeats looked for faeries in the hills;   15

Joyce contemplated unpaid bills;
Yeats, the realist, wrote in fire
The alchemical heart's desire;
Joyce, the mystic, kept his head
Concerned with coin, and booze, and bread,   20
Finding a thousand epiphanies
In each day's banalities;
He wrote what each man thinks who sits
And reads the tabloid as he shits.
Yet in the style of each there lurks   25
Civility like Edmund Burke's.
I, who grew as corn is grown,
In Hanrahan's mad song
And saw the river Liffey dance
In Brooklyn, in a kind of trance,   30
When I was only seventeen,
And yet believed what I had seen,
I was damned by Yeats and Joyce:
I swear I never had a choice.
At the age of fifty, then, I came   35
As any moth to any flame
Back to the land of Finn Mac Cool.
I know I was a proper fool.
Now twice a year, at standard rates,
I go and lecture in the States   40
And the one remark I always hear
Is "You grow more Irish every year."
Back in Dublin, every street
Once was walked by Grandad's feet
But this is the nails that pierce my hands: 45
I am alien, exiled, in both lands.
Romantic Ireland's all around me
To perplex me and confound me.
Rational Ireland we may see
In, perhaps, a century: 50
Joyce was often seen quite pissed;
O'Casey died a communist;
O'Brien drowned his brain in stout;

Beckett learned to live with doubt;
Synge disappeared into the mist;   55
It's a long and dreary list.
Yet Joyce, who looked at death and doom,
Answered them with Molly Bloom—
Yes I said Yes I will Yes—
And now perhaps I should confess: 60
Romantic Ireland can't be beat.
In the P.O. on O'Connell Street
I, a pacifist, feel pride
For the ghost of John MacBride,
For Connolly, and all the rest   65
Who gave their lives for the oppressed,
Who inspired Nehru, Ho Chih Minh
And all who fight the cruel machine
In Africa today, or Salvador.
And I, with genes of Lachlann Mor,   70
Know my soul is crucified
By fanatic Ireland's pride.
As Wilde found, wit is no defense,
Nor skeptic Joyce's common sense:
Defeat itself becomes a joy   75
In the last three bars of **Danny Boy**.

Cisatlantic notes for transatlantic readers:

4. Ballinspittle: a town in Kerry where, in 1985, a statue of the Blessed Virgin was perceived by thousands to move, jump, dance, make "imploring" gestures etc. over a period of about four months. The statue was finally smashed by Protestant iconoclasts who denounced the Catholic worshippers for "idolatry." Sinn Fein: a political party with an ideology so close to the Irish Republican Army that it is widely considered a "front" for the IRA. The name **Sinn Fein** means "ourselves alone" and is the slogan the Citizen shouts, in *Ulysses*, before throwing the biscuit box at Bloom.

62. The P.O. on O'Connell Street is the Post Office seized by the rebels during the Easter 1916 rebellion. To get them out of the PO, the British shelled downtown Dublin and killed thousands of innocent civilians.

64. John MacBride: See the interview with Sean MacBride.

65. Connolly: James Connolly, founder of the Irish Socialist Party. When he ran for Parliament in 1905, the Catholic Bishops sent out a pastoral letter to be read from every pulpit, announcing that anyone who voted for him would be excommunicated. In 1916, Connolly initially opposed the Uprising as "bourgeoise revolution," but after the British began killing civilians *en masse*, Connolly joined the rebels, was wounded and captured, and was executed by firing squad. His flag for the Irish socialist movement, the plough with a band of stars, inspired the title for O'Casey's great play about 1916, *The Plough and the Stars*.

THE POET AS
DEFENSE EARLY WARNING
RADAR SYSTEM

The following article is not just "about" Allen Ginsberg, whom I regard as our major living American poet. It is also "about" my concept of what a writer should be doing with his or her talent in a world like this.

Forty years ago, Ezra Pound made his celebrated boast of the social function of art: "The artist is the antenna of the race, the barometer and voltmeter." Allen Ginsberg* is nothing if not contemporary. He brings the boast up to date with a stunning effectiveness:

> I am the Defense Early Warning Radar System
> I see nothing but bombs

These lines are typical of Ginsberg's unpolished-looking verse. He seems to work in poetry the way Rouault worked in paint: hacking his way savagely, with crude and sweeping strokes, toward an image of maximum ferocity. Look at Rouault's "Three Judges," those faces of moronic evil plastered on the canvas as if in rage and colored with the darkest, smeariest

---

Kaddish and Other Poems, by Allen Ginsberg. City Lights Books, 1961, 100 pages.

blacks and browns this side of downtown Passaic; this is the typical "feel" of a
Ginsberg poem. Actually, of course, neither Rouault nor Ginsberg work in a
frothing frenzy. Ginsberg in particular probably spends as much effort
sounding "uncivilized" as Henry James ever spent in sounding "civilized."

There has been little technical analysis of Ginsberg's verse thus far; the
job requires an ear delicate as Pound's and the patience of an elephant. It
generally takes me three or four readings aloud to feel my way toward
Ginsberg's music; his great bass, as Pound would call it, is strong as a Watusi
drum, but, like a Watusi drum, full of surprising polyrhythms and
unexpected variations. I have heard that the poetry reviews in the *Saturday
Review*, New York *Times*, etc. are actually written by machines; and, from the
reviews Ginsberg has gotten in those and similar publications, I would
gather that the machines in question, like most university poetry teachers,
are not yet capable of following a meter more challenging than the
traditional umpty-umpty-umpty (followed occasionally by *umpty-umpty-UMty*.)

Let's take a closer look at one of Ginsberg's oral constructions. A poem is a
statue in sound, or "frozen architecture," or anyway you slice it it's basically a
structure, a form *manufactured* by a man. The chief thing about Allen Ginsberg
as a poet is that he always shows you his form emerging, the way it builds
up, a thing created out of ordinary speech but suddenly, by the height of its
emotion, transcending ordinary speech. *Kaddish* begins with words you or I
might speak:

> Strange now to think of you, gone without corsets & eyes, while I walk on
> the sunny pavement of Greenwich Village

Like most modern poetry, this cannot be broken down into a traditional
meter, but has to be considered in terms of Pound's Second Law of Imagism:
"to write in the sequence of the musical phrase." There are three phrases
above, the second syncopating slightly with the first, and the third a
prolonged complication on both of the first two. It's rather like Charlie
Parker taking off and searching for his theme. In a few lines Ginsberg finds
his basic beat:

> . . . and I've been up all night, talking, talking,
> reading the Kaddish aloud, listening to
> Ray Charles blues shout blind on the phonograph
> the rhythm the rhythm

We are still in the area of normal American speech, but Ginsberg is
beginning to pick out of it his own building blocks. "And I've been up all
night, talking, talking" . . . "Ray Charles blues shout blind on the phonograph/

the rhythm the rhythm:" these lines syncopate beautifully, and the internal phrase, "reading the Kaddish aloud" picks up on the initial "Strange now to think of you." Allen Ginsberg sifts through the resources of American English like a placer miner going through his dust, carefully lifting out a nugget at a time.

Once he has found what he's looking for, he hammers it out with the remorseless monotony of Beethoven, or perhaps I should say of Bizet in the *Arlesienne Suite*. *Kaddish* moves towards its close through a hymn to the God who allowed the poet's mother to go mad:

> In the house in Newark Blessed is He! In the
> madhouse Blessed is He! In the house of
> Death blessed is He!

Even the tragedy of the poor old woman is blessed:

> Blessed be you Naomi in Hospitals! Blessed be you
> Naomi in solitude! Blest be your triumph! Blest
> be your bars! Blest be your last years' loneliness!

But an even stronger rhythm breaks in to mourn the all-too-true truth that there is nothing blessed, only pain, in the story of Naomi Ginsberg:

> only to have seen her weeping on gray tables in long wards of her universe
> only to have known the wierd ideas of Hitler at the door . . .
> only to have seen the time-jumps, memory lapse, the crash of wars, the
> roar and silence of a vast electric shock

and the reality, the lack of blessing and triumph, is therupon hammered like Pound's rock-drill till it almost bursts the reader's brain:

> with your eyes running naked out of the apartment screaming into the hall
> with your eyes being led away by policemen to an ambulance
> with your eyes strapped down on the operating table
> with your eyes of the pancreas removed
> with your eyes of appendix operation
> with your eyes of abortion
> with your eyes of shock
> with your eyes of lobotomy

The theme beats into the soul like a drum:

> with your eyes
> with your eyes

—and then suddenly turns around on itself and bursts forth into a line of sheer genius:

with your Death full of flowers

From "Strange now to think" through "the rhythm the rhythm" the poem has gradually created, just through the integrity of its own emotion, the justification from the drum-beat and thunder of "only to have, only to have" and "with her eyes, with her eyes." If anybody else repeated the "formula," it would only be a trick, because the emotion is in the words and the discovery of the words is the discovery of the emotions. It is Ginsberg's personal Golgotha that we meet here, and if you or I were to tell our own stories we would have to find our own words and emotions. That is why a great work of poetry is always so original as to seem "formless" at first glance. It appears to have no form because it is a new form, manufactured in heart's agony, a shape cut in the air as a sculptor cuts.

The last movement opens with a bird call:

> Caw caw caw crows shriek in the white sun over grave stones in
>   Long Island

The crows seem to burst onto the page with the vividness of real life; we actually hear them before we see them. But Ginsberg, with the audacity of genius, has another trick for us in the next line:

> Lord Lord Lord Naomi underneath this grass my halflife and my own
>   as hers

The tom-tom is back again, this time in a half-rhymed fugue with "Caw caw caw" chasing "Lord Lord Lord" down the page. It is "only to have" and "with your eyes" picked up into greater urgency than before:

> Lord Lord great Eye that stares on ALL and moves in a black cloud
> caw caw strange cry of Beings sung up into sky over waving trees

The ending is pure fugue, pure as Bach:

> Lord Lord Lord caw caw caw Lord Lord Lord caw caw caw Lord

The harsh monosyllables of American speech have dominated the poem from "Strange now to think" right through to "caw caw caw Lord." Pound showed us how to do this forty years ago, with his "Blue jade cups well set" etc., but he has had no student to apply him half so well as Allen Ginsberg. And the economy and magnificence of using "Lord Lord Lord" against "caw caw caw"—an implied identification picked up in the montage-like shift from God as "black cloud" to the black cloud of crows—this is balancing a poem as skillfully as Roebling balanced the Brooklyn Bridge.

Among the shorter poems in this volume, particularly good are "Poem

Rocket," "Death to Van Gogh's Ear," "The Lion for Real," and "Ignu." "Poem Rocket" contains a line that evokes extra-terrestrial beauty better than the best of the science-fiction writers: "Which way will the sunflower turn surrounded by millions of suns?" And "The Lion for Real" brings the Spirits of Terror to the page in a way that makes one think of Dante; you can't laugh off Ginsberg's Lion anymore than you can smile at Dante's hell, or Blake's Tyger, or Melville's Whale. Ginsberg has *seen* the Lion, and by God, he makes you see it, too. Naturally, *Life* magazine describes his vision as "sick" and "warped"; the System which is willing to create twenty thousand abnormal babies everytime it sets off a nuclear bomb cannot afford to listen to the reports of this extremely delicate instrument, the "Defense Early Warning Radar System" that is the soul of the poet today.

COINCIDANCE: PART TWO

Death and Absence
in James Joyce

... the time is come wherein a man of timid
courage seizes the keys of hell and of death, and
flings them far out into the abyss, proclaiming
the praise of life, which the abiding presence of
truth may sanctify, and of death, the most
beautiful form of life.

The time was 1 February, 1902: the place, the Literary and Historical
Society room in University College, Dublin. The speaker, who would be
twenty years old the following morning, 2 February, was James Joyce; and it
does not take great perspicacity to observe that his style was not yet equal to
the task of containig his vision. Dublin students, who are always great wits,
had a wonderful time parodying "timid courage" in the following days, but
one of them (whose name has been, alas, lost) had even more fun with the
final strophe, satirizing it as "absence, the highest form of presence."

As Richard Ellman has noted, Joyce was no man to back down from a
paradox, and two of the stories in his first book of fiction, *Dubliners*, seem
intended to drive home the points that death and absence can be higher and
more beautiful than life and presence. As for "timid courage," that also
remained a theme in everything Joyce wrote.

Joyce's first use of death and absence as positives, in *Dubliners*, is the marvelous short story, "Ivy Day in the Committee Room." A group of minor political hacks are sitting around drinking Guiness's stout and carefully avoiding talking about anything serious. Gradually we discover that it is Ivy Day—October 6th, the anniversary of the death of Charles Stewart Parnell—and that all of them had, in one way or another, betrayed him. It is Parnell, still called "the Chief," who is physically dead and absent but very much alive and present in the haunted consciences of every man in the Committee Room.

(Parnell organized the rent strikes of the 1880s, which for a time made it impossible for English landlords to collect Irish rents. He did not invent but popularized the *boycott*, which cut deeply into English profits in Irish markets. He became the leader of the "Home Rule" party and the most popular man in Ireland, called "Erin's uncrowned king," but fell from power after being denounced by the Roman Catholic clergy as an adulterer. After his political downfall he died quickly of pneumonia and, with what now seems prevision of 20th Century psychosomatic medicine, his few loyal followers insisted bitterly that "the Chief" had died of a broken heart.)

"Ivy Day" ends, with superb Joycean irony, when a loyal Parnellite named Joe Hynes arrives and reads a poem in praise of the dead Chief. The poem is wretched, mawkish, awful, shot through with every dreadful cliche of popular Victorian verse; and, precisely because it is not great literature but the simple expression of genuine emotion by a simple man, it is strangely moving. The closing line of the story gives the reaction of Crofton, the most vehement anti-Parnellite in the Committee Room:

Mr. Crofton said that it was a very fine piece of writing.

The evasion of the meaning of the poem is obvious; whether Crofton is also hypocritical in praising the non-existent literary merits of the piece is unclear; maybe, like the author, Joe Hynes, Crofton is ignorant enough to think the verse is well written. Joyce, who believed ambiguity is the prime feature of human existence, loved to leave his readers with little mysteries like that. What is important is that the lyric, trite and dreadful as it is, makes Parnell the hero of the story:

He is dead. Our Uncrowned King is dead.
O, Erin, mourn with grief and woe
For he is dead whom the fell gang
Of modern hypocrites laid low

In palace, cabin or in cot
The Irish heart where'er it be

Is bowed with woe—for he is gone
  Who would have wrought her destiny

They had their way: they laid him low.
  But Erin, list, his spirit may
Rise, like the Phoenix, from the flames,
  When breaks the dawning of the day

Oscar Wilde, another Irishman, said it would take a heart of stone to read the death of Little Nell (in Dickens) without laughing. In "Ivy Day in the Committee Room," Joyce drenches the sentimentality of Joe Hynes in mockery, producing exactly and precisely the bad poem Joe himself would write if asked to collaborate on the story, and then proceeds to cap the absurdity with Crofton's doubly-ambivalent hypocrisy; but who can sneer as the ghost of Parnell indubitably rises, even clothed in journalistic "verse," to haunt and afflict those who betrayed him? The dead and absent is stronger than the live and present, and Joyce has vindicated his paradox.

That Joe Hynes is a man of "timid courage"—he has to be prompted several times before he will consent to read his subversive poem—indicates that another paradox from the 1902 lecture was still on Joyce's mind. Joe's hesitation is not only motivated by the fact that he is the only loyal Parnellite in the room, but is also necessary because he included a line (not quoted above) about the "rabble-rout of fawning priests" that will not go down smoothly with any Irish Catholic audience.

In "The Dead," the last story in *Dubliners*, Joyce returns to and enriches the themes of death, absence and timid courage. Gabriel Conroy, the protagonist, is an intellectual who is nervous, or timid, all through the story, because he knows that his opinions are not shared by his middle-class relatives. Nonetheless, he does state his opinions, even though hesitantly; and he has the courage to commit the "social sin" of marrying a woman from Connacht, even though Dubliners regard Connacht people as *declasse*. Courageous in his timidity, Gabriel is timid in his courage, and when asked directly if Gretta is from the West, he answers evasively that "her people" were.

The real hero of "The Dead," we only learn at the end, is not Gabriel but Michael (the angelic names are no coincidence, anymore than the Phoenix in the "Ivy Day" poem was an accident). Michael Furey, specifically, loved Gretta before Gabriel did, and Michael even died for love—in a Romantic, absurd, Irish way, of course. Michael Furey died of pneumonia, which he caught standing all night in an Irish rainstorm singing love songs beneath Gretta's window. It is he, not Gabriel, who has dominated Gretta's thoughts and feelings all through the story: dead and absent, he is very alive and present in her heart. The dead, Joyce is here proposing, cannot only psychologically displace us but even metaphorically cuckold us.

This story is autobiographical. Nora Barnacle, Joyce's mistress 1904-1931 and his wife 1931-1941, had been courted in Connacht by a Michael Bodkin, who actually did die of pneumonia after singing lovesongs to her in a rainstorm. Joyce changed Bodkin to "Furey" to add violent, fiery connotations to the ghost that afflicts Gabriel Conroy. In 1909, Joyce even went to Galway to look at his dead rival's grave, and found beside it a grave for one "J. Joyce"—an incident that left him with a lifelong preoccupation with synchronicity long before Carl Jung named that phenomenon.

In *Ulysses*, the dead and absent are not only present but omnipresent. Stephen Dedalus is afflicted with what psychiatrists would call clnical depression; Stephen with his medieval erudition, prefers to call it "agenbite of inwit"—the incessant gnawing of rat-toothed remorse. His sin? He refused to kneel and pray when his dying mother asked him, an act not motivated by atheism but by anti-theism: Stephen fears that there might be a malign reality in the God he has rejected, and that any act of submission might open him to invasion and re-enslavement by that demonic Catholic divinity. Probably, only another ex-Catholic can understand that anxiety, but any humane person can understand the dreadful power of the guilt that, personified by Stephen's mother, haunts him all through the long day's journey of 16 June 1904 into night.

Stephen is the overture, and, later, the anti-chorus. The major theme of *Ulysses* is Leopold Bloom, Irish Jew, timid hero, solid wanderer in the formless abyss, the greatest comic and tragic figure in modern literature. If Stephen is haunted by a dead mother, Bloom is equally preoccupied with a dead son: Rudy Bloom, dead at the age of 11 days, absent from the public world of Dublin, alive and ever-present in Bloom's memories.

If the dead have power over our imaginations, the absent have even more power. Conspicuously absent form the text of *Ulysses*—he only appears on stage once, to utter banalities to a shopgirl—is Hugh "Blazes" Boylan, who is also over-conspicuously absent from Bloom's thoughts most of the day. Only about two-thirds of the way through the book, on first reading, do we discover why Bloom's private inner conversation with himself (which we are privileged to share) always wanders into chaotic images and a wild search for a new topic of interest whenever Boylan's name is mentioned by another character. Bloom knows, but does not want to know, that Blazes Boylan is having an affair with Bloom's wife, Molly. By being absent from Bloom's consciousness, Boylan acts like an invisible magnetic field governing thought processes that we can see, but cannot understand, until we know Boylan is there, unthought of, deflecting and determining the conscious thoughts we do see. That the name Blazes Boylan suggests devils and hell reminds us that Joyce's "man of timid courage," Bloom, will seize "the keys of hell and death" before the book is over.

Concretely, Bloom earns his living cadging ads for a newspaper; on 16 June 1904, he is trying to secure an ad for Alexander Keyes, whose company logo is a pair of crossed keys, suggesting the Coat of Arms of the Isle of Man. With typical Irish indirection, Mr. Keys is also advertising his loyal Parnellism: the House of Keys on the Isle of Man is the local parliament, independent of England, and Parnell's "Home Rule" party used that example as an argument that the Irish were entitled to their own parliament also. Symbolically, the crossed keys indicate everything associated with Celtic crosses, Christian crosses, Egyptian Tau-crosses and all crossed emblems of rebirth; and the Isle of Man symbolizes humanity's isolation and solidarity at once (another Joycean paradox): every man is an island, but we are all crossed or linked with each other, as Stephen Dedalus and Leopold Bloom are crossed and linked in ways neither understands. (It is no accident that the first sentence of *Ulysses* has 22 words, one for each letter of Cabala, and that the last is "crossed.")

Indeed, *Ulysses* is made up of crossed keys in time as well as in space. In the first chapter, Stephen Dedalus broods on his agenbite of inwit, eats breakfast, and replies with dry, bitter wit to the more robust, blasphemous and outrageous jokes of Buck Mulligan. Only when we discover the parallelism of Homer's *Odyssey* that explains Joyce's title do we realize that Stephen is reliving the experiences of Telemachus, who at the beginning of the *Odyssey* awakens in a tower, as Stephen does, and is mocked and bullied by Antonioos as Stephen is mocked and bullied by Mulligan. When Stephen, in chapter two, is given pompous and pontifical advice by the Ulster Protestant, Mr. Deasy, we are again watching trans-time synchronicity: Telemachus was similarly given advice by Nestor in the similar section of the *Odyssey*. The parallels follow throughout: Bloom is Ulysses, Molly is Penelope, the Catholic Church is the island of the lotus eaters, the newspaper office where everybody quotes their favorite political speeches is the Cave of Wind, etc. Dead and absent for 3000 years, Homer's images are alive and present, in some sense, in Dublin.

In what sense (as the impatient may ask)? Is Stephen literally the reincar-nation of Telemachus and Bloom of Ulysses? Or is the connection one of Jungian synchronicity (not yet discovered when Joyce wrote *Ulysses*)? Or might one posit Dr. Sheldrake's morphogenetic resonances in time? Joyce does not answer. He exhibits the living presence of the absent dead and lets us draw our own conclusion.

That the simple models of reincarnation or metempychosis* will not quite

---

*Which is deliberately hinted at by Joyce in Chapter 4, when Molly asks Bloom the meaning of "met-him-pike-hoses" and Bloom tries to explain "the transmigration of souls" to her.

cover the case is indicated by the secondary level of parallels with *Hamlet* which underlie and reinforce the parallels with Homer. In the first Chapter, the Martello tower is compared to Elsinore, and Stephen wears a "Hamlet hat." He is asked his theory about *Hamlet*, and evades the question for the moment, to answer in full in Chapter 9. A whole stream of symbols linking Stephen with Hamlet, Bloom with the ghost of Hamlet's father, Molly Bloom with Gertrude etc. gradually emerges on re-readings of the book. What Joyce is exhibiting to us is, in fact, a *coherent synergy* or *knot*, as Bucky Fuller would say: a pattern that co-exists in many places and times. The dead and absent will be again live and present, in this context, because history repeats the same stories endlessly, just changing the names of the players.

But *Ulysses* is also a mock-encyclopedia, with every chapter corresponding to one human science or discipline; and the discipline emphasized in chapter one is theology, as Joyce's notes indicate. This begins with Buck Mulligan's burlesque of the Mass, runs on through Stephen's tortured reflections on the "mystic oneness" of Father and Son in the Trinity, comes back in Mulligan's hilarious "Ballad of Joking Jesus," and permeates every paragraph in subtle ways. If Stephen = Telemachus as son disinherited (Stephen's father, a drunk, has sold at auction the properties Stephen expected to inherit) and Stephen = Hamlet as son haunted (by a mother's ghost, not a father's, but still haunted), the theological context of the chapter implies that Stephen = Telemachus = Hamlet because all young men, at some point, are obsessed with a father who is either dead or missing-in-action: namely, God the Father. *Ulysses* is set exactly 18 years, or nearly a breeding generation, after Nietzsche announced that God was dead. Stephen as young rebel or *puer aeternis* is a perennial archetype; Stephen as individual is representative of the first generation to arrive at maturity with that grim Nietzschean autopsy on their minds.

This is why Mulligan remarks that he and Stephen are both "Hyper-boreans." He is almost certainly referring to the startling opening paragraph of Nietzsche's *The Antichrist*:

> Look me in the face. We are Hyperboreans; we know very well how far out we have moved. "Neither by land nor by sea will you find the Hyper-boreans"—Pindar already knew that about us. Beyond the north, beyond ice and death, lie our life, our happiness. We have discovered joy, we know the way, we have the exit out of the labyrinth of history.

Nietzsche's labyrinth of history, which Stephen later calls the nightmare of history, is the rules laid down by State and Church. Mulligan has indeed found his way out of the labyrinth; but Stephen has not. He is named after the maker of labyrinths, remember, and he remains trapped in the labyrinth of his own narcissistic agenbite until Bloom delivers him.

This is why Stephen tells the fatuous Englishman, Haines, that the Irish artist is the servant of two masters—the imperial British State and the Roman Catholic Church. In this sense also, the dead live: the Irish writer of Joyce's day made his obedience to the dead invaders and traitors who made Ireland a colony of Rome and of England, or else he was forced to choose Joyce's path of exile: as did Shaw and O'Casey and Beckett and a dozen lesser lights along with Joyce.

For Bloom, as for Stephen, God is either dead or missing-in-action; but Bloom, at 38, has been a freethinker longer and is no longer hysterical about it. Approaching middle-age (by 1904 standards, when average life expectancy was 50), Bloom has lost faith, successively, in Judaism, Protestantism, Catholicism and Freemasonry; one feels that his attachment to Socialism is precarious also. In the abyss of uncertainty, Bloom remains a modern Ulysses steering his way diplomatically and prudently among such hazards as drunken Catholics (Simon Dedalus), anti-semitic Nationalists (the Citizen) and unctuous undertakers who may be police informers (Corny Kelleher). Mourning his dead son, ashamed of and yet attached to his father who died a suicide, knowing his wife is "unfaithful," Bloom retains equanimity and practises charity discretely and inconspicuously: feeding the seagulls, helping the blind boy across the road, negotiating to protect the rights of Paddy Dignam's widow, visiting Mina Purefoy in hospital. Lest we think this kindly chap a paragon, Joyce keeps Bloom in the same precise naturalistic focus as we watch him defecate, urinate, peep into a masochistic porn novel and masturbate. Joyce announced that he did not believe in heroes, and Bloom is no hero: just an ordinary decent man. There are a million like him in any large city: Joyce was merely the first to put him in a novel, with biological functions and timid courage unglamorized and uncensored.

The climax of *Ulysses*—the brothel scene in which Stephen, drunk, actually sees his mother's ghost cursing him, and Bloom, exhausted, dreams in hypnogogic revery of his son not at the age of his death (11 days) but at the age he would be if he had lived (11 years)—brings us back to the living presence of the absent dead. But in that scene also, Bloom's *timid* courage becomes timid *courage* as he risks scandal, gossip, disgrace and even associating with the possible informer, Corny Kelleher, in order to protect Stephen from two drunken and violent English soldiers. This is the pivot-point of the novel, and, since Joyce carefully avoids revealing Bloom's actual motivations, critics have had endless entertainment "interpreting" for us.

My own guess is that, even if Bloom is looking for a substitute son, as some say, or has unconscious homosexual urges as others claim, or is hoping to procure for Molly a lover less gross and offensive to Bloom's sensibilities than Boylan, as Marilyn French recently suggested, the answer lies in a four-letter word that each of Joyce's three major characters speaks once at a crucial point in the narrative. Stephen speaks it first, in the library, when asking himself what he left out of his theory of *Hamlet*; he answers, "Love, yes. Word known to all men." Bloom speaks it to the Citizen, offering an alternative to politics and national hatreds:

—Love, says Bloom. I mean the opposite of hatred.

And Molly concludes her ruminations of What's Wrong With Men by repeating the theme of the two major male voices in the narrative:

they don't know what love is

When Bloom brings Stephen home to Eccles Street to feed him, they share "Epp's massproduct"—Epp's cocoa—but Joyce the punster is telling us what can seize the keys of hell and death, proclaim the praise of life, and make the absent present. The cocoa is not only massproduced but is for Stephen a new Mass produced: a Mass of humanity to replace the Mass of God who may be dead or missing-in-action. "The physician's love heals the patient," wrote the psychiatrist Ian Suttie; Bloom's love, I think we are meant to believe, heals Stephen's agenbite of inwit. The point of Bloom's charity is precisely that it has no reasons. Beneath the *Odyssey, Hamlet* and *Don Giovanni* (recently discovered), *Ulysses* also parallels the most effective and memorable of the parables of Jesus: the story of the Good Samaritan.

The dead and absent survive, then, because we love them. *Ulysses* itself, the most complexly intellectual of comedies, is a testament to love: to Alfred Hunter, a man of whom we know only a few facts: he lived in Dublin in 1904; he was Jewish; his wife was, according to gossip, unfaithful; and one night he took home a drunken, depressed, impoverished and totally embittered young man named James Joyce and sobered him and fed him. All else about Alfred Hunter is lost, but those facts plus artistic imagination created "Leopold Bloom"; and if Hunter is dead and absent, Bloom remains forever alive and present for students of literature.

The curiosity of Joyce's mature technique is that while on first reading *Ulysses* seems only intermittently funny and consistently "naturalistic" (realistic), on successive re-readings it becomes progressively funnier and spookier. None of Joyce's 100 or more major and minor characters knows fully what is going on in Dublin on that one extraordinarily ordinary day of 16 June 1904. The first-time reader is similarly ignorant, navigating through 18 chapters and 18 hours of "realism" that is often as squalid and confusing "as real life." Beneath this surface, as we have already seen, the ghosts of Homer, Shakespeare, Mozart, and (if I am right about the Good Samaritan theme) Jesus are present-although-absent as the archetypal themes of their works are reflected in this everyday bustle of ordinary early 20th Century city.

Everybody in the story is involved in misunderstandings or ambiguities that become clearer and more hilarious on each re-reading. This existential fact—that every mind creates its own reality-tunnel—is the abyss of which Joyce spoke, at nineteen, in the lecture on absence and death from which we began. Stephen invokes the abyss again in his theory of *Hamlet* (Chapter 9), saying fatherhood is like the universe itself in being founded "upon the void, Upon incertitude." Various Dublin gossips (all male) have different theories about how many lovers Molly Bloom has had; the reader who believes them is terribly deceived. In Chapter 17, we are given a list of Molly's lovers which we are apt to consider definitive; on re-reading, we discover it is not a list of real lovers but of Bloom's suspicions. Molly's monologue should resolve the mystery, but only adds to the ambiguity; she is not as promiscuous as gossip paints her, but the exact number of her infidelities is still uncertain.

By the middle of the book, almost everybody in Dublin thinks Bloom has won a great deal on the horse race that day. On first reading, we are likely to think so, too, and wonder why he hasn't gone to pick up his winnings. Only on careful re-reading do we discover the confusions out of which this inaccurate rumor got started. A dog who appears vicious and ugly to one narrator appears "lovely" and almost "human" to another narrator, and a third narrator claims the dog actually talks. Alf Bergan sees Paddy Dignam at 4 p.m. but Paddy was buried at 10 in the morning; we are to decide for ourselves if Alf saw a ghost or just shared in the general fallibility of human perception. Some Dubliners think Bloom is a dentist, and discovering the source of that error is amusing to the re-reader. Bloom thinks Molly doesn't know about his Platonic "affair" with Martha Clifford, but Molly knows more than he guesses about that and all his other secrets. Nosey Flynn, the first Dubliner to tell us Bloom is a Freemason, is wrong about everything else he says; it takes careful study to discover that this font of unreliable gossip is right about that particular detail.

The tradition of the realistic novel, at this point, has refuted itself, in a classic Strange Loop. Joyce has given us more realism than any other novelist and the upshot of it is that we don't know what's real anymore. If Dante's epic was informed by the philosophy of Aristotle, whom he called The Master of Those Who Know, Joyce's epic, as Ellman commented, is dominated by David Hume, the Master of Those Who Don't Know. Is the man in the brown mackintosh who continually gets entangled with Bloom a significant figure in Bloom's past (or future?) or is this repeated conjunction "mere coincidence"? We are privileged to peep into the mind of a typist named Martha (who works part-time for Blazes Boylan) but we don't know if she is thinking about Bloom or about the hero of a novel she has been reading. Since Bloom's thoughts, like everybody's, contain wishful thinking and self-deception, we cannot believe him totally, but the other narrators are so prejudiced pro-Bloom or anti-Bloom that we can't trust them either. We have seen Reality and found it an abyss indeed; Blake only *claimed* to see infinity in a grain of sand, but Joyce has shown us the infinity by opening every hour of an ordinary day to endless interpretations and re-interpretations.

Things become even more interesting, and weirder, when we begin to count the coincidences in this very, very average day: a day so banally normal that early critics complained chiefly that many chapters are boring and pointless. On the first page, Mulligan is performing a parody of the Catholic Mass* and whistles to summon the Holy Spirit; a mysterious returning whistle answers from the street. Mulligan, a devout atheist, is not impressed by this coincidence, but it is the overture to a rising crescendo of synchronicity throughout the day. A few pages on, Mulligan mentions working at the Mater hospital; Bloom lives on the same street with that hospital. Mulligan then talks of a friend named Bannon who is courting a girl in a photo shop in Mullingar; at the same time, but three chapters away in the text, Bloom is reading a letter from that girl, who happens to be his daughter, Milly. Bannon arrives in Dublin at 11 that evening, just in time to see the meeting of Stephen and Bloom in conjunction with another appearance of the enigmatic man in the brown mackintosh. Moses is the topic of conversation in the newspaper immediately before and after Bloom enters, and when Bloom arrives at the library two hours later, Mulligan anti-semitically calls him "Ikey Moses"; at the end of the day, Bloom suddenly guesses the answer to the child's riddle, "Where was Moses when the candle went out?" Other coincidences connect Bloom and Moses throughout the day; a secondary string of synchronicity links bloom with Elijah; a third famous Jew, Jesus, gets linked to Bloom in Chapter 12, where the narrator's favorite oath is "Jesus" and the Citizen threatens to "crucify" Bloom.

Weirder and more wonderful: in the newspaper office, Bloom reflects that William Braydon, the editor, looks like Jesus and then remembers that Mario "the tenor" also looked like Jesus. Giovanni Matteo Mario (1810-1883) was famous for looking like most popular portraits of Jesus, but equally renowned for his role as Lionel in Flotow's opera, *Martha*. Jesus was associated

---

* And don't forget that the climax comes when Bloom and Stephen share the "massproduct," Epp's cocoa.

with Martha (of Bethany) and Bloom is corresponding flirtatiously with Martha Clifford. Four hours later, in Chapter 11, Bloom sits down in the Ormonde Hotel restaurant to write a letter to Martha, and Simon Dedalus sings the aria, *Martha*, from Flotow's opera, for which Mario was famous. Bloom notes the synchronicity *in part*, and dismisses it; but Bloom is to become, temporarily at least, a spiritual father to Stephen Dedalus, a role which Simon Dedalus has alcoholically abandoned. When in the next chapter, Bloom tells the anti-semitic citizen that Jesus was a Jew and so was his father, the citizen replies that Jesus had no father: Jesus, Mario, Martha, Stephen's reflections on the mysteries of fatherhood in Catholic theology and *Hamlet*, Joyce's preoccupation with incertitude and the void, have dovetailed so neatly into multiple synchronicity that one hardly notes that the next song to be sung in the musical Chapter 11, by Ben Dollard, is "The Croppy Boy," which contains a line, "And forgot to pray for my mother's rest," which brings us back to Stephen's guilt.*

The Irish critic Sheldon Brivic has counted over 100 coincidences of that complexity integrating the banalities and confusions of 16 June 1904 into a patterned harmony that none of the characters consciously apprehend, although their thoughts and actions are creating or co-creating it in collaboration with each other and with the dead and absent. As Brivic says (*Crane Bag*, VI, 1):

> The unconscious Joyce represents is not merely an area within the brains of his creatures. It is a network of connections through time and space that extends beyond any awareness but the most absolute.

The presence of the absent and the dead in this network of connections is the theme of Joyce's last, greatest work, *Finnegans Wake*. Where *Ulysses* is an epic of the day, *Finnegans Wake* is an epic of the night; where the former dislocates our normal notions of "reality" only indirectly and on careful re-reading, the latter makes no concession to day-time "reality" at all and plunges us, from the first page to the last, in Altered States of Consciousness. "Joyce's prose," Timothy Leary has said (in *Flashbacks*) "prepared me to enter psychedelic space."

The "nat language"† of *Finnegans Wake*, in fact, can best be described as hologrammic prose. Just as a hologram is so structured that each part

---

* The mother also comes in to balance the heavy fatherhood theme, just as the first coincidence linking Stephen and Bloom is Mulligan's employment at the Mater hospital.

† A specimen of the text that describes the text. Norwegian "nat" = night, so this means *night language* on one level. But this Norse word, "nat" is pronounced "not," so the expression also means *not language*. In either case, it is not the language of the day-light tunnel-realities.

contains the whole, *Finnegans Wake* is structured in puns and synchronicities that "contain" and reflect each other, creating the closest approximation of an infinite regress ever achieved in any art-form. The absent is ever-present, the dead are all alive, and the abyss of uncertainty appears in every multi-meaningful sentence. (This will be illustrated below.)

The revolutionary nature of this dream-book can be indicated by the fact that Joyce's notes include four separate symbols to stand for that which in a day-time novel would be the hero or protagonist: E , m , ɯ and Ǝ . There is, as we have said, no "character" dominating this book, but rather what mathematicians would call a *system function*. The first person "dead" or missing in *Finnegans Wake* is the conscious ego we normally take for granted. We can only deduce him, as it were, from the system of which he is part.

The ego (Joyce's E), we know, is one Humphrey Chimpden Earwicker, a publican (inn-keeper) in Chapelizod, a western suburb of Dublin. Probably, he was a sea captain for many years before settling down; almost certainly, he is having this dream in 1921 or when the Irish Revolution was at its most violent and any stranger in the park might be an I.R.A. terrorist, any three British soldiers might arrest you "on suspicion." Earwicker is terrorized, throughout the dream, by ambiguous strangers in the park and three accusatory British soldiers.

To try to "understand" *Finnegans Wake* in terms of the life of E or Earwicker, the conscious ego, is entirely mistaken, however. The Ego that seems so real in day-light is "dead" or comatose in the dream-world, and *Finnegans Wake* is dominated by those trans-Ego functions Joyce abbreviates as m , ɯ and Ǝ .

m has some of the qualities of Freud's personal unconscious and also of his "censor band." Joyce identifies it also with Stonehenge and other Celtic monoliths (because of shape?) and, by association, with human sacrifice, religion, guilt, anxiety and the fear of authority-figures. On this level, you will find on every page of *Finnegans Wake* disguised, distorted and sometimes deeply hidden ("repressed") images of everything that is taboo in Catholic Ireland, especially incest, homosexuality, voyeurism, exhibitionism, urination, defecation, masturbation, patricide, regicide and cannibalism. In Jungian terms, this is the Shadow of the waking Mr. Earwicker; it is the Mr. Hyde within every Dr. Jekyl.

ɯ is the "collective unconscious" of Jung, the "phylogenetic unconscious" of Grof, the "neurogenetic archives" of Leary and/or the "morphogenetic field" of Sheldrake—to use four modern scientific metaphors. In older mystical languages it is called the "Akashic records" in Theosophy, the "long memory" in Hermetic texts, the *aliyavijnana* ("treasury mind" or "storehouse mind") in Buddhism. On this level, every page of *Finnegans Wake* is drenched with human and pre-human "memories" unknown to the conscious E (Earwicker-Ego). The heroes of Ireland are all there: Parnell and O'Connell and Silken Thomas Fitzgerald and Brian Boru; and so are Napoleon and Charlemagne and all the emperors of Rome; and the Hebrew prophets and Noah and Abraham and Sarah and Adam and Eve; and Confucius and Buddha and Mohammed; and all the dead-and-resurrected gods of Frazer's *Golden Bough*: Tammuz and Adonis and Hyacinth and Osiris and Attis and Dionysus, etc.; and chimpanzees and other mammals and salmon and whales and insects and trees and flowers. On this level, *Finnegans Wake* is like *The Outline of History* and *The Origin of Species* talking to each other in rich Dublin brogues.

It is of this level of being that Freud wrote, mystified, "The unconscious is not aware of its own mortality," and Aleister Crowley, more perceptively, wrote, "The unconscious is aware of its own immortality." Joyce also identifies this Ш with mountains because mountains symbolize eternity and, coincidentally, Ш is the Chinese ideogram for "mountain"; he also identifies Ш with the Hebrew Ш identified by Cabalists with the descent of "spirit" into "matter," an occult metaphor which is understood by Christian Cabalists to refer to the incarnation of God in Jesus and by pantheistic Cabalists to mean that the history of life itself is the autobiography of God. Chinese Ш is pronounced *shan*, Hebrew Ш is pronounced *sheen* (and usually spelled shin) and *Finnegans Wake* contains a Shaun, a postman,* who is perpetually trying to deliver a letter containing undefined good news. The letter was found in a garbage-heap which becomes, in turn, Dublin, an archeological dig, all human history, and Ш itself or the living presence of our dead ancestors.

The fourth function, Ⅎ , of the system-function EⅎⅢ seems to have been *named* only twice before Joyce (the Buddhists call it "void" and the Taoists call it *wu-hsin* or no-mind) although described by all mystics. To use the Taoist metaphor Ⅎ is no-mind because it is the class of all possible minds, which is not a mind for the same reason that the class of all possible mammals is not a mammal. It is speaking of this level that mystics say such "paradoxical" things as existence and non-existence are the same, the real is the unreal, all is illusion but the poplar tree in the courtyard is Buddha, etc. Obviously, here ordinary language breaks down and Joyce was compelled to invent his own language to write *Finnegans Wake*.

Quantum physicists, meanwhile, have gotten beyond ordinary language

---

* Shaun the postman is a character in Dion Boucicault's 19th Century melodrama, *Arrah na Pogue*. The Gaelic title means "Nora of the kiss' and coincidentally invokes Joyce's life companion, Nora Barnacle. Dion Boucicault suggests Dionysus, one of the dead-and-resurrected gods who haunt *Finnegans Wake*; and there is a Finnegan in *Arrah na Pogue*, too.

by using special mathematics, and they have also discovered that an $\exists$ level is necessary to complete description of existence. To the Copenhagen school of quantum theory, $\exists$ is the multiple-reality of an atomic "particle" before we measure it and constrain it to one value. To the "hidden variable" theorists like Bohm, who deny that the act of measurement can magically transform a multiple reality to a single reality, $\exists$ is the hidden variable (they write it c_1) which constrains particles even when we aren't measuring them. To the quantum logic school of von Neumann, $\exists$ is the indeterminate function between Aristotelian true and false, the "maybe" in which quantum systems spend most of their time when we are not constraining them by experimental meddling. To Heisenberg, $\exists$ is the multiple true-false-maybe forward-and-backward-in-time condition of *potentia*, which only becomes "reality" after our participation as experimentalists. Finally, in the Everett-Wheeler-Graham, or EWC, model, $\exists$ is every possible state that a "particle" or a "universe" can get itself into, all of which are considered equally "real," not just mathematically but physically, even though we only participate in one "reality" at a time.

It is evident that these conflicting interpretations of quantum experiments, despite differences in technical philosophical niceties, all agree that ordinary everyday "reality" is only an aspect of a more complex function of multiple realities. If we ask why this quantum ontology agrees so conveniently with the teachings of Buddhism and Taoism, and why both physics and Eastern mysticism agree with *Finnegans Wake*, the only answer seems to be that the deep structure of matter, experimentally investigated, contains the same paradoxes as the deep study of mind, when experimentally investigated by the techniques of meditation and Altered States of Consciousness. In the depths, we do not find One Mind and One Reality, as Theists and Materialists both imagine, but something so different from day-time concepts that it can only be categorized in contradictions—No Mind (Taoism) and Many Realities (EWC model) or mathematical fictions that only become "real" when we interact with them (Copenhagen/Heisenberg views) or the three-valued von Neumann logic (True/False/Maybe) which resolves all Zen riddles and Sufi puzzles if you apply it to them.

Before the reader cries (as Byron did of Wordsworth) "I wish he would explain his explanation," let us look concretely at some of the hologrammic prose of *Finnegans Wake* and see how the systems of E , $\sqcap$, $\sqcup$ and $\exists$ apply to it. We try the first sentence:

> riverrun, past Eve and Adam's, from swerve of shore to bend of bay, brings us by a commodius vicus of recirculation back to Howth Castle and Environs.

On the level of E or daily Ego consciousness, the dreamer is mingling geographic details of his everyday experience. The river Anna Liffey runs ("riverrun") past the Church of Adam and Eve on Merchant's Quay in downtown Dublin; the Liffey empties into Dublin Bay ("bend of bay") which in turn swerves southward past Vico Road between Dalkey and Kiliney ("vicus of recirculation"); on the north rim of the bay is the hill of Howth and Howth Castle. The daily Ego has even inserted its initials: **H**owth **C**astle and **E**nvirons: **H**umphrey **C**himpden **E**arwicker.

On the level of **m** or the Freudian unconscious (Mr. Hyde) we find infantile obsessions on urination and defecation: the river is a urine symbol, "commodius" suggests commode or chamber-pot, and recir*cul*ation includes *cul*, French ass-hole. Voyeurism and/or exhibitionism are also implicit in Adam and Eve, via the popular tag, "naked as Adam and Eve." Howth Castle atop Howth Hill is, of course, a Freudian phallic symbol.

On the level of **ш** or the collective unconscious ("Akashic records") Adam and Eve are male and female archetypes, the river and hill are Chinese images of *yin* (generalized femaleness) and *yang* (generalized maleness), the "vicus of recirculation" contains the turning wheel and/or Jungian mandala that most mystics have visioned, and several of the dead and absent are alive and present within the multiple language: the Roman emperor Commodus and the Neapolitan philospher Vico, for instance.

On the level of **Ǝ** or multiple realities (no-mind), we are in the Garden of Eden with its four rivers while we are simultaneously in Dublin with its one river ("riverrun . . . Eve and Adam"); *vicus* (Latin road, later town) coincidentally links the dreamer, Earwicker (it is part of the eymology of his name) with the historic locale, because Dublin was originally Baile-atha-Cliath, "the town of wicker bridges"; the *cul* in "recirculation" includes not just a Freudian anal reference but introduces the themes of Finn Mac Cool and *felix cupla* which hologrammically appear in every part of the book, virtually in every paragraph.

That was a brief introduction to the hologrammic structure of the first sentence of *Finnegans Wake*; the reader can see how, like a hologram, this prose contains the whole in each part—as the universe does, according to the recent theories of the physicist David Bohm. The reader may also begin to fathom why Lao-Tse said, "The largest is within the smallest."

Let us try a simpler example, from Chapter 2:

cross Ebblinn's chilled hamlet

On the **E** level, dreaming Earwicker recalls, all night long, the songs the customers in his pub like to sing; here he is half-remembering "Molly Malone"—"In Dublin's fair city" / cross Ebblinn's chilled hamlet . . . the rhythm gives us the tune, while the reversed initials (E.c.h./HCE) remind us that the day-time Ego is only present-by-absence in the dream world. On the **ɯ** level, "chilled hamlet" suggests Byron's *Childe Harold* and the rumors of incest and homosexuality that surround the poet; "hamlet" alone brings in Oedipal themes. On the **ɯ** level, Childe Harold is the archetype of the Wanderer, Hamlet is the *puer eternis* with overtones of the trickster-god (Hamlet feigns madness and speaks in riddles), the "cross" again invokes death/resurrection, and, since the historical Hamlet was governor of Dublin during the Danish occupation of Ireland, "racial memory" or Sheldrake's morphic resonance are again present. Since Eblana was the first Latin name for Dublin (on a map by Ptolomy c. 100 AD), Ebblinn also contains the living presence of the absent dead. On the **Ǝ** level, the "ham" in Hamlet connects with the three sons of Noah (Shem, Japhet and Ham) who recur periodically; ham also associates with Bacon, who coincidentally is thought to be the real author of *Hamlet* by some; Bacon in Old High German is *Bach* and the initials E.C.H. are backward and Bachward also, in the manner of Bach's more intricate melodies.

Of course, the very name of the Crimean War combines crime and war and this reflects the whole dark, Shadow side (**ɯ**) of humanity. Buckley is from a Gaelic root meaning "youth," so the story, like *Hamlet*, has Oedipal overtones. Defecation and war are connected by anal sadism on the **ɯ** level, according to Freud; they are also connected by territorial imperatives on the **ɯ** level, according to ethologists who tell us mammals defecate to claim territory and war is a continuation of mammalian territorial dispute. On the E level, the story of the General reflects Earwicker's personal shame about an incident in Phoenix Park (foenix *cul*prit) in which three British soldiers saw him taking a crap in the bushes. (Dublin didn't have many public toilets in those days.) On the **Ǝ** level, the story indicates quantum indeterminacy: just as a "particle" is only "spin up" or "spin down" when we measure it and in every state or no state when we aren't measuring it, the General is only "human" with his pants down and is an "Enemy" with his pants up.

A more lyrical passage illustrates the same principles amusingly:

> In the name of Annah, the Allmaziful, the Everliving, the Bringer of Plurabilities, haloed be her eve, her singtime sung, her rill be run, unhemmed as it is uneven.

The reader may find it enlightening to disentangle the four levels of **E** , **ɯ**, **ɯ** and **Ǝ**, as an exercise. It is worth noting that we have two patriarchal prayers combined, with a matriarchal underlay. "In the name of Allah, the Allmerciful" is the Islamic sunset prayer; I assume anybody can find the Lord's Prayer of Christianity easily enough. On a deeper level of the psyche, the Great Mother still reigns: *Annah* is "mother" in Turkish; the female river Anna Liffey appears "Annah . . . living"; the special Anima or Great Goddess of *Finnegans Wake*, Anna Livia Plurabella, combining river and woman emerges from "Annah . . . living . . . plurabilities." The first woman, present in the first sentence ("riverrun . . . ") is still present below the surface although absent on the surface: we can dig her out of "*Ever*living," "haloed be her *eve*" and "un*even*." The Maize Mother or Corn Mother, earliest form of the goddess according to Frazer, is there hiding in "Allmaziful." Just as she was there, intangible as a tune, in "cross Ebblinn's chilled hamlet," where she is the ghost of Molly Malone; and just as, in the first sentence, she was not only the river but the *vicus* which gave English *wicce*, a turning, a turning dance and craft of wicca, the one faith which kept the worship of the Goddess alive in the patriarchal aeon.

It should be clear that in *Finnegans Wake*, past, present, future, space, time and Ego-reality are all dissolved into the multiple "realities" described by mystics and quantum physicists; that Joyce, a man of timid courage, has seized the keys of hell of death, by showing that the Ego dies and is reborn more continually than we realize, and that absence or death are as unreal in this context as the famous Schrodinger equations which demonstrated in quantum theory that a cat may be dead and alive at the same time.

As Philip K. Dick wrote in *VALIS*:*

> Apollonius of Tyana, writing as Hermes Trismegistus, said "That which is above is that which is below." By this he meant to tell us that our universe is a hologram, but he lacked the term.

Joyce's equivalent is:

> The tasks above are as the flasks below, saith the emerald canticle of Hermes . . . solarsystemised, seriolocosmically, in a more and more almightily expanding universe under one, there is rhymeless reason to believe, original sun.

The emerald canticle of Hermes brings us backward and Bachward to Humphrey Chimpden Earwicker again, that day-time Ego. Above and below, like absence and presence, are equivalent in this hologrammic field; Bach again invokes Bacon and Ham and Hamlet and pork and P'ork (Padraic), Ireland's patron saint and Saint Patrick's Cathedral where Swift, the melancholy Dean was a melancholy Dane in Dublin brogue; "seriolcosmically" refers not only to Joyce's serio-comic style but to *The Serial Universe*, in which J.W. Dunne attempted to demonstrate mathematically that each

---

* *VALIS* is Dick's equivalent of Joyce's **ⴹ** or the Chinese no-mind; it means **V**ast **A**ctive **L**iving **I**nformation **S**ystem.

mind was part of a bigger mind, in infinite regress (an approximation of
Joyce's hologrammic Ⅎ); the original sun is the Big Bang combined with
the original sin which brings us by a commodius vicus of recirculation back
to Adam and Eve and *felix culpa* and Phoenix culprits and Finn Mac Cool and
the Russian General showing his culious epiphany to Buckley; and, if Bach is
bacon in Old High German, returning us to pork and ham, Bach in modern
German is "brook," bringing us back to Anna Livia Plurabella, the river-
woman who is Joyce's ultimate symbol of permanence in change, change in
permanence, life in death, presence in absence.

INTRODUCTION TO

Three Articles From
THE REALIST

Paul Krassner's iconoclastic journal, *The Realist*, has published more of my writings than any other American magazine, and there was a period in the late 1950s and early 1960s when I might have given up writing entirely if Paul had not gone on publishing my work. I think everybody in the "counterculture" owes a great debt to Paul Krassner, but I perhaps owe him more than anyone else.

The first two of these three pieces were written in the 1960s; the third is newer, and was written in 1985. I will speak more about the third piece later, but now I find it illuminating that the 1960s articles deal with, respectively, the most savagely Darwinian of Tennessee Williams's dramas and with the Marquis de Sade. The reader might think I was rather morbidly preoccupied with violence and sadism at that time; and, indeed, I was.

Although I became a pacifist so far back I cannot exactly date my "conversion" (if that's what it was), my opposition to warfare escalated in the 1960s in exact proportion to my horror at the non-governmental violence that was becoming more and more common in America then and has continued to proliferate. It seemed to me, and still seems to me, that sado-masochism plays a far larger role in "normal" psychology than most commentators realize; my fascination with the theories of Dr. Wilhelm Reich is largely based on the fact that he explored this subject with more insight and courage than most Freudians, who are aware of it but prefer not to notice or speak about its political implications.

Let me make it clear that I am not the same kind of "pacifist" as Gandhi or Joan Baez. I am not as "moral" as those noble souls, and certainly not as dogmatic and self-righteous; I do not feel comfortable sitting on a perch of assumed "moral" superiority and lecturing down at the "sinners" below me. I have always had a basically scientific worldview (however eccentric it is is some respects) and have never believed in metaphysical "evil." I tend to think that all the violent sadism in the world, which horrifies me emotionally, is still perfectly natural and is the inevitable product of the past 3 billion years of evolution. I suspect that all viable planets pass through similarly bloody stages in the evolution upward to higher and higher consciousness. I am almost entirely lacking in "morality" in the conventional sense, and find it hard to despise any organism—fish, reptile or mammal. Since I am also a relativist rather than an absolutist, I have no hesitation about being violent in self-defense, and Gandhi and Ms. Baez would regard me as a very sinful chap indeed.

My brand of pacifism is based, first of all, on my own emotional repugnance for cruelty toward women and children (modern warfare being increasingly destructive to civilians, including women and children). Such an emotional prejudice is admittedly personal and subjective and not expected to move anybody who sincerely likes the idea of bombs and napalm dropping on defenseless populations; but my pacifism is also based upon factors which I believe can be proven to be in the rational self-interest of all. That is, I agree with Einstein and Bertrand Russell and the whole band of radical scientists who assert that we are very unlikely to survive a nuclear war.

Even here I am a heretic. I think we as a species might **possibly** survive one nuclear war, if it is a short one and limited. I believe Hermann Kahn is right in claiming that such a limited nuclear war is statistically slightly more likely than the Holocaust predicted in professional pacifist agit-prop.

Nonetheless, it seems obvious to me that we cannot survive a **series** of nuclear wars—at some point, the death of Earth will become inevitable— and I am not **sure** that even a limited nuclear war will remain limited when one side sees that it is losing. In short, I think if we are to survive, we have to ban warfare eventually, and the risk gets worse every year as more and more scientific brains work on the problem Bucky Fuller defined bitterly as "delivering more and more explosive power over longer and longer distances in shorter and shorter times to kill more and more people." Before that process culminates in Armaggedon, we must learn the arts of peace, and we better start studying them avidly right now. We should have started the day after Hiroshima.

This seems so obvious to me—and I note that even Neanderthals like Ronald Reagan give occasional lip-service to it—that I have been driven repeatedly over the years, but especially when the following two essays were written, to ask the inevitable question: if rational self-interest does demand that we abandon our traditional violent approach to international relations, why is it that most people still passively tolerate the growing nuclear stockpile that moves us closer to annihilation every day? The only answer to that which makes sense to me is Freudian and perhaps Reichian, and the Vietnam War brought all this home to me even more than the Nazi horrors had, because in Vietnam it was my countrymen and contemporaries who were happily toasting women and children with napalm. Any theory about Eichmann that eased my anxieties broke down when I tried to apply it to Lt. Calley, who was the product of the same socio-economic-cultural environment that had produced me.

I began to fear that people are **not** guided by rational self-interest; sadism and masochism may play a larger role in human psychology than we like to admit. The masochism of the masses may even, as Reich claimed, summon the most sadistic "leaders" who can be found. People tolerate weapons of megadeath not just because they like the idea of Russian women and children being toasted and roasted and barbecued in nuclear hell, but because they like the idea of this being done to women and children generally, including "our" "own"—**and because they like the thought of it being done to themselves**. In short, the "moral majority" likes nuclear war for the same reason it likes hellfire-and-damnation sermons. It enjoys wallowing in the imagery of ultimate sadism and ultimate masochism both. Maybe Hell is so popular, and nuclear war (man-made Hell) is so popular with the people who dig Hellfire theology, because the masses want to suffer more than they want anything else.

These anxieties run through all my novels and even haunt the one play I have written. I am sourly amused that some critics complain that I am "too optimistic" or "too Utopian." I guess critics of that ilk only read every second page. My "optimism" is an act of will—a revolutionary act of defiance, perhaps—but it is not based on any innocent illusions about what human beings have been doing to each other since the dawn of history.

The Doctor
With the Frightened Eyes

---

*"Queegqueg no care what god made him shark . . . wedder
Fejee god or Nantucket god; but de god what made shark
must be one dam Ingin."*

—Herman Melville, *Moby Dick*
Chapter 66, "The Shark Massacre"

Tennessee Williams' new move, *Suddenly, Last Summer*, seems to have
infuriated more wowsers than any literary work since Joyce's *Ulysses*. From
north, south, east and west the impassioned voices resound, declaring that
Williams is "sick," "morbid," "unwholesome," and generally a sad blend of the
unheimlich and the *mashugga*.

"Almost intolerably evil," fulminates *Parents* magazine. "Clinical, distasteful,
morbid, extraordinarily shocking," howls *McCall's*. The weeping and
gnashing of teeth from other sources is even more heart-rending. One
would think that the wisdom of Christ or the immaculate conception of
Eleanor Roosevelt had been challenged.

Actually, all that Williams has done is to confront some of the issues
which great tragedy has always raised, from Sophocles through Shakespeare,
right up to Melville. *Suddenly, Last Summer*, far from being sick, is Williams'
healthiest work—because it is his bravest.

It doesn't see human suffering as an illustration to a theory by Freud or

Marx. It doesn't pretend that evil is always due to economics or Oedipus complexes. It will probably not be popular with people who think that Arthur Miller, or Maxwell Anderson, or William Inge, are important playwrights.

Like *King Lear*, this new Williams tragedy does not pretend to have all the answers; but, like *King Lear*, it is brave enough to ask all the questions.

The difference between a great writer and a minor one is fundamentally this: that the minor writer always has answers—glib answers, slick answers, memorably-worded answers, resounding and pretentious answers. The great writer dares to stand before you naked, armed only with his questions.

Villon is great because he doesn't pretend to know what he doesn't know. What he does know he tells us in direct language—language so simple that stupid critics have debated several hundred years now on what makes his poetry so strong.

What he knows is that hunger makes the wolf devour sheep, and hunger makes the man kill another for his money, and that people who end up on the gallows are not much different from those who die quietly in bed. He knows these things, intimately, and he says them. He knows that most whores are not glamorous but ugly, and he says that.

Villon doesn't know a damned thing about Professor Lutkopf's essay on Dr. Kleindenken's commentary on what Marx wrote to Engels in 1872. Or, if he does know, he doesn't care—anymore than he cares about Aquinas' commentaries on Aristotle.

Villon is not really much like Tennessee Williams, and I really shouldn't have dragged him into this article, but the two men do have this thing in common, that they are not running for President. Arthur Miller, for instance, is a writer who is always running for President.

Death of a Salesman is to drama what an Eisenhower speech is to rhetoric. There is in it none of the really frightening, terrible, unspeakable quality that makes a great tragedy. Everybody knows why Willy Loman suffered and died; they knew before they went into the theatre.

Death of a Salesman offers, really, nothing but a bland uplift. It tells the Broadway audience what they want to hear, that the liberal left-wing philosophy of the '30s was true after all. It has all of the answers, so it doesn't really ask any of the questions.

The great writer creates situations so true and so urgently significant that he himself often doesn't "understand" them. I mean that very seriously. When Achilles suddenly weeps, in the great interview with Priam at the end of the *Illiad*, Homer is probably as surprised as the rest of us.

Nobody knows why Achilles wept, but we all know that he *must have* wept;

just as we know that Lear *must have* prayed for the "poor hungry wretches" that night on the moor. A Homer or a Shakespeare creates such scenes without knowing why they must be just as they are; and we weep over them without knowing how we are sure that they are true.

Suddenly, Last Summer is this kind of a story. It has no "message," no religious or economic or psychological theory to sell, no relaxing answer to the unbearable tensions it creates. All it has is mystery and horror and a lyric poetry that is shot through with pain and wonder. All it has is the pulsating life of the naked soul of a man who is the greatest dramatic artist since Ibsen.

The story is really quite simple. A psychiatrist with an unpronounceable Polish name that he translates as "sugar" is offered a fantastic sum of money to perform a lobotomy upon a psychotic young girl. The woman who offers the money is Violet Venable, a "southern lady," mother of a recently dead poet, Sebastian Venable.

Dr. Sugar interviews the psychotic young girl, Cathy. He decides that he can cure her without resorting to lobotomy. Through narco-analysis he gradually learns what has driven Cathy into the hiding place we call insanity. Cathy, it seems, has seen Sebastian's death, and it was a gruesome one.

Sebastian was a homosexual who had used Cathy as "bait" to attract young men. He did this once too often, the last time on a tropical island where most of the population is living in that state of starvation which is so common in the world today—and which we rich Americans try so hard to blot out of our consciousness.

Sebastian "caught" several of the ragged, ugly, filthy, starving adolescent boys on this island, using Cathy as "bait." But, with cool selfishness, he used these boys and then carelessly tossed them aside. They were of primitive and ignorant people. They finally united against Sebastian, came for him in a mob, took him, murdered him . . . and devoured his body.

When Cathy is able to remember this and tell it to "Dr. Sugar" she is cured.

This is the whole story. But, of course, to tell it this way is to obliterate its significance. The gruesome act of cannibalism which forms the climax is only the strongest of a series of disturbing images which are the real elements of the dark poem Williams has constructed.

The hospital in which Dr. Sugar works is called *Lion's View*, for example.

The island where Sebastian dies is called *Cabezo de Lobo*—head of a *wolf*.

Violet Venable has an insectivorous plant, given to her by Sebastian, and we see it being fed in the course of the story.

The dinosaurs, one character remarks (inaccurately, but with artistic meaning), perished because they were vegetarians—"the earth belongs to the carnivores."

Violet's garden has in it a statue of a winged skeleton, and this comes between her and Dr. Sugar at a significant moment.

Finally, the place where Sebastian is killed is "the ruins of an old temple," that looked "horrible . . . as if it had been the scene of terrible sacrificial rites."

Sebastian is, indeed, a sacrificial victim, and the winged skeleton reappears briefly in a surrealistic half-image on the screen just before the murder is consummated. Sebastian, actually, is a self-elected sacrifice, like Christ, testifying to a very non-Christian vision of God.

That Sebastian had had a "vision of God" we learn very early in the story. Violet tells us about it, in the longest and most poetic speech Tennessee Williams has ever written. Sebastian saw God in the Galapagos Islands at the breeding-time of the turtles.

Every year at this time the female turtles crawl out of the sea, laboriously lay their eggs, and, hideously tired, crawl weakly back into the sea. In a while the eggs hatch and the young come out and begin their run toward the sea.

But the great birds of the Galapagos know all about the breeding-time of the turtles and they wait for this moment every year. As the young turtles race toward the sea, the birds descend from the sky, thousands of them, in a great black cloud. They attack the infant turtles, turn them over, tear their bellies and devour them.

Of the hundreds of turtles that hatch each year, only about one-tenth of one percent ever reach the sea. The rest are eaten.

When Sebastian saw this natural process he knew in a poetic flash that "God is cruel and creation and destruction are the same." The God he worshipped, the God to whom his poems are henceforth written, was the God of Melville's "shark massacre," the Hangman God of Joyce's *Ulysses*, the sadistic Nobodaddy of Blake's prophetic poems, the God of Greek tragedy, the God who, in *King Lear*, kills men for sport.

That Sebastian's vision of God was a true one is the dark, hidden fear of every religious person. The non-dualistic Orient accepts such a thought with equanimity: when Ramakrishna saw the goddess Kali give birth and then devour her own child, he took the vision as a true revelation of the oneness of creation and destruction.

To Buddhist Tibet, this is the unity of *yab* and *yum*; to Taoist China, the unity of *yin* and *yang*. The Occident perennially seeks to repress this thought, and perennially is haunted by half-awareness of it.

It is the symbolic meaning of the scar that bisects Ahab in *Moby Dick*, and of the half-obliterated body of "the Runner" in Faulkner's *Fable*. It recurs again and again in Euripedes, Sophocles, Shakespeare, Joyce and dozens of others.

With this clue in mind we can see that the world of *Suddenly, Last Summer* does, indeed, belong to the carnivores.

Shortly after Sebastian's death, two loathsome relatives turn up to attempt to scavenge as much of his clothing and other possessions as they can get their hands on. (This type of emotional cannibalism also appears in Williams' *Cat on a Hot Tin Roof*.)

Sebastian's homosexuality, we eventually learn, had resulted from his mother's attempts to enforce the neurotic condition she calls "chastity" upon him. (This type of cannibalism by parents upon children is, of course, the chief feature of organized religion, and the principle theme of most of Williams' works.)

Cannibalism is even a characteristic of societies, as well as individuals—the deplorable conditions of the hospital where Dr. Sugar treats Cathy are depicted unblinkingly by Williams; and anybody at all aware of the treatment of the psychotic in this great, rich nation knows that the best that most states do for these unfortunates is precisely as inadequate and horrible as this movie indicates. Some state hospitals are even worse than *Lion's View*.

The only literary work to confront these issues as boldly as *Suddenly, Last Summer* is Melville's *Moby Dick*. The classic description of a sea-battle—"men cannibally carving each other's live meat on deck" while the sharks "carve the dead meat" of the bodies thrown overboard—would be just the same if you turned it upside down and put the men in the water and the sharks on the deck, "a shockingly sharkish business enough for all parties." Ishmael, reflecting on this, considers "the propriety of devil-worship," just as Williams' Sebastian does.

While the sharks eat a whale in the water, Stubb eats steak off the same whale in his cabin. "Go to the meat-market," Melville tells the reader: "Cannibal! Who isn't a cannibal?"

The all-time classic in this chain of thought also occurs in *Moby Dick*, in the great scene where the "grandfather whale" is harpooned and killed. Melville writes:

> From the points where the whale's eyes had once been, now protruded blind bulbs, horribly pitiable to see. But pity there was none. For all his old age, and his one arm, and his blind eyes, he must die the death and be murdered . . . to light the gay bridals of men, and also to illuminate the solemn churches that preach unconditional inoffensiveness by all to all.

We begin to realize that, once these issues are raised, it doesn't really matter whether a man "believes in God" or not. "God," after all, is just a short-hand symbol for our attitude toward the nature of the universe.

Most *soi-disant* "freethinkers" and "atheists" can't accept the notion that Ultimate Reality is really this sharkish, anymore than religionists can accept it.

The *Book of Job* dares to raise the question—that is its eternal glory—but then hastily buries it under a cloud of meaningless rhetoric. Only the greatest works of art have dared to stare unblinkingly at the question without attempting to smooth it over or bury it—works like *Medea, King Lear, Moby Dick,* Beethoven's *Fifth,* Goya's *Saturn Devouring His Children* and *The Disasters of War.*

The theological writings of Kierkegaard and Tillich make honest attempts to confront this question; and I respect these two men more than I respect the banal flow of bilge that issues forth from the "philosophers" of the American Humanist Association.

(If the Reverend Schaef wants to write to the *Realist* again and renew his charge that I am a theologian in disguise, I will admit that he's not completely wrong—but I'm only a theologian in the sense that Antonin Artaud was.)

But, is everything completely black and sharkish in Williams' view of the universe? Well, it has to be granted that it is not. Dr. Sugar does, finally, cure Cathy, through that discipline of unmitigated psychological honesty which is the essence of psychotherapy; and a universe in which such honesty and such cures are possible cannot be all bad.

Indeed, the East which accepts the unity of good and evil, *yin* and *yang,* with such equanimity, has never forgotten that if the evil is omnipresent, why, then, so must be the good.

And even Melville's vision—at the climax of *Moby Dick,* when the great Whale Armada comes before us—includes the significant detail that, with slaughter rampant all around them, the young whales at the center of the school are copulating and the mother whales are suckling their young.

"And thus," Melville writes, "surrounded by circle upon circle of consternations and affrights ... the creatures of the center fearlessly indulge in peaceful concernments . . . yea, in dalliance and delight."

A few sentences later, Melville boldly declares the Oriental doctrine of the undefiled essence: " . . . and while planets of woe revolve around me, deep down and deep inland I still bathe in eternal joy."

But Melville was no fatuous optimist, as we have seen. At the end, Ahab and whale destroy each other and, in ironic last testimony to the unity of the opposites, Ishmael returns to *life* floating on a *coffin.*

And, similarly, Williams' Dr. Sugar, though he can cure one girl, has obviously no ilusions about himself or his science. *The doctor has frightened eyes.* Montgomery Clift's sensitive portrayal brings this home to us in scene after scene, and two of the characters remark upon it.

Nietzsche once wrote: "When you gaze into the abyss, the abyss also gazes into you." And the mystic Eckhart is even more direct: "The eye with which I see God is the eye with which God sees me."

Sebastian Venable spoke of the young boys he preyed upon as "tasty" and "delicious"; he used them selfishly, then cast them aside. He could only know the carnivorousness of the creative principle so well if it was *within* himself—in the depths of his own perverse and poetic heart.

That is how Dr. Sugar understands his patients, also; and that is why he, too, has frightened eyes.

"All these people who go around protesting against the nuclear tests," a friend of mine once said to me—"they never have the guts to face the problem in the only place where it can be handled—by facing the thing in themselves, in all men, that wants the Bomb to go off."

This is a far cry from the fatuous liberalism and optimism of the old-fashioned "humanist" and "freethinker," but perhaps the *Realist* is sufficiently aware of 20th Century history and 20th Century psychology to allow it to be expressed by one Negative Thinker.

Thirteen Choruses
For The Divine Marquis

FIRST CHORUS
"You are afraid of the people unrestrained—
how ridiculous!"

— Sade*

I dreamed I called Rita Hayworth on the phone and asked her if she hears the babies of Hiroshima screaming in the night.

"No," she said, "I useta have kinda kooky problems like that but my analyst cleared them all up."

But—I insisted—after all, it was your picture that was painted on the Bomb. Not Harry Truman, or Einstein, or even Marilyn Monroe. You.

"Well, yeah, if you wanna look at it that way," she said. "But, Christ, they was sticking my picture on everything those days."

But, but—I shouted—don't you feel any sense of responsibility?

"Waita-minit, Mac," she said, "what are ya, some kinda nut? Nobody ever asked me nothing about it. They just went ahead and dropped it."

---

* Quotations identified as Sade are from *Marquis de Sade*, Grove Press, 1965. Those identified as Marat/Sade are from *The Persecution and Assassination of Marat as Performed by the Inmates of the Asylum at Charenton Under the Direction of the Marquis de Sade*, by Peter Weiss, Athenium, 1965.

But, but, but—I screamed—all those people—550,000 of them, according to one estimate I read—blown apart by a picture of you—

"Look, Clyde," she said firmly. "My analyst told me it don't do no good to brood over such things."

And the line went dead with a hollow click, like a coffin closing snugly on Dracula as the morning sun throws its white and ghastly nuclear radiations into the cool darkness of dream.

SECOND CHORUS
Why do the children scream
What are the heaps they fight over
those heaps with eyes and mouths
                                              — Marat/Sade

And we, we Hiroshima-makers, are now finally, more than 150 years after his death, tentatively beginning to look at the unexpurgated de Sade.

I dreamed I called Dwight Eisenhower on the phone and asked him if de Sade should be banned.

"I don't know," he said. "I'll have to ask Postmaster General Summerfield. If he says it's a filthy book, then of course it should be banned. America must maintain its purity and its God-given heritage."

And I dreamed I called him back two nights later and he had consulted with Summerfield and the verdict was n.g. "Summerfield says dee Sayd was a pinko pervert."

And the phone went dead with a sudden dull click like the last sound Hemmingway heard when he put the gun to his head and said, ah, shit, now, not any other minute but this minute, right *now*.

THIRD CHORUS
... and as if I were a naughty little boy, the idea
is to spank me into good behavior?
                                              — Sade

Prof. B.F. Skinner of Harvard, ripe with years and wisdom, rich with degrees and honors, says that a world without punishment is operationally conceivable. That is, speaking as a scientific psychologist, Skinner does not know of any behavior that can't be increased or decreased without the use of punishment.

Desirable behavior (from your point of view, whatever your point of view is)?—reinforce it through a system of rewards. It will increase.

Undesirable behavior (again, from whatever your point of view is)?—no need to punish it; just reinforce *incompatible* behavior, again through a system of rewards. The incompatible behavior will increase, and the "undesirable" behavior will decrease.

Simple as a proof in geometry.

But there is something in mankind which profoundly resents Prof. Skinner and his rationalism and his technology and his simplicity. The name of that something is the name of the divine Marquis, Donatien Alphonse Francois de Sade.

I dreamed I called J. Edgar Hoover on the phone and asked him, hey, dig, man, what do you think of a world without punishment?

"(Get a tap on this line,)" he said away from the phone, "(I got a pinko bleeding heart here.)"

"I'll tell you, sir," he said, "we are just a fact-finding agency; we don't draw any conclusions. But I Will Say This! There Is Only One Language the Godless Communists Understand And That Is The Language of Superior Power."

But, but—I cried—can you put the whole world over your lap and spank it?

"If the world had one ass, you can be sure we would," he said. "As it is, the spankings will have to be administered jointly and severally."

And the line went dead with an empty click, like a whip being pulled from its sheath and flicked, testingly, in the air.

FOURTH CHORUS
Marat
these cells of the inner self
are worse than the deepest stone dungeon
and as long as they are locked
all your revolution remains
only a prison mutiny
to be put down
by corrupted fellow prisoners
         — Marat/Sade

Eventually we begin to realize that Sade has never been understood. He cried out for liberty, and we accuse him of being a forerunner of Hitler. He dreamed of a world without punishment, and we attribute brutality to him. He spoke for the spirit of love, and we project every viciousness onto him.

We are afraid of being seduced by him, we Hiroshima-makers.

He showed us our own face in a mirror and we have screamed for 150 years that it was his face.

Nothing could be more explicit than his actual words:

Laws should be "flexible," "mild" and "few" (Sade, p. 310).

We must "get rid forever of the atrocity of capital punishment" (Sade, p. 310).

Women must be equal with men: "Must the diviner half of humankind be laden with irons by the other? Ah, break those irons, Nature wills it" (Sade, p. 322).

Property should cease to be monopolized by a few (Sade, p. 313-314).

The present system of property-and-power rests on "submission of the people . . . due to . . . violence and the frequent use of torture" (Sade, p. 11).

He gave up his post as magistrate rather than administer capital punishment—"They wanted me to commit an inhumane act. I have never wanted to" (Sade, p. 29).

His principles are, as he says, quite correctly, not those that lead to tyranny but "principles to whose expression and realization the infamous despotism of tyrants has been opposed for uncounted centuries" (Sade, p. 311).

Even against the clergy, he maintains a solidly libertarian position: "I do not, however, propose either massacres or expulsions. Such dreadful things have no place in the enlightened mind. No, do not assassinate at all, do not expel at all. . . . Let us reserve the employment of force for the idols; ridicule alone will suffice for those who serve them" (Sade, p. 306).

But these words are ignored. Because he committed one crime—the crime of *reporting accurately* the secret day-dreams and longings of the psyche of men and women in this civilization, men and women reared in the crucible of authority-and-submission, discipline-and-punishment—he has been portrayed as the *endorser* of these extremities.

More truly than Flaubert said "Je suis Bovary," Sade could have said (*did* say, for those who read between the lines), "Je suis Justine." It is his voice that cries out continually in Justine's speeches, "Oh, monsters, is remorse and dead in you?" Just as it is his voice, undeniably, in the "Dialogue Between a Priest and a Dying Man" which says simply, "Reason, sir—yes, our reason alone should warn us that harm done our fellows can never bring happiness to us . . . and you need neither god nor religion to subscribe to [it]" (Sade, p. 174).

I dreamed I called Jesus Christ on the phone and asked him, say, Man, did you *really* forgive them for they knew not what they did?

"Verily, verily, I say unto you," he replied, "I made my position on authority-and-submission as clear as I could: 'You know that the princes of the Gentiles exercise dominion over them, and they that are great exercise authority upon them. But it shall not be so among you.' —Matt. 20:25. 'Every kingdom divided against itself is brought to desolation.' —Matt. 12:25. 'If the blind lead the blind, both shall fall into the ditch.' —Matt. 15:14. 'For they bind heavy burdens and grievous to be borne, and lay them upon men's shoulders; but they themselves will not move them with one of their fingers.' — Matt. 23:4. They be blind leaders of the blind, baby, and mechanical laws of punishment-and-conditioning lead them in little grooves of robot-life."

But, but—I protested—is there anything outside conditioned behavior? Is there a real freedom, Man? Is there?

"Find the place where Sade and I agree," he said, "and there you will find the beginning of a definition of liberty."

And the line went dead with a sudden click like the sound of a bedroom door closing as a little boy is pushed outside.

FIFTH CHORUS
"They declaim against the passions without bothering to see that it is from their flame philosophy lights its torch."
— Sade

The Castle, somebody pointed out, is a Sadean novel: Kafka's scene is a typical lair of Sadean monsters lying in wait for the innocent traveler. *The Trial* is even more Sadean I would argue, because the two thugs who haul Joseph K. off to an empty lot to slit his throat "like a dog" are, like Sade's images, revelations of the reality of our civilization. Capital punishment presented as a more nudely naked lunch than even Burroughs has fed us.

What happens to Joseph K., what happens to Justine, are very slight distortions* of what happens to each man, each woman, in a society based on authority-and-submission.

What Sade saw—what Marat did not see—the hidden meaning of Peter Weiss's noisy and Sophoclean circus of a play—is that Man as we know him, Man in historical time, is entirely the product of punishment. That punishment defines his character, contours and structures his character, *is* his character. That sado-masochism is not a perversion, or a "way of life," but the meaning of our civilization.

Sade's drive for liberty—i.e., his attempt to understand himself—led him to the scene in the brothel in which he buggered and was buggered, whipped and was whipped. That scene, and the seven years imprisonment it cost him, has given his name to perversion, and yet one feels there has been a mistake somewhere, Sadeanism isn't Sadism, the two forces met head-on, but Sade was going in one direction and the true Sadist is going in the other.

Open any schlock newspaper and read the personal ads in which S-M people grope for each other: "Docile young man seeks woman experienced in discipline . . . " "Male, interested in leather and uniforms, seeks male of

---

* "Two of the commonest types of hallucinations are the obscene epithet and the deadly injunction. Both the accusation 'You are homosexual!' and the command 'You must kill them!' may be safely regarded as revived and *not very much distorted* memories of pareental utterances." *Transactional Analysis in Psychotherapy*, by Eric Berne, Grove, 1961 (italics added).

dominant disposition . . . " "Interested in leather on women. . . . "

But this is not Sade's direction, my God, it is the direction of General Hershey and LBJ; it is the direction of our civilization; it is the *essence* of our civilization, dragged out into hideous visibility. Uniforms and discipline. "Kill for freedom, kill for peace, kill Vietnamese, kill, kill, kill!" The hallucinatory parental voice that says "You are homosexual" and "You must kill him." Uniforms and discipline. The blind leading the blind.

Albert Ellis is more general than Dr. Berne. According to Dr. Ellis, in a lecture at the N.Y. General Semantics Society, most neurotics—i.e., most civilized people—go around with a little internal voice saying "You are a no-good shit." ("You are homosexual," "You are a coward," and "You are a helpless neurotic" are only three variations on the main theme. The main theme is always "You are a no-good shit.")

Eric Frank Russell, the science-fiction writer, propounded a riddle once: "If everybody hates war, why do wars keep on happening?" Remember the S-M ads: "seeks discipline," "seeks uniforms," "seeks leather and rubber."

Authority-and-submission is the chief structural fact about feudal, capitalist and socialist society. Punishment-and-obedience is the defining gesture, as Stanislavsky would call it, of such societies. To illustrate it in one flash: Orwell's "boot stamping on the human face forever." And that is de Sade's theme, always.

I dreamed I called Fulton Sheen on the phone and asked him, I read in your column that "A child needs a pat on the back to encourage him— provided it is applied hard enough, low enough and often enough." You believe that crap, man?

"Without discipline," he intoned, "our whole civilization would fall into anarchy. 'I will chastize him with my rod,' says the Good Book."

But, but, man—I protested—you're supposed to be anti-sex. Don't youknow some cats get their rocks off that way? Ain't you read about spanking orgies and people coming in their pants during it? Ain't you against anybody coming, ever, anywhere, anytime, in any way?

"Argggh!" he said, like the dying villain of a comic book, and I couldn't tell if he was having an orgasm or a heart attack.

The line went dead with a weird like a bomb-bay door opening to drop Rita Hayworth's picture (Gilda, the whore, beckoning from her golden bed . . . on little bronze heathens who didn't believe in Jesus.

SIXTH CHORUS

Marat
forget the rest
there's nothing else
beyond the body

—**Marat/Sade**

So: after 150 years, we are ready to look de Sade in the face, eyeball to eyeball. He comes on, always, like a Zen Master, shouting right into our ears: "Tyranny or Anarchy—you must choose. Answer now!"

He was the first one mad enough and sane enough to accept the *given*, the immutible, to start from man-in-history rather than from man-in-theory. Well, he says, I don't believe in the "noble savage," I even doubt that he is "inherently good," but taking him as he is I still say: Freedom. He deserves liberty because nobody else is good enough to take it away from him.

He looked into anarchy, he looked past the voluntarily organized anarchy of Proudhon and Tolstoy, he looked into chaos itself, and he said, yes, even that, I will accept even that, before I will bend the knee to any Authority that claims to own me.

I dreamed I called LBJ on the phone and I said, look, man, you're not taking my son for one of your damnfool wars.

"You are mistaken," he said smoothly. "That boy is not *your* son. He belongs to society and the State, and I am society and the State. I will take him anywhere I want, I will order him to do anything I care to have done, and I will shoot him if he disobeys."

But, but, man—I said—like, wow, man—do you think you *own* us?

"Read your law books, son," he chuckled. "Ownership is the right 'to use *or abuse.'* "

And the line went dead with a cold little click like an IBM machine punching a hole in a card somewhere in the vast and infinite halls of bureaucracy.

SEVENTH CHORUS

"Although the prodigious spectacle of folly we
are facing here may be horrible, it is always
interesting."

— **Sade**

I called the world up on the telephone and I implored them:

How much of you belongs to the Combine? If they can take your money in taxes and your sons in wars, how do you differ from the cow who is milked or the pig who is eaten? Do you breed for them like a stallion in a pasture? Is the get of your loins theirs to dispose of? Even a no-good shit afraid that Daddy will come and slice it off has some rights, doesn't he? Or does he? Is there any sacrifice you will not make? Is there any discipline you will not accept? Is there any order you will not obey? Is there any shit you will not eat?

Who got the Indian Sign on you? How did it start? At age 12, worrying that J. Edgar Hoover was watching you jack off through his Washington telescope? Was it the bogey-man they scared you with? "Don't make dirty-dirty in your pants or ogres will come and eat you"? Circumcision the most cruel and inhuman attack on the genital accepted by your doctors; why? Schedule feeding that fucked up the minds of a generation; why? Is that how they get the soldiers for their wars? The whip-and-belt boys, the uniform-and-discipline boys, the Pentagon boys, all one big happy spanking-orgy?

And the operator said, "I'm sorry, sir. The world is not answering the phone anymore. It's watching television."

And the line went dead with a loud and unearthly click like the sound of a boy pulling his zipper up when he hears Father's footstep in the hall.

EIGHTH CHORUS

> A mad animal
> Man's a mad animal
> I'm a thousand years old and in my time
> I've helped commit a million murders
>
> — Marat/Sade

Rita Hayworth's picture on the Bomb.

What do we really want from them? What drove Garbo into hiding, Monroe into suicide, Lamaar into shoplifting, what struck Harlow down and sent Garland into the booze bottle?

And what happens in a Playboy Club? Have you stood there, like me, vodka-and-tonic in hand, looking down a bunny's cleavage and thinking suddenly of Lon Chaney as the Wolf-Man: "Even a man who is pure of heart / And says his prayers by night / Can turn to a wolf when the wolfbane blooms ? and the moon is full and bright. . . . " If you turned the fantasies of each person in the room onto the wall in LSD stereo what would it look like—a friendly little orgy, the Rape of the Sabine Women, or Mass Murder?

I dreamed I called a bunny on the phone and asked her, dig de Sade?

"But the most, darling," she cooed.

But, but—I asked—what do you really think of men?

"But, hon," she said innocently, "what do cattle think of butchers?"

And the line went dead with an abrupt click like a diaphragm falling from a purse onto a cold metal floor.

NINTH CHORUS
"My neighbors' passions frighten me infinitely less than do the law's injustices, for my neighbors' passions are contained by mine, whilst nothing checks the injustices of the law."
— **Sade**

A civilization based on authority-and-submission is a civilization without the means of self-correction. *Effective* communication flows only one way: from master-group to servile-group. Any cyberneticist knows that such a one-way communication channel lacks feedback and cannot behave "intelligently."

The epitome of authority-and-submission is the Army, and the control-and-communication network of the Army has every defect a cyberneticist's nightmare could conjure. Its typical patterns of behavior are immortalized in folklore as SNAFU (situation normal—all fucked-up), FUBAR (fucked-up beyond all redemption) and TARFU (Things are really fucked-up). In less extreme, but equally nosologic, form these are the typical conditions of any authoritarian group, be it a corporation, a nation, a family, or a whole civilization.

Produhon was a great communication analyst, born 100 years too soon to be understood. His system of voluntary association (anarchy) is based on the simple communication principles that an authoritarian system means one-way communication, or stupidity, and a libertarian system means two-way communication, or rationality.

The essence of authority, as he saw, was Law—that is, fiat—that is, effective communication running one way only. The essence of a libertarian system, as he also saw, was Contract—that is, mutual agreement—that is, effective communication running both ways. ("Redundance of control" is the technical cybernetic phrase.)

Sade saw this, before Proudhon. "The rule of law is inferior to that of anarchy; the most obvious proof of what I assert is the fact that any government is obliged to plunge itself into anarchy whenever it aspires to remake its constitution. In order to abrogate its former laws, it is compelled to establish a revolutionary regime in which there is no law; this regime finally gives birth to new laws, but this second state is necessarily less pure than the first, since it derives from it" (Sade, p. 46).

The conflict, Marat/Sade (which should really be Marx/Sade, except that the ingenious Mr. Weiss was not quite ingenious enough to devise a historical conjunction between uncle Karl and the Marquis), is the conflict between anarchy and tyranny. Sade, not Marat or Marx, is the true revolutionary, for he aims at a world outside the crucible of punishment-and-submission, while they aim at a new world still within that crucible.

I dreamed I called Ignatz Mouse on the phone and asked, why do you always throw bricks at Krazy Kat?

But Krazy answered instead and said, "Little Dahlink... he's always faithful."

And the line went dead with a dreadful click like Captain Queeg rolling his little marbles together.

TENTH CHORUS
The guillotine saves them from endless
** boredom**
Gaily they offer their heads as if for
** coronation**
Is not that the pinnacle of perversion?
                                    — Marat/Sade

Ralph Nader writes incredulously, in his study of automobile safety, *Unsafe at Any Speed*, "If one were to attempt to produce a pedestrian-injuring mechanism, the most theoretically efficient design would closely approach that of the front end of some present-day automobiles." Mr. Nader has never read Sade. He takes this as an oversight on Detroit's part.

I dreamed I called Batman on the phone and asked, any truth in those rumors about you and Robin?

"Our relationship is 100% platonic," he replied stiffly. "We *sublimate*. Why do you think we're always out looking for 'bad guys' that we can punish?"

And the line went dead with a quick click like handcuffs closing on a thin wrist forever.

ELEVENTH CHORUS
"If you are timid enough to stop with what is natural,
Nature will elude your grasp forever."
                                    — Sade

There is much sadism in popular culture these days, but little Sadeanism. One rare example of Sadeanism is the old movie, *The Most Dangerous Game*, and another is Ken Kesey's novel, *One Flew Over the Cuckoo's Nest*.

The heroes of both of these works are trapped in situations where superior power seeks remorselessly to destroy them. Both heroes, pure

Sadeanists, accept the situation at once—without complaining about its "immortality" or "injustice"—and set out systematically and cold-bloodedly to turn the tables.

This is the doctrine of the bandits in *Justine*—"Nature has caused us to be equals born, Therese; if fate is pleased to upset the primary scheme of things, it is for us to correct its caprices" (Sade, p. 481)—and the doctrine of Stirnerite anarchism. DeSade's proletarian heroes, like the glorious anarchist bandit, Ravechel, believe instinctively that "crime alone opens to us the door to life" (Sade, p. 482).

To anyone who doesn't like this doctrine, Sade's answer is blunt: "The callousness of the Rich legitimates the bad conduct of the Poor; let them open their purses to our needs. . . . We will be fools indeed to abstain from [crimes] when they can lessen the yoke wherewith their cruelty bears us down" (Sade, p. 481). This sounds horrible, it seems, only to those whose conscious or unconscious wish is to be oppressors. Sadean man merely refuses to be oppressed; *he can only be killed, but never subjugated.*

I dreamed I called Adolf Hitler on the phone and asked him, What was your gimmick?

"They believed it was wiser to obey anyone, even me, than to risk anarchy," he said with a ghoulish laugh.

And the line went dead with a sharp click like boot-heels snapped together.

TWELFTH CHORUS
I'm a mad animal
Prisons don't help
Chains don't help
I escape
through all the walls

— Marat/Sade

B.F. Skinner envisions a world without punishment. Nobody is interested.

Guns are now available—they are used in Africa by game wardens—that will stun without killing. Armed with these, an army could capture a town without shedding one drop of blood. Have you heard of any government plotting to wage its future wars with these guns?

Punishment, discipline, obedience—these are the keys to such mysteries, and to the mystery of war itself, and to all oddities of behavior in Man and the other domestic animals. Sade saw it, and was banned for 150 years. He saw the genital fever, the need for embrace, dammed up at the center of man. Another reason he was banned.

The actors are going nuts playing in Marat/Sade. "There is not a single member of the cast who does not hate with a deep loathing every single performance he is required to do of this play," says Ian Carmichael, who plays Marat. "It gets harder and harder," says Patrick Magee, who plays Sade. So far, the company has had one case of acute depression, one fit of "raving screaming" after the show, one actor who almost lost control on stage (Dick Schaap, N.Y. *Herald Tribune*, March 4, "Inmates of the Asylum").

I dreamed I called D.A.F. de Sade on the phone and asked him, "Jesus told me that he and you agree on at least one thing and it explains freedom. What is that one thing?"

"Quite simple," he replied, "don't be afraid of the Cross. *The fear of death is the beginning of slavery.*"

And the line went dead with a triumphant click like a barred door falling open.

THE MARRIED CATHOLIC PRIESTS' CONVENTION

Ariccia, Italy, is one of the hottest places on earth in August, but the convention room in the Hotel Cavalcanti was even hotter than the streets outside, where the dogs were too prostrated by heat to bark at the cats. The air-conditioning system sputtered and cackled, and occasionally some foul-smelling smoke oozed out of it, but the repairmen who returned twice a day never did succeed in getting any cold air out of the vents; usually, they produced only a temporary increase in the vile smoke, or smog, or viscous vapor, or whatever it was that made everybody smell vaguely like a dead skunk on the highway. It was about as restful as a poke in the eye with a sharp stick.

The Irish priest, Father Malachi Mulligan of Galway, was sweating like a boxer who's fought twelve rounds already and knows he lost eleven of them on points. He still wouldn't sit down. "By Christ," he cried passionately, "if you're a married man, and everybody calls you Father, it's only natural to have children, is it not? And, faith, have we forgotten the Vow of Poverty? Every time my wife starts swelling up again, I can *feel* myself getting poorer. Now surely that is living up to the Vow of Poverty and learning to identify with the poor, is it not?" He had his eye on the Liberation Theologians, who make a big thing about living like the poor; he knew how to score debater's points, being a Jesuit.

What the hell am I doing in this furnace of a room with these crazy Catholics, I asked myself for the hundredth time, *and can Paul Krassner ever pay enough to compensate me for four days of this?*

"The reverend Father is out of order," the chairentity droned (I am trying to avoid the humanism of "chairperson"). "Move to the next point of business."

The Fathers who were not fathers made feeble sounds of support. They were too blasted by the heat to be really enthusiastic about anything, even the prospect of shutting up Father Mulligan. The children were getting noisier by the hour and the mothers were out of their heads, or close to it. Rumors were circulating that the air conditioning had been deliberately sabotaged by the Knights of Malta, and that sort of story always creates high paranoia in Catholic countries, since liberal Catholics feel about the K of M about the way liberal Americans feel about the C.I.A. ("Those bastards are capable of anything.")

This was the second annual convention of the Married Roman Catholic Priests Association (International), representing 70,000 R.C. priests who, in defiance of the Vatican, had married during the last two decades. The MRCPA (I) had called the convention in Ariccia because that is only about 30 kilometers from Rome and right next door to the Pope's summer home in Castle Gandolfo. Only 150 priests were able to attend because of that Vow of Poverty mentioned by Father Mulligan; the Church, which provides travel expenses for "worthy" projects, did not think a convention of heretics was very worthy, especially if it was to be held right in the Pope's backyard as it were. Nonetheless, the actual attendance was closer to 750 than 150, because the Traditionalists had somehow raised the cash to bring their families along. That and the defective air conditioning caused most of the horrors to come.

The Traditionalists in the MRCPA (I)—led by Father Mulligan, who has fifteen children himself (and a wife, Dierdre, who, to say the least of it, looks haggard)—refuse to admit they are heretics at all and are adamantine in their allegience to all Vatican teachings except the one about clerical celibacy. CONTRACEPTION IS CONTRA-GOD said a huge banner they had erected in the convention hall on Day One. Their position paper, distributed at the door and thrown away immediately by most delegates, had the title "Let Not The Issue of Celibacy Become the Thin Entering Wedge to Theological Anarchy." They wanted all the married priests with small families or no families thrown out of the MRCPA (I) as *real heretics*. They said such priests were "half-way to Protestantism and Freemasonry already." They wanted to keep the MRCPA (I) *respectable*.

The Liberals, as usual, vacillated between trying to placate these loonies and spreading gossip about them behind their backs. They whispered (I eavesdropped at every opportunity) that Father Mulligan could afford his fifteen children only because his wife was "on the dole" (the Irish name for Welfare). This offended the Liberation Theologians, who were otherwise in sympathy with the Liberals, but who insisted that there was nothing contemptible about being on the dole, especially when the Church only gave Father Mulligan living expenses for one person, refusing to recognize his wife or brood. The Liberals then spread rumors that Mulligan and the other Traditionalists were secretly in league with Archbishop Lefebvre, the French nut-case who believes the Vatican was taken over by the Freemasons and Satanists during the 1960s and who inspired Father Juan Krohn, the oddball who tried to assassinate John Paul II at Fatima in 1982. It was even muttered in corners that the Traditionalists were infiltrated by the nefarious Knights of Malta who had flummoxed the air conditioning.

The Knights of Malta, as I said, create real terror in Catholic countries, especially among Liberation Theologians. The K of M are one of the oldest secret societies in the world, dating back at least 600 years, and yet even the most ardent conspiracy buffs do not know much about them—does Mae Brussell have a file on them?—even though they inspired part of the plot of *The Maltese Falcon*. William Casey, the current head of the C.I.A., is a K of M. Licio Gelli, who headed the "P2" conspiracy (which turned the Vatican Bank into a laundromat for Mafia heroin money, took over the Italian secret police, and infiltrated 951 agents into the Italian government), was and is a K of M. Alexander Haig is a K of M. When Gordon Thomas, a British journalist, claimed (in his *Year of Armageddon*) that the K of M's act as couriers between the Vatican and the C.I.A., the paranoia quotient among Liberation Theologians went up about 2000%. It didn't help when Archbishop Romeros, a leading Liberation Theologian, was assassinated, evidently with C.I.A. connivance. When the current Pope, John Paul II, visited Romeros' turf afterward and told Liberation Theologians to keep their noses out of politics, some thought that was the equivalent of what the Mafia calls "letting the other guys know where it came from."

By the second day of the convention a rumor was circulating that the K of M, not satisfied with ballocksing the air conditioning, was planning to poison the food. Everybody pretended not to believe this, but I noticed that the delegates began boycotting the dining room. When I followed some of them, I found they were grabbing quick sandwiches at working class bars in the vicinity.

The heat, by then, was producing dizziness, the general indefinite wobblies and (I think) altered states of consciousness. Quarrels broke out among the conspiracy buffs, some of whom alleged that the K of M was too involved in C.I.A./Vatican politics to waste time sabotaging this convention; the ones who had really fucked up the air conditioning, they claimed, were the nefarious Opus Dei. This is a Catholic secret society formed in Franco Spain about 50 years ago which is so fascist that not even Pope Pius XII would touch it with a ten-foot pole; it was ignored or rebuffed by all the other popes since then, too, until suddenly the current pontiff, John Paul II, recognized and blessed it in 1983, to the consternation of liberal Catholics everywhere.

Mrs. Roberto Calvi, the widow of the banker found hanged in London in 1982, claims Opus Dei simply bribed the pope by making a huge donation to the Vatican Bank, which rescued it from bankruptcy. But Mrs. Calvi also says it was Archbishop Marcinkus of the Vatican Bank, not her late husband, who embezzled the 55 million dollars that disappeared somewhere between the Vatican Bank and Mr. Calvi's Banco Ambrosiano, and that the Vatican hired the men who killed her husband, and all sorts of scandalous things like that. Conservative Catholics prefer to think she's just a hysterical widow. It must be hard to have your husband hanged by persons unknown for reasons equally unknown.

I heard part of an interesting debate about whether Opus Dei was or was not likely to be poisoning the food. "You know what sort of *creeps* that Opus Dei gang is," an excitable young Dominican was telling an elderly Jesuit, while their wives sipped Singapore Slings and discussed the latest Sophia Loren film.

"Well," the Jesuit said carefully, "they are admittedly into ah er um medieval 'mortifications.' "

"Mortifications, my ass," the Dominican cried. "The word is *perversions*. You've read Freud, for Christ's sake. Whips and chains! My God, they make the Marquis de Sade look like a pussycat."

"One must be charitable in thought as well as deed . . . the religious impulse takes many forms . . . "

"Yeah, well why won't you eat the food here? Remember what happened to Papa Luciani, maybe?" (The reference is to Pope John Paul I, born Albino Luciani, who was taken suddenly dead after ordering an investigation of the Vatican Bank, and got buried without an autopsy. If Mrs. Calvi is right, Opus Dei now largely owns the Vatican Bank.)

That's the way it always starts. By the third day of the convention, half of the delegates were having whispered conversations about which of the others were agents of the Knights of Malta or Opus Dei. There was even a rumor (I couldn't get it confirmed) that some of the delegates hired *food tasters*, gaunt pitiful children from the slums of Naples, even when they traveled to the other end of town for a sandwich.

The Condom Caper blew the roof off, metaphorically of course. It was the fourth and last day, and the air conditioning still wouldn't work. The children were louder and more unruly than ever. The mothers were frantic, and one of them got the mike for a while to denounce Sexism Among the

Allegedly Liberated. The Fathers who weren't fathers all had expressions, by then, which reminded me of W.C. Fields looking at Baby Leroy and contemplating mayhem. "Why couldn't they leave their brats home with baby-sitters?" one of them muttered audibly.

Father Mulligan, for the Traditionalists, recaptured the mike and launched another, typically Irish, glorification of the Bodaceously Huge Catholic Family. There were boos and catcalls and more cries of "point of order" than I've heard since the Army-McCarthy hearings. Mulligan was sweating more than ever and, while saying something about the family being the backbone of the Church, pulled a handkerchief from his pocket to mop his brow.

Out of his pocket, with the handkerchief, came several condoms, which fell to the floor and were seen by all. I noticed that one was a French Tickler and another, evidently Japanese, had a dragon's head on it.

Father Mulligan sputtered and cackled—an uncanny imitation of the sounds of the air conditioner—and turned the exact sunset-red of a garden-fresh tomato. It was a chilling, terrible moment: we all thought he was having a heart attack or stroke. When he fell over backwards (landing on a tray of antipasto which nobody had tasted for two days), most of the delegates mournfully made the Sign of the Cross, convinced he was dead. It turned out later that he was only suffering heat prostration and shock, but the damage was done. He recovered, but the convention never did.

Some said later that the Knights of Malta had planted the rubbery witnesses of lubricious hypocrisy on the poor man; others blamed Opus Dei; some of the Traditionalists close to Mulligan remained bitterly convinced the Liberals had done it as a cruel joke. Perhaps we shall never know the truth. Suspicion and paranoia reached new heights.

The children, you can be sure, were beyond control now. Some had been terrified when Father Mulligan keeled over; a second group were hilarious, thinking evidently that a man falling into antipasto is as funny in real life as in a Laurel and Hardy comedy; it was impossible to quiet either group, especially with the younger children howling that they wanted to play with "the pretty balloons, especially the ones with feathers and dragon's heads."

Two hours later I saw one elderly Franciscan, so damp with perspiration that he actually looked guilty, surrounded by ten others, who claimed he was Licio Gelli in disguise. "But I am Father Dino Lo Bello, of Nola," he kept protesting, while the others snarled at him and snapped pointed questions such as "Why did you poison John Paul I?" and "How did you get out of that Swiss prison?"

In fact, although Father Lo Bello had a beard, the heat must have been getting to me, too, because I thought he did look like Gelli might look with a beard. But would Gelli (hiding out in Uruguay to avoid extradition to Italy, where he is wanted for murder, fraud and conspiracy, among other things) dare to come back in so thin a disguise? Why not? Audacity was always Licio Gelli's trademark. He was once on the payroll of the C.I.A. and the K.G.B. simultaneously (see David Yallop's *In God's Name*): such men are capable of anything, including disguising themselves as married priests. But would the Knights of Malta (of which Gelli was admittedly a member) bother with Yippie-style pranks like buggering up the air conditioning or planting rubbers on a Jesuit?

"Tell us about Klaus Barbie and ODESSA," one of the inquisitors barked.

"I don't know Klaus Barbie, I don't know ODESSA . . . "

I went up to my room to take a shower, cool off and clear the contagious paranoia from my brain. Of course, the shower wouldn't work. Well, I told myself, Italian showers are as unreliable as Irish phones, and I am not going to blame this on the Knights of Malta. They (and their associates in the C.I.A. and ODESSA) are too busy stomping out liberation movements in Latin America to waste time on a bunch of eccentric priests who decided to get married.

Voices drifted up from the convention room. They were singing the Monty Python song with the chorus, "Every sperm is sacred / Every sperm is great / If a sperm is wasted / God gets quite irate." At first I thought it was the Liberals mocking the Traditionalists, then I recognized some of the voices. It was the Traditionalists singing. They were so humorless themselves that they didn't even know the song was a parody, and why should they? It is, in fact, merely a blunt statement of the orthodox Vatican dogma on procreation. It only seems funny if you're not Catholic. I thought about that. I thought about it a great deal. The song went on: "Every sperm is sacred / Every sperm is good / Every sperm is needed / In your neighborhood." The Knights of Malta were probably just as humorless, I thought. To them, a crowd of married priests was as much a threat to the Catholic Way of Life as ten regiments of *godless Russian communists* landing on the Italian beaches. Maybe David Yallop was a bit of a sensationalist and poor old Luciani (John Paul I) died of natural causes, after all; but Pecorelli, the editor who first exposed the "P2" conspiracy (run by Licio Gelli of the Knights of Malta) was shot dead by machine-gun fire a few months later. And two public prosecutors have been shot dead, also, during the "P2" investigations. And Gelli himself escaped from a Swiss prison only three days after being arrested there, which makes one wonder how much power do Knights of Malta have to protect their members anywhere on earth.

I began to develop that peculiar sensation which Raymond Chandler, I believe, once called the acute awareness that one is not bullet-proof. I even began to think that the antipasto tray had a smell of *bitter almonds* about it.

I packed my bags and crept quietly down the stairs of the Hotel Cavalcanti.

As I passed through the lobby, I heard the delegates in the convention hall smashing chairs and other furniture. Hoarse, impassioned shouts of "Fascist," "Communist," "Mariolatry," "Spermolatry," "Manicheanism," "Arianism" and "Don't give me that Jesuit equivocation, you sonofabitch" were drowned in inarticulate screams of rage and pain. I gathered that the debate had grown acrimonious, as theological discussions so often do.

Sounds of shattering glass and a pongoid cry of "Take that, Socianist*— Unitarian dog!" followed me into the dusty, sunbaked Italian street.

I decided to get the hell out of Italy.

---

* Not a typo. Socianist: a rational theology that denied Papal infallibility, the Trinity and the efficacy of sacraments. Condemned as heresy, of course.

SELF-REFLEXIVE SURREALIST HAIKU

**READING NEWS HEADLINES
CAUSES BRAIN TO SHRINK:
SCIENTISTS FIND HAIKU ALSO "RISKY"**

The Godfathers and
The Goddess

As some of you have guessed by now, that last *Realist* article contained a great deal of put-on.

Well, I warned you this book was a Head Test, didn't I?

Actually, there really was a convention of married Catholic priests in Ariccia in August 1985, but I wasn't there; I was on a lecture tour in the midwestern United States at the time. The previous article is the same kind of fiction you find in most of my novels—that is, my imagination runs wild but it also runs along the tracks of historical records. Almost everything in the piece you have just read is based on something real, even if I have given it my own surreal flavor.

The following article deals with some of the same subjects, and contains no hoaxing or deliberate deception at all. Where I am guessing, I say so clearly. Where I do not specify that I am guessing, there are several sources for what I say, and I have reason to believe these sources are trustworthy. If what follows nonetheless sounds as bizarre as what you've just read, the explanation can only be that the world of modern power politics is, as Paul Krassner, editor of *The Realist*, keeps saying, much crazier than anything we satirists can invent.

The first paragraph of this article, in which I go through some spaghetti-like convolutions to express what I mean without actually using the words "fuck" and "suck," was necessary because I was writing for an Irish news magazine.

The secret of the Mona Lisa smile may never be explained, but the equally famous and more sensual smile of Marilyn Monroe has finally been elucidated. Marilyn projected that hypertumescent expression by looking tenderly into the camera lens and whispering softly to herself two old Anglo-Saxon words that rhyme with "duck" but have nothing to do with waterbirds at all, at all.

This is one of the many revelations in *Goddess*, Anthony Summers' new book about the life and death of our century's most enduring sex symbol. Mr. Summers also informs us of how the girl born Norma Jeane Mortenson, an attractive-but-ordinary brunette, transformed herself into "Marilyn," the Blonde Bombshell who could make *castrati* chew a hole through the walls of St. Peter's: starting at 19, Norma Jeane studied anatomy the way Napoleon studied war, learned how to use every muscle, jogged every day (20 years before that became a fad) and even lifted weights. By the time she had become "Marilyn," Norma Jeane not only had her dresses specially designed but sometimes had the literally sewn on her body for maximum advertising of her natural resources, and she always had those Anglo-Saxon monosyllables to hype-or-hypnotize herself into public arousal every time she saw a photographer on the horizon.

The creation of "Marilyn Monroe" was one of the great artistic and engineering feats of U.S. history: after the technology had been acomplished, there was great art and shrewd psychology in animating the myth with a numinous blend of little-girl innocence and mature, shameless eroticism. A true Goddess had been manufactured, as any Jungian psychologist will agree. Behind the Goddess was an intelligent and intuitive Actress and behind the Actress was Norma Jeane, a woman who had never been innocent, never became mature, and wasn't even shameless. Norma Jeane was, in fact, guilt-ridden, insecure, haunted by the father she had never known, terrified of inheriting her mother's insanity, and seldom free of crippling anxiety for two minutes at a time. She was also a compulsive liar whose ability to believe her own fantasies reminds one inescapably of that other self-made American Archetype, Ronald Reagan, and she was prone to bouts of paranoia and the anxiety-neurotic's ever-escalating alcohol and drug dependence. She surely must have been some kind of genius, too, because it takes more than talent to create and maintain the Goddess image while in the dark night of your soul the shadows of nightmare howl and gibber around you.

Norma Jeane's childhood would have been enough to cripple a water buffalo. Anthropologist Ashley Montagu, not quoted by Summers, has statistics in his *Direction of Human Development* showing that orphans have more mental, emotional and physical illnesses throughout life than parented children, are more prone to crime and drugs, die younger and even measure several inches shorter on average than the norm for their gender. In Norma Jeane's case, her father did not have the decency to die but simply walked out, and her mother went yodelling off to the "Asylum"; the girl-child, shunted from orphanage to foster-home and from foster-home to orphanage for 16 years, was psychologically more orphaned than most orphans. Understand that, even a little, and you will be astonished at the gay charm and sly humour in even her most lightweight comedy roles; with the demons that haunted Norma Jeane, those sexy-funny girls were performances as miraculous as a three-legged giraffe learning to dance the can-can. By comparison, her "serious" dramatic roles, such as the schizophrenic baby-sitter in "Don't Bother To Knock" or the ambitious hustler in "Bus Stop," required less art. Schizophrenia and ambition were closer to the real Norma Jeane than gaiety or humour ever were.

It is noteworthy that Norma Jeane could bring the Goddess to life occasionally even when off screen. Summers shows that there is some doubt about the famous incident of sexual molestation or rape at age 12—Norma Jeane told several conflicting versions of it and lied so often that everything she said needs to be taken with caution—but she could even be funny about that assault or fantasy, or whatever it was. Once she claimed that she first had sexual intercourse at seven, and when asked "My God, how old was the man?", she replied, abruptly shifting to her sly bedroom whisper, "Younger." I don't think Groucho Marx ever became "Groucho Marx" so convincingly in real life as Norma Jeane played "Marilyn" at that moment; but we still don't know what real incident or hallucination was the basis of both her pathetic tales of rape and that obvious Send Up. We are in *Roshomon*, as Mailer concluded desperately at the end of his biography of her: whenever Norma Jeane almost comes into focus, up pops the Actress holding up the Goddess masque to blind and bewilder us.

On the question of having sex with producers to advance her career, "Marilyn" said, "It was no great tragedy. Nobody ever got cancer from sex." Did Norma Jeane believe that? One or other, anyway, wrote poetry with occasional brilliant lines in it (*"I am both your directions / Existing more with the old frost / Strong as a cobweb in the wind."*) and believed that, because she was a Gemini like her idol, Walt Whitman, she was doomed to be two persons. Norma Jeane was converted to Christian Science early on and, whenever she came out from hiding behind the Actress and the Goddess, was still trying to believe she could cure her terrors with Faith; "Marilyn" bluntly called herself an atheist. She read Joyce, Proust, Emerson, Rilke, art criticism, everything she could get her hands on, and studied how to improve her acting with the grim determination of a terrorist plotting Apocalypse in a garret. She suspected all her lovers and husbands of betrayal and even suspected her female friends of weaving Lesbian plots to seduce her. Booze and pills, and more booze and more pills, and some Christian Science, kept her moving like a missile toward the target of Success, and when an audience or camera appeared, she trampled her anxieties like Atilla trashing a village and became, while the performance lasted, the sexiest and funniest woman in the world.

Was there some kind of cover-up connected with Marilyn's death? Summers presents a convincing case that there was a conspiracy in which Marilyn's death was concealed for three hours while persons unknown carefully removed from her house all evidence of her love affairs with John and Bobby Kennedy. I think Summers also proves that this cover-up was instigated by actor Peter Lawford, brother-in-law to John and Bobby, who had previously provided his house as a discrete trysting place for the lovers. It is not perfectly clear that Lawford ever suspected, or allowed himself to suspect, that he might be conspiring to conceal clues to a murder; he probably thought, or wanted to think, that he was only covering up politically embarrassing sexual dalliances.

The possibility of murder remains only a possibility, although often raised by the tabloids, once accepted by Norman Mailer and still insisted upon by the award-winning journalist Hank Messick (former consultant to the New York Joint Legislative Committee on Crime). Messick claims that unnamed informants in the Mafia and the Justice Department both believed that the mob killed Marilyn to lure Bobby Kennedy into a trap and then blackmail him. Summers is skeptical of this, and so am I. The mob, as Summers documents, already had enough on Bobby to blackmail him, because they had used electronic bugs to acquire several tapes of Marilyn and Bobby making the-beast-with-two-backs. Since the cover-up obliterated real evidence, the possibility of murder cannot be ruled out, but the probability is that only the romantic proclivities of John and Bobby were being whitewashed. And yet . . .

A few months after Marilyn's death, a woman named Mary Pinchot Meyer became another of John Kennedy's mistresses. She was also a dear and good friend of the Harvard LSD researcher, Dr. Timothy Leary, and, curiously, the wife of Cord Meyer, a top CIA official who was the only man ever to receive the agency's Distinguished Intelligence Medal three times. In 1964, about one year after the JFK assassination, Mary Pinchot Meyer was shot to death on a Washington street. Clearly it was statistically somewhat hazardous to be a mistress of the President of the U.S. in those days.

According to Dr. Leary's autobiography, Flashbacks (Tarcher, Los Angeles, 1983) Mary Pinchot Meyer informed Leary as early as 1962 that the CIA was engaged in its own LSD research and wanted to stop him and other scientists from publishing the results of open LSD research. She also told Leary of a vicious power struggle in Washington between the Kennedy faction and the old-guard CIA faction. Leary claims there was a cover-up in the death of Mary Pinchot Meyer and names two Washington sources as confirming that opinion.

Another of President Kennedy's mistresses, Judith Exner, later came to the attention of the House Select Committee on Assassinations in 1978 because at the time of her affair with the President she was also the mistress of Sam Giancana, Chicago Mafia leader, who had once, according to informants, discussed the desirability of assassinating the President. The Committee took seriously the possibility that Giancana had put Ms. Exner in the President's bed in order to blackmail him; the Committee also examined seriously the possibility that Giancana had gone ahead with his assassination plot and masterminded the events in Dallas on 22nd November 1963. In its published report, the Committee concluded only that there *was* a conspiracy and that possible Mafia involvement deserved further investigation; but the Chief Counsel for the Committee, Prof. Robert Blakey went further and said for the record, "I am now firmly of the opinion that the mob did it. It is a historical truth."

Sam Giancana was believed to be heavily involved in heroin traffic. He wanted John Kennedy dead because he believed Bobby would be replaced as Attorney General under a new administration (as indeed happened) and Bobby had been spending millions to break up the heroin racket and send Giancana personally to prison. Giancana himself was shot dead in June 1975.

Dr. Leary was sentenced to 37 years imprisonment in 1970 for alleged possession of one cannabis cigarette, a crime then usually punished in the States by six months. He was released in 1976, amid a carefully orchestrated rumour campaign claiming he had become an informant for the FBI. He is now engaged in the manufacture of computer software. LSD has become, like heroin, a monopoly of the CIA and the Mafia.

Johnny Roselli, Mafia king-pin of Las Vegas, was also accused of involvement in the JFK assassination by Prof. Blakey and others. He was shot to death in July 1976, after talking once to the Assassination Committee and while waiting to be recalled to testify again.

In the same vein, George de Mohrenschildt, a close associate of Lee Harvey Oswald in Dallas, who has also been linked to the CIA and the Mafia, died of gunshot wounds in March 1977 while under subpoena to testify before the Assassinations Committee; in this case, the coroner ruled suicide. De Mohrenschildt and Sam Giancana were both shot through the mouth, traditional Mafia punishment for informers.

The most provocative moment in the Watergate tapes occurs when Nixon agrees to pay E. Howard Hunt $1,000,000 not to spill "that whole Bay of Pigs thing." It is hard to imagine what Bay of Pigs "thing" has not yet been revealed in Congressional hearings; yet the implication of Nixon's willingness to pay Hunt $1,000,000 for silence—better than a poke in the eye with a sharp stick, you must admit—is that some damned Bay of Pigs "thing" has not come out into the light of day, even yet.

Part of the answer to this curiosity may be found in Anthony Summers' earlier book *Conspiracy* (Fontana, London 1980) and in Prof. Carl Oglesby's *The Yankee And Cowboy War* (Berkeley, New York, 1976) wherein one finds that Sam Giancana and Johnny Roselli, the above-mentioned now-defunct Mafiosi, were engaged with the CIA in several plots to assassinate Fidel Castro, which may have been known to President Kennedy, and that Mr. Hunt, while involved in these murderous conspiracies with the Mafia, was also involved with other CIA officials in clandestine raids on Cuba which were *definitely* concealed from the President. Another part of the answer may be discerned in Penny Lernoux's *In Banks We Trust* (Doubleday, New York, 1984) which tells of a bank called the World Finance Corporation in Miami, Florida, which went belly up after the local District Attorney indicted its top officials for knowingly engaging in the laundering of billions of dollars of money from the cocaine trade.

The President of the WFC was Hernandez Cataya, who had also been involved with Giancana, Roselli, Hunt and the CIA in clan destine anti-Castro activities, and two other officers of the bank turned out to be former, or allegedly former, CIA agents. Lernoux concludes that the CIA now wields a major influence on the cocaine trade, which it operates in association with the neo-fascists in Italy and South America and the pseudo-Freemasonic conspiracy called P2.

Lernoux carefully documents that the WFC laundered the cocaine money by sending it on a merry-go-round through the Cisalpine Bank in the Bahamas, owned by Archbishop Marcinkus, the Vatican Bank, managed by Marcinkus, and the Banco Ambrosiano, managed by the late Roberto Calvi but owned in effect by the Mafia and the P2 conspiracy. She also documents that Licio Gelli, Grandmaster of P2, had been a CIA agent since the 1940s. Funny coincidence, that.

Members of the Hierarchy in Ireland have been so vociferous in defense of the other-worldly naivete of Archbishop Marcinkus that I hesitate to draw any conclusions about his part in all this. It is *possible* that his innocence was so extra-mundane that he thought all the time that he was dealing in baby booties. Back in the early 1970s, however, Archbishop Marcinkus received from the Johnny Roselli Mafia family (there's that name again) $1,000,000,000 in counterfeit stock, as documented by *NY Times* reporter Richard Hammer in *The Vatican Connection* (Bantam, New York, 1982). It is possible that even on *that* occasion the Archbishop thought he was dealing in baby booties, but as a profound layperson I can only wonder why he didn't comment enquiringly when he received counterfeit stocks instead of kiddie ware; but, then, the mysteries of the Faith are beyond human reason.

In 1978, *Osservatore Politico* sent Pope John Paul I data on the Mafia/P2 infiltration of the Vatican Bank. That particular pope, as all readers of David Yallop know (see *In God's Name*, Bantam, New York, 1984) was taken suddenly dead under mysterious circumstances; the editor of *Osservatore Politico*, Mino Percorelli, was subsequently shot dead in Rome. Percorelli, like Roselli and De Mohrenschildt in America, was shot through the mouth.

Klaus Barbie, the Nazi war criminal who was so curiously protected by the CIA for 30 years, was also associated with P2's financial and political activities in South America. Licio Gelli, the CIA agent who founded P2, was arrested in Switzerland, but made an unexplained escape from a maximum security prison and is at large in Uruguay.

Bobby Kennedy, after being removed as Attorney General by President Johnson, decided to run for President himself in 1968, posing more potential problems for the Mafia, but fortunately for them there was another deranged lone assassin on hand. Since Bobby's death, the Mafia has had little real heat in the US: Michele Sindona, Mafia lawyer and P2 member, was at Nixon's inauguration, an honoured guest, and Licio Gelli, the Grandmaster himself, is in photos taken at Reagan's second inauguration. He and Reagan are smiling, as if at some private and intimate joke.

From all this we can extrapolate three outstanding facts that are almost synecdoches of our increasingly clandestine world. 1.) The cocaine money laundered by Archbishop Marcinkus helped finance the death squads that killed Archbishop Romeros, who served the same God and the same church as Marcinkus: we are all living in a Le Carre novel. 2.) In the symbiosis between the Mafia and the CIA the mob thinks it is using the spooks, and the spooks think they are using the mob and one of them is terribly deceived. 3.) Bobby Kennedy broke off his affair with Marilyn when he learned, from FBI wiretaps, that the Mafia was taping his boudoir adventures. Contemplate that: while the Justice Department wiretaps the Mafia, the Mafia wiretaps the head of the Justice Department. It is more than a synecdoche; it is a Joycean epiphany.

And Norma Jeane, the neurotic woman who created and became "Marilyn Monroe"? She grew up with a typically American adoration of Abraham Lincoln, a perfect father-symbol for orphans everywhere; I suspect that when she climbed into bed with Jack Kennedy she really thought she was climbing into bed with Lincoln and history. Nobody had warned her that History is a blood sport, and the only one in which innocent bystanders are the principle victims.

She was as beautiful as the Parthenon by moonlight, as goofy as a surrealist painting and as hard to ignore or forget as a kangeroo in a symphony orchestra. I, for one, still mourn her, tantalized by the wish that she had found something better than booze and pills to get through the noon's unease and the nights alone. Which leaves just one haunting note on which to conclude this odyssey through the undergrowth of American and international intrigues: where the hell does all the heroin on the streets of *Dublin* come from?

Goddess by Anthony Summers is published by Victor Gollancz Ltd, London IR£16.

THE PHYSICS OF SYNCHRONICITY

The following article originally appeared in *Science Digest* and inspired a heated rebuttal from some chap hiding behind a pen-name (I forget if he called himself Dr. Crypton or Dr. Matrix, but it was something like that.) This excited, agitated and emotional chap was very offended by my ideas—or my popularization of the ideas of several prominent physicists—and therefore claimed that I was irrational. If I remember correctly, he said I was "groveling in awe" before "inscrutable gods" or something of that sort. I leave it to the reader to decide whether there are inscritible gods invoked here or if that polemic was just another example of the hysterical anxieties that beset Rationalists when their dogmas are undermined.

Synchronous events have long fascinated leading scientists.
Are these unexpected occurrences . . .

MERE COINCIDENCE?

For over 100 years, various heretical scientists have been studying the so-called paranormal—strange events that are attributed to extrasensory perception, precognition or telekinesis. And, every step of the way, this research has been attacked by critics who explain the positive results as "mere coincidence" or (even worse) "sheer coincidence." Now there appears to be a possibility that coincidence may be more important scientifically—and may change our scientific paradigm much more radically—than telepathy would. Coincidence may be more earthshaking than telekinesis. There have been coincidences so dramatic, so symbolic or so wildly improbably that they have aroused feelings of the uncanny in scientists and laymen alike for generations.

Could such things happen by chance alone? There must, it seems to some, be an underlying logic to these bizarre juxtapositions of events in time and space. Among those who have seriously considered the logic of coincidence was Paul Kammerer, the German biologist who was one of the last of the Lamarckian evolutionists. (Kammerer killed himself soon after one of his crucial experiments in support of Lamarckian evolution was found to be a fraud. Einstein, however, was impressed with Kammerer's work on coincidence, calling it "original and by no means absurd.") Other interested scientists have included Carl Gustav Jung, disciple of Freud and one of the great psychologists of the century, who mapped the unconscious mind with an eye to the mystical; and Wolfgang Pauli, the Nobel laureate physicist and discoverer of the neutrino who, in the words of Arthur Koestler in *The Roots of Coincidence*, extended "the principle of noncausal events from microphysics (where its legitimacy was recognized) to macrophysics (where it was not)."

Let us examine a few cases, moving gradually from the only moderately peculiar to the increasingly bizarre.

1. English novelist Dame Rebecca West was writing a story in which a girl finds a hedgehog in her garden. As West wrote this passage, she was interrupted by servants who informed her they had just found a hedgehog in the garden.

2. When Norman Mailer began his novel *Barbary Shore* there was no Russian spy in it. As he worked on it, a Russian spy became a minor character. As the work progressed, the spy became the dominant character. After the novel was finished, the Immigration Service arrested a man who lived one flight below Mailer in the same building. He was Colonel Rudolf Abel, named as the top Russian spy in the United States at that time.

CRACKING THE CODE?

3. While the Allies were planning the Normandy invasion of June 6, 1944, the following code words were used (and were among the best-kept secrets of the war): *Utah* and *Omaha*, the beaches where the American troops would land; *Mulberry*, the artificial harbor to be used after the landing; *Neptune*, the naval operations plan; *Overlord*, the entire invasion. On May 3, 1944, the first code word, *Utah*, appeared as an answer to the *London Daily Telegraph* crossword puzzle. On May 23, *Omaha* appeared in an answer to a *Telegraph* puzzle. On May 31, *Mulberry* appeared. And on June 2, four days before the invasion, *Neptune* and *Overlord* both appeared.

British Intelligence investigated this matter extensively. They found that the man who created the crosswords was innocent of espionage, had no knowledge of the invasion and was as puzzled as they were. Verdict: mere coincidence.

4. When Hart Crane was living in Brooklyn Heights, he decided to write a poem about the Brooklyn Bridge, which he could see from his window. It is the poem for which he is chiefly remembered. Only a year later did Crane discover that the address where he had lived while writing *The Bridge* was the address at which Washington Roebling, chief engineer on the bridge, had lived.

5. One day in 1909, Sigmund Freud and Carl Jung were in Freud's study, having an argument about extrasensory perception. It is worth noting that Freud was Jung's hero, virtually his substitute father, at that time. As the argument grew heated, emotions crackled. Suddenly, for no obvious reason, there was an explosive noise from Freud's bookcase.

"There," said Jung, "that is an example of a so-called catalytic phenomenon."

"Oh, come!" Freud exclaimed. "That is sheer bosh."

"It is not," Jung answered, seized by an uncanny certainty he could not explain. "You are mistaken, Herr Professor. And to prove my point, I now predict that in a moment there will be yet another loud report!"

Boom! It happened just as Jung predicted. Freud was aghast, and Jung was gripped by an inexplicable guilt.

6. Sequel to the above: In 1972, Dr. Robert Harvie, a psychologist at London University, was reading aloud to a friend Jung's account of the experience. When Harvie came to the second explosion in Freud's bookcase, a lamp inexplicably fell over with a loud crash.

7. Second sequel: Margaret Green, of London, was riding a train and reading Arthur Koestler's *The Roots of Coincidence*. When she came to Koestler's account of Freud's noisy bookcase, the window of the train suddenly smashed as if somebody had thrown a rock at it. Note that even if there were a rock thrower, it is eerie that he launched his missile just at that time, as if to prove "the roots of coincidence" are everywhere.

8. I was discussing the Harvie and Green sequels to the Jung-Freud incident with my wife in a restaurant. I thought it was amusing that I had discussed this and written about it many times without triggering anything explosive. At that point, my wife spilled her water. The waiter rushed over to mop the table—and accidentally knocked over my water.

UNEXPECTED PRESENCE

9. Jung had a patient who was telling about a dream in which an Egyptian scarab beetle appeared. This was of great interest to Jung, since he believed dreams often contain images from the collective unconscious, and the scarab beetle was sacred to the ancient Egyptians. At that point, something banging against the window caught Jung's attention. It was a scarab beetle, a species rather rare in Zurich, where Jung lived.

10. Jung himself later had a dream about Liverpool, England, that he considered so important that he analyzed it and wrote about it at length. (Liverpool was a pun on pool of life, he decided, and signified rebirth.) Years later, Peter O'Halligan, of the World Coincidence Center in Berkeley, analyzed the dream more carefully and decided the details fitted only one street intersection in Liverpool. At that place was the cafe where the Beatles first performed. And on the same spot, later, was the Science Fiction Theatre of Liverpool, where my play *Illuminatus* appeared. A large part of the play takes place aboard a yellow submarine, inspired by a Beatles song. And Jung himself is a character in the play.

11. Novelist William Burroughs, while living in Tangier in 1958, had a conversation with a Captain Clark, who mentioned that he had been sailing 23 years without an accident. That day, Captain Clark had his first serious accident. In the evening, while thinking about this, Burroughs flipped on the radio and heard a bulletin about a crash of an airliner. The flight number was 23 and the pilot was also a Captain Clark.

12. Sequel: Burroughs later decided to write a screenplay about the Prohibition Era gangster Dutch Schultz. In researching it, he found the number 23 over and over again. Schultz had put out a contract on a rival, Vincent "Mad Dog" Coll, and Coll was shot on Twenty-third Street in Manhattan when he was 23 years old. Schultz himself was shot to death on October 23, 1935.

13. When my play *Illuminatus* opened on the Liverpool street so strangely linked with Jung-beetle-Beatle coincidences, the premiere was November 23. British playwright Heathcote Williams made a guest appearance as a walk-on. Later, Williams and I talked about other writers we knew, and Burroughs was mentioned, along with the 23 coincidences he had collected (only a few of which are mentioned above). Williams told me that when he met Burroughs this subject came up, because Williams had mentioned that he was 23 years old at the time. When Williams returned to his flat that night (he had recently moved), he noticed for the first time that the building across the street was number 23.

14. After Koestler's *Roots of Coincidence* was published, Professor Hans Zeisel, of the University of Chicago law school, wrote to Koestler about a whole chain of 23s that had haunted his life: he lived at Rossaurerlaende 23 in Vienna, he had a law office at Gonzagagasse 23, his mother lived at Alserstrasse 23. Once Zeisel's mother was given a novel, *Die Liebe Der Jeanne Ney*, and took it with her to Monte Carlo. In the book, a character wins a great deal by betting on 23 at roulette. Zeisel's mother decided to bet on 23 at roulette. Twenty-three came up on the second try.

15. This whole area, as if it weren't bizarre enough already, took on even more exotic aspects after a celebrated experiment by Robert Harvie and biologist Sir Alister Hardy that attempted to demonstrate the reality of telepathy so totally that the last skeptic would be overwhelmed. The experiment, conducted in London in 1967, involved 110 trials with 20 subjects in each. Using every possible safeguard to ensure rigorousness, Harvie and Hardy obtained marvelous results. The subjects, trying to guess or "telepathically" read target cards they could not see, scored well above what might have been expected from chance.

Then, as a control, Harvie and Hardy randomized the response sheets. That is, instead of just comparing the responses of 20 people who were trying to "see" an invisible target card, as in the experiment proper, Harvie and Hardy made up groups of 20 response sheets from different people in different trials. This, they hoped, would prove that chance alone could not account for the results of the telepathy trials.

SHOCKING CORRELATIONS

What appeared was more shocking than what came out of the initial experiments. Correlations above chance were found again—correlations wildly beyond what could be expected according to probability theory.

What we have here is worse than telepathy from the orthodox viewpoint. Randomizing should have produced fewer correlations, according to one application of the second law of thermodynamics, which says that disorder always increases in random processes. Here, randomizing produced more order instead of less.

Hardy and Harvie could only suggest that probability and coincidence needed to be reexamined.

Actually, this reexamination had begun as early as 1919 in a book called *The Law of Series*, by Dr. Paul Kammerer. As a biologist, Kammerer not only studied strange coincidences but developed a taxonomy of them. For instance, his brother-in-law went to a concert at which he had seat number 9 and cloakroom ticket number 9. By itself, that would be a "series of the first order," in Kammerer's terminology. The next day, however, the brother-in-law went to another concert and got seat 21 and cloakroom ticket 21. That makes a "series of the second order."

Kammerer went on to list and give examples of series of the third order, fourth order, etc. He also provided a morphology involving powers (number of parallels in a coincidence) and a typology (coincidences of numbers, names, events).

He concluded that coincidence represents an acausal principle in nature, as distinguished from the causal principles science had hitherto studied. He compared the acausal coincidental principle (ACOP, we shall call it for short) with gravity, noting that gravity acts on mass, while ACOP acts on form and function. He concluded, in words that foreshadowed some current speculations in quantum physics, "We thus arrive at the image of a world-mosaic . . . which, in spite of constant shufflings and rearrangements, also takes care of bringing like and like together."

Jung eventually collaborated with Nobel physicist Wolfgang Pauli in developing a theory of coincidences that they called *synchronicity*. Pauli was attracted to the subject because he himself was haunted by malign coincidences that his fellow physicists jokingly called "the Pauli effect." As a theoretical, as distinguished from an experimental, physicist, Pauli did not spend much time in laboratories. It happened however that—more often than mere chance could explain—whenever Pauli was in a laboratory something got smashed or broken. It was not that he was clumsy; these accidents usually happened many yards away from him.

TWO CONNECTIONS

What Jung and Pauli suggested was that there are two kinds of connecting principles in nature. The first connecting principle is ordinary causality, which is what science usually studies. Causality is structured linearly in time: if A causes B, then A must occur in time before B. The other connecting principle is acausal, as Kammerer believed (though neither Jung nor Pauli appear to have read his book). The ACOP (acausal coincidental principle) Jung and Pauli called synchronicity because they assumed it was at right angles to causality and structured in space, not time. That is, the synchronicities (from the Greek, *syn*, together, and *chronos*, time) happen at the same time.

The relation between synchronous events, according to Jung, is basically psychological. The logic, in other words, is the logic of the deep psyche, which Jung (and Freud) had found in dreams and myths.

Barbara Honegger, a leading student of these matters, has pointed out a basic defect in the Jung-Pauli theory. ACOPs are by no means only synchronous. They are often separated by days or even years.

A new light was shed on ACOPs in 1964 by the Scots physicist John Bell. Bell's theorem holds that if quantum physics is accurate, particles that were once in contact continue to influence one another, no matter how far apart they move. This influence is instantaneous, according to Bell, even if the particles are at opposite ends of the Universe.

This makes a nasty problem for physicists because Bell's conclusion directly contradicts Einstein's special relativity, which holds that any influence between particles must require an energy transfer, and energy cannot move instantaneously. Energy only moves at the speed of light or less. Bell's theorem provides a possible mechanism at the quantum level for the acausal interaction of apparently unrelated events. Whether it can be applied beyond the strange world of subatomic particles is a question so far without a firm answer.

Four experiments have confirmed Bell's math; two have cast doubt on it; research is continuing. Meanwhile, some physicists have started reflecting on how to reconcile Bell with Einstein, if both are right. Dr. Evan Harris Walker has suggested that the "influence" in the Bell connection does not involve energy and hence does not contradict Einstein. The influence, Walker proposes, is consciousness itself.

Dr. Jack Sarfatti offers a different interpretation. The medium of the Bell interconnectedness, he says, is not consciousness but information. Now, information is very abstract in communication theory: it is the negative reciprocal of entropy, which means roughly that it is the opposite of disorder. It is almost what we call system or organization in daily speech. Information, Sarfatti proposes, is not bound by the same laws as energy and not subject to Einsteinian limits.

This would explain a great many of the ACOPs collected by Jung, Kammerer, Koestler and others; it might even explain the Hardy-Harvie experiment, in which randomizing led to more order rather than more disorder. And it throws all of the data of parapsychology into a new perspective: instead of separate paranormal abilities such as ESP, precognition and telekinesis, there might just be one ACOP—acausal coincidental principle—appearing to us in many forms to which we give those names.

Another angle on the problem comes from Dr. David Bohm's hidden-variable theory, developed from some ideas of Einstein's. According to Bohm, below the quantum level there is a subquantum world of hidden variables. This is a metaphor. Bohm does not mean below in the ordinary sense but, in a logical sense, what Bohm means is that the space-time world observed in physics is an epiphenomenon, a phenomenon caused by another phenomenon; underlying it is a spaceless, timeless realm from which the events of ordinary reality emerge. Bohm uses this theory to explain, or transcend, the notorious indeterminacy of the quantum realm (where ordinary causality breaks down), but it could also explain the acausal coincidences we are discussing.

Whether we take Bell's interpretation of quantum mechanics or Bohm's, we seem to arrive at a world in wich all things are very intimately connected, no matter how far apart and seemingly unconnected they may appear in ordinary space and ordinary time. This may sound like Buddhism or other mystic teachings, but other quantum theorists have come to similar conclusions by other avenues. Nobel laureate Erwin Schrodinger decided, as early as 1945, that the only sane explanation of quantum wave mechanics was that "The mind . . . is something we simply cannot conceive of as plural."

Barbara Honegger has a model that united all these approaches with current neurology. The brain, in a general, way has two hemispheres. The left hemisphere seemingly does all the talking (except in dreams and schizophrenia); it is the seat of the conscious ego. The right hemisphere is often called the silent hemisphere because it talks much less. It is also very active in hypoexcitation (deep yogic trance), in hyperexcitation (LSD trips, wild dancing, etc.) and while listening to music.

Honegger believes that the right hemisphere ego consciousness is continually trying to assert its existence and communicate with the left hemisphere ego, which Western adults think is their only ego. The right-side ego usually communicates via dreams, as noted by Freud and Jung, but if the left-sided ego remains deaf to these messages, the right hemisphere creates Freudian slips or hysterical symptoms to get the ego's attention. And, if nothing else works, it produces an ACOP. It does this, Honegger suggests, by means of connecting principles such as those suggested by Bell and Bohm. According to Honegger, we should analyze such ACOPs the way Freud and Jung analyzed dreams to see what unconscious messages they contain.

SPACE-TIME UNLIMITED

The uncanny, then, is just the right hemisphere's way of violently capturing our attention.

Of course, recent evidence suggests that the right brain-left brain dichotomy is not as absolute as once believed; Honegger's model is only the latest, not the last, word on this subject. But the growing convergence of data from coincidence hunters and the latest theories in quantum physics suggest that the model that will tie all this together will be much more revolutionary than proof of ghosts or of UFOs or even of thought transference would be. We seem to be dealing with a force that is, as Kammerer said, as universal as gravity and without limitations in either space or time.

COINCIDANCE: PART THREE

Semper as
Oxhousehumper

A is the first letter of most European alphabets and is thus associated with beginnings or origins. The Hebrew A is pronounced **aleph** and spelled ALP by Cabalists writing in English, ALP being the English equivalent of the spelling of aleph in Hebrew, which is, in full **aleph-lamek-pe**. Cabalists have found many mystical meanings in this A or ALP, but not nearly as many as Joyce finds in *FW*.

ALP is Joyce's abbreviation for Anna Livia Plurabelle, the anima figure who combines all women and all rivers. In Joyce's notebooks ALP is symbolized △, which is pronounced delta in Greek, a nice coincidence since rivers have deltas and the Greeks traditionally regarded △ as a symbol of the vagina. ALP or △ is thus a pure yin force in the Chinese sense, female and watery at once.

Anna Livia Plurabelle takes her name, in part, from the Dublin river, Anna Liffey. Livia Svevo, wife of Joyce's friend Italo Svevo, was also told that she was a partial model for ALP, and Joyce scholars have found the Roman Empress (and poisoner) Livia also included in ALP. This last is appropriate because as Joyce's anima, ALP should be the female part of his own personality and his middle name was **Augusta**, due to clerical error. (His parents intended Augustine, but the clerk was Irish and these things happen.)* **Augusta** was the title of the Roman Livia, wife of Augustus Caesar, so Livia=Augusta=the woman inside James Joyce.

Plurabelle (or sometimes Plurabella) seems more simple and just means "many beauties" or "many women" in Joyce's mixed Latin-Italian. However, it also includes a reference to Vico's repeated phrase "O pura et pia bella" (Oh pure and holy wars), an expression used often in his *Scienza Nuova* and entirely typical of his Neapolitan trickiness. Norman O. Brown in *Closing Time* takes the phrase at face value and thinks it expresses religious piety, but J. Mitchell Morse in *A Conceptual Guide to Finnegans Wake* thinks the expression contains veiled irony and as much sarcasm as Vico dared to show with the Inquisition looking over his shoulder. As somebody said, it is hard to translate Vico into English because English is a basically honest language.

Anna Livia Plurabelle is thus a very feminine and yin symbol, containing its own opposite—the yang (or macho) warfare imagery that links Vico to the brawl at Finnegan's Wake in the balad. (Similarly, ∃ or HCE, Joyce's male or yang force, has a hidden female element, as in "Hag Chevychase Eve," where he has become bisexual. Chevychase invokes bear-goddess and huntress Artemis, or the virgin; Eve is the mother of us all; and Hag is the Crone or Wise Woman. We thus have the three aspects of the ancient Moon Goddess, virgin-mother-crone, within the male HCE.)

Permutated, ALP becomes APL which brings us back to the apple in the Garden of Eden, the Fall theme and Adam and Eve who are always lurking below the surface from the first sentence onward: "riverrun, past Eve and Adam's . . . " (For instance, "a tum" page 7, with Adam mixed with Atum; "eddams . . . aves" page 69, "Hoddum and Heave" page 296, etc. etc. Especially delightful is "atoms and ifs," page 455, where quantum indeterminacy appears.) APL, however, also forms the initials of Alice Pleasance Liddell, the model for Alice in Wonderland.

As is well known, Lewis Carroll (Charles Dodgson) loved Alice very warmly but perhaps not wisely—not wisely enough to avoid the speculations of Freudians. Thus Alice and Lewis Carroll link to the "incest" or Paedophilia theme in *FW*, as well as to Humpty Dumpty, the warring twins theme (Cain and Abel or ⊏ and ∧, who appear in Carroll's masterpiece as Tweedledum and Tweedledee), and the "nat language" which Joyce and Carroll both employ for non-aristotelian modes of mentation. It is appropriate that "Jabberwocky," Carroll's most Joycean verse, is recited by Humpty Dumpty

---

* By a similar clerical error, Joyce's Leopold Bloom in *Ulysses* acquired Paula instead of Paul as a middle name.

in *Alice in Wonderland* but was originally published under the title "Mishmosh."
(Nor avoice from afire belowsed mishe mishe . . .)

Alice first appears with the initials ALP and her family name, Liddell, on
the second page of *FW*

he addle liddle phifie annie (emphasis added)

She recurs hundreds of times, and is even in the famous prankquean
riddle, "Why do I am alook alike a poss of porterpease?" **Alike** is Greek for
Alice, and "like as two peas in a pod" suggests the warring twins ($\wedge \sqsubset$)
again, while "I am" brings us back to the E at Delphi and the voice from a fire
that bellowed **Moishe Moishe** and then identified itself as **I AM**.
Coincidentally, Dodgson invented the mathematical symbol ∃, which
Joyce uses for nonlocal consciousness. (Of course on the E or ego level, "why
do I am alook alike a poss of porterpeece" just echoes customers in
Earwicker's pub calling for a pint of porter, please.)

Charles Dodgson, the rationalist-mathematician, and "Lewis Carroll" the
fantasist and child-lover, are often presented as one of Joyce's Jekyll-Hyde or
split man teams ($\wedge$) but on one occasion they get expanded into a full
triplicity or $\wedge \sqsubset \wedge$ system: "Dogfather, Dogson and Coo," which sounds
like a British partnership company but invokes the Holy Trinity—Father,
Son and Pigeon. We are back at the Pigeon House again, where Stephen
Dedalus thought of Mary's bizarre sexual coupling with the Pigeon and
Bloom masturbated while virginal Gerty McDowell exhibited her **bloom**ers
(a verbal synchronicity). After the "immaculate" (no touching) sexual
encounter of Gerty and Bloom, Bloom wrote in the sand, I AM A — and
stopped. We will never know if he was going to write A VOYEUR, in
shameful confession, or ALONE, in anguish (or maybe even A JEW in
defiance?) In any case, he accidentally wrote "I am aleph" in Hebrew or "I am
alpha" in Greek and thus invoked *Revelations* 1:11, "I am alpha and omega, the
first and the last, saith the Lord." This 1:11 business turns out to be more
curious than we realize at first, even if we note that it is connected with
Bloom's son, who died at age 11 days, Shakespeare's son Hamnet who died
at 11 years and the 22 (2×11) letters in the Hebrew alphabet or the 22 words
in the first sentence of *Ulysses*.

If ALP and APL invoke all this, the LAP, a further permutation, invokes
the LAP where a Freemason wears his apron, as in Aleister Crowley's
BOOK OF LIES, Chapter 54, in which some Freemasons guess that the lost
Mason Word is AMO, whose number is 111, and some guess that it is LAP
which also has the number 111. (By Cabala, AMO=A which is 1, M which is
40, and O which is 70, 1+40+70=111, while LAP=L or 30, A or 1, and P or 80,
and 30+1+80 also=111.) William York Tindall, a Joyce scholar who likes to
count, has noted that many of the long sentences in *FW* have 111 clauses.

Anna Livia Plurabelle's untitled "mamafesta" in Chapter Five has 111 alternative titles; when sad, she is described as "wan wan wan"; in Chapter 8, she has 111 children. Most books on Cabala hint at transcendental meanings in the fact that the Hebrew A or aleph=ALP=111 when spelled in full as aleph-lamek-pe. I think Crowley is hinting in Chapter 54 of *The Book of Lies* that the Mason Word also=111 by Cabala, but it is curious that Joyce often identifies ALP with the number 54, because she is basically Anna Liffey and in Roman numerals LIV=54. (But as "livvy" on the bottom of the first page she is Mark Twain's wife, Olivia, whom he called "Livvy," as well as being the Roman historian, Livy, who inspirec Vico's theories of class war, which in turn inspired Marx, who is usually involved in Joyce's King Mark/Mark Twain puns.)

Joyce combines that Freemasonic lap theme with the Marriage Ceremony in the "Tavern" chapter of *FW*, which happens to be chapter 11:

Him her first lap, her his fast pal, for ditcher for plower, till deltas twoport.

Delta ($\triangle$) as a symbol of the vagina here combines also with Hamlet's notorious puns to Ophelia on lap meaning vagina and "nothing" meaning 0 or another symbol of the vagina. The 0 and its role as link between Leibniz's binary and *I Ching* is a subject to which we will return.

But we started from ALP and that word features prominently in a famous, oddly Joycean passage from Marx: "The weight of the past presses down on the brains of the living like—" Like what? Marx wrote "**Alp**," which in German can mean a nightmare or a mountain. Some translators make this "like an incubus" and some say "like an Alp." Since *FW* is a nightmare in which a mountain (Howth, **ш**) is a prominent character, and since Joyce lived in Switzerland near the Alps for many years, this is all wonderfully appropriate.

We are not quite finished with the ALP-APL-LAP system yet. Another permutation gives us PLA, which is Dublin slang for Portlaois Lunatic Asylum, which many of Joyce's contemporaries predicted would be his ultimate destination. (Carl Jung, on first looking into *FW*, said it indicated "either mental illness or a degree of mental health inconceivable to most people." Salvador Dali, the painter whose work so often resembles Joyce's prose, liked to say, "The only difference between me and a madman is that I am not mad.")*

* There are at least two tributes to Dali in *FW*. Joyce's "furloined notepaper" combines Poe's purloined letter with Dali's fur-lined teacups and bathtubs (and our animal anatomy: fur-loined). I also think Joyce's accusation that Earwicker was guilty of "covert meddlement with the drawers of his neighbor's safe" conflates the commandment against coveting one's neighbors wife with Dali's quite Joycean painting of a lady who

The second letter of most European alphabets is B and if you put our A and B together you get AB, or **ab**, which is the Indo-European root for "river," and appears in the name of the Punjab in India as well as in the Gaelic origin of Joyce's (or Dublin's) Anna Liffey, which is spelled **abhe life** and means "dark river." It also appears in numerous rivers between India and Ireland, including (by way of Grim's b-v switch) Shakespeare's Avon. We can't seem to get away from the "riverrun" with which *FW* begins, but that word probably owes something to Coleridge's

> *Where Alph, the sacred river, ran*
> *Through caverns measureless to man*
> *Down to a sunless sea*

In fact, the original Alph or Alpheus ran through Arcadia in Greece, which means "the place of the bear-god" and brings us back to that ursine archetype again. But Alph or alpha is just the Greek version of the Hebrew aleph or ALP or Joyce's Anna Livia Plurabelle . . .

The **ab** root may or may not be historically linked to Abel, but it is linked in the unconscious, and thus we are back to the battling twins again—Shem the Penman and Shaun the Postman, Cain and Abel, ∧ and ⊏ , Mutt and Jeff, Dodgson and Carroll, Jekyl and Hyde etc. These begin to seem like the two hemispheres of the brain, as discovered long after Joyce finished *FW*. As "cainapple," Joyce unites the Cain/Abel opposites, just as "the Hindu Shimar Shin" incongruously present at the battle of Waterloo unites them in their Shem and Shaun incarnations and Bruno of Nola unites them in their Brown and Nolan polarity. **Ab** also suggests Abraham—and Abraham and Sarah appear almost as often as Adam and Eve in *FW* as male/female or yang/yin archetypes.

Sara in Sanscrit means "salt" and this may explain why the Abraham/Sarah puns are especially thick on the closing pages of *FW*, where the freshwater Anna Liffey (**AB**, river) mingles with the salt water (**sara**) of Dublin Bay. Abraham Lincoln, who also appears, had a patriarchal name, a patriarchal beard and presided over the American Civil War, a magnified battle of brothers, or Cain and Abel Writ Large, or the brawl at Finnegan's Wake as a recurrent historical pattern. Ulysses Grant finally won that war for Lincoln and had appeared already in *Ulysses* as a living synchronicity with the title (Molly Bloom remembers seeing him on a visit to Gibralter). The hard-drinking author of the disreputable *Ulysses* seems to have had a strange sympathy for the hard-drinking and disreputable Ulysses Grant, who

---

had wooden (bureau) drawers where she should have ordinary lingerie drawers. Incidentally, Dali was as preoccupied with the fact that his first name, Salvador, means Saviour in Spanish as Joyce was with the fact that his name implies a joyous one or one who makes jokes.

appears as a "Grant, old gardner" in one part of *FW*—blending with Adam, whom Tennyson called "the grand old gardner"—and whose name is also cunningly hidden in "grand uproar style" (emphasis added) and several other Joycean arabesques you might enjoy discovering for yourself. The Blue and the Grey of the Civil War also appear frequently, but ultimately appear part of the Glues and the Gravys—two odd family names Joyce noted in the graveyard at Sidlesham where he found the Earwicker tombstone.

If **Abhe life** is identified with Eve in the opening clause of *FW* ("riverrun, past Eve and Adam's . . . ") this is also fortunate, since Eve in Hebrew means **life** (as Adam means **earth**.)

The "Anna" got into "Anna Liffey" because the English did not understand the Gaelic **abhe** (pronounced more like awa) but is quite appropriate for Joyce's purposes. Anna, in the New Testament, was the grandmother of Jesus and thus, in Catholic theology, the grandmother of God, which makes her a good symbol of that which is most ancient and primordial. The Tuatha de Danaan, early inhabitants of Ireland, worshipped a goddess named Danu, seemingly cognate with Diane-Artemis (the bear goddess who was a bare goddess) and also with the ancient Near Eastern goddess Anu and the Egyptian Nuit. Considering these and other etymologies, Robert Graves in *The White Goddess* concluded that "Anna" is the best of all alternative names for the ancient Moon Goddess, who combines virgin, mother and crone.

The "Anna" root also appears in the Russian, Anastasia, which means "resurrection" and fits perfectly into the symbolism of *FW*. As usual, when you look for synchronicity, synchronicity looks for you. While Joyce was writing *FW* in Paris a woman surfaced there who claimed to be the lost Grand Duchess Anastasia. She appears on page 28 Gaelicized as Anna Stacey, but then Anna Liffey becomes Judaized on page 253 as Hannah Levy. Each of Joyce's "characters" is a local example of a non-local function, as all women are aspects of the non-local Δ

A and B in Norse, meanwhile, are Ask and Embla, which mean Ash and Elm and are also the names of the Adam and Eve of Norse mythology. They appear on *FW* page 4 in the lovely Freudian/Jungian cluster,

elms leap where askes lay. Phall if you but will, rise you must (emphasis added)

Although Joyce has given it a detumescense/retumescense reference, the second line echoes McPherson's *Fingal*, a Scots version of the Finn MacCool epic: "If I must fall, my tomb shall rise."

ABC or Hebrew Aleph-beth-gimmel recurs constantly in *FW*, usually symbolizing the "three quarks" of page 383 (∧ ⊏ ⋏) who later got incorporated into quantum mechanics by Nobel laureate Dr. Murray Gell-Mann. "Alfred, Bertie, Charlie" and similar disguises usually conceal these three who include the warring twins ($\wedge$ $\sqsubset$) and their reconciliation ($\nwarrow$), but especially delightful is Abraham Bradley King who is three in one, being a real Lord Mayor of Dublin whose initials suggest the ABC team, and whose name opens with the pregnant **ab** root. As Joyce comments, "It's as semper as oxhousehumper." Since Latin semper=eternal, this means simple as ABC or eternal as ABC or eternal as the Hebrew letters aleph-beth-gimmel, which mean ox, house and camel. The camel becomes a "humper" to remind us of Humphrey Chimpden Earwicker and Humpty Dumpty.

But by now we should be ready to examine the family relationships between Joyce's major system-functions: $\triangle$ $\exists$ m $\wedge$ $\sqsubset$ $\dashv$ $\vdash$

The underlying principle of *FW* seems to be the non-local $\exists$ or the class of all possible minds, cognate with the Chinese no-mind (**wu shin**) or the Tao. When non-local $\exists$ appears in space-time it takes the form of the polarity of male or yang **w** energy and female or yin $\triangle$ energy. The first sentence, to look at it again, shows these yin/yang polarities neatly:

> **riverrun, past Eve and Adam's, from swerve of shore to bend of bay, rings us by a commodius vicus of recirculation back to Howth Castle and Environs.**

Eve and Adam are human forms of the yin/yang balance; the river Anna Liffey and Howth hill are geographic forms of the same polarity (the Chinese consider rivers yin and mountains yang); there may even be masculine energy in the rocky "swerve of shore" and female energy in the smooth "bend of bay." This yin/yang runs through the book in countless forms:

ancients link with presents as the human chain extends

FW is already startlingly isomorphic with *I Ching*. But we have already seen that the male or yang energy takes the opposite forms of $\wedge$ and $\sqsubset$, while the female or yin energy takes the opposing forms of $\dashv$ and $\vdash$ (the two Isoldes, the two Esthers, the two Alices—Alice Liddell and Isa Bowman, who played Alice on the stage and also became a subject of great affection to Dodgson/Carroll). This is isomorphic to the origin of *I Ching*, which is known as King Wen's Arrangement and looks like this

active yang   passive yang   active yin   passive yin

The cosmology of *I Ching* can be abbreviated as

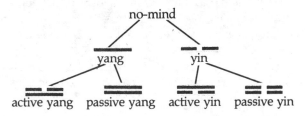

where the cosmology of *Finnegans Wake* is

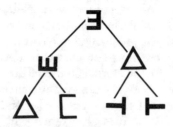

The isomorphism of the two systems is the more remarkable because there is nothing in Joyce's letters to indicate that he ever read, or even heard of, the *I Ching*; but this only repeats the isomorphism, or synchronicity, in which Leibniz also recreated *I Ching* in the form of his binary notation. As is well known to mathematicians, Leibniz lived long enough to see the first European translation of *I Ching* and to note the "coincidence" and be astounded by it. It was this isomorphism, in fact, which led Leibniz to postulate a kind of universal logical language below all forms of consciousness, a concept like and yet unlike Jung's "collective unconscious."

The Chinese yang or ⸺ is isomorphic to Leibniz's I and the yin or ⸺ ⸺ isomorphic to his 0. Substituting the binary symbolism in King Wen's Arrangement we get

The rule by which *I Ching* was generated out of King Wen's Arrangement is: out of these four elements, make all possible combinations of 3 each. If you will try this with King Wen's elements, you will get the 64 hexagrams of *I Ching*, since $4^3=64$. If you try it with Leibniz's terms instead of King Wen's, you get the first 64 numbers of the binary system (0 to 63), because, of course, 4^3 still$=64$.

Joyce seems to have known something of Leibniz, since he refers to the Leibniz's monad once, turning it into a confectionary "Prince Le Monade" (lemonade) who appears in a sugary fantasy involving girls in "sundae dresses." More interestingly, on page 261, ⨆ and △ become "that upright one and that naughty besighed him zeroine," which has a Freudian meaning (phallus and vagina) but also seems to refer directly to Leibniz's 1 and 0. The Chinese yang and yin, of course, reconcile this double-meaning, since they are both mathematical and sexual.

Leibniz predicted modern computers after the isomorphism between his binary numbers and *I Ching* became clear to him; it was obvious to his fine mathematical mind that such a symbolism could be mechanically reproduced and we would then have something akin to a "thinking machine." It is amusing that those who think computers think (or will soon think) generally consider themselves materialists, while those who claim *I Ching* thinks call themselves mystics, but if thought is defined in these terms, then both computers and *I Ching* must be considered to be thinking. (The fact that the human nervous system operates on a similar binary code may account for our occasional impression that humans also think, at least outside the areas of politics and religion.)

The implied thesis of these notes is that Joyce, Leibniz and the authors of *I Ching* all found this system independently and in different ways because it does, in fact, exist on the level of the non-local "mind" or system (**∃**) underlying all individual minds or Egos (**E**). This is the I AM or A Ham which appears in Gaelic, Hebrew, Sanskrit and about 60 other languages throughout the pages of *FW*: Plutarch's explanation of the E at Delphi.

There is one feature of *I Ching* which appears in Joyce but not in binary—the moving lines (—✕— and —✕—) which transform active yang to passive, active yin to passive, or vice versa. These are, of course, Joyce's non-aristotelian functions, ⋏ as hidden unity behind ∧ and ⊏ , and ⟂ as hidden unity behind ⊣ and ⊢ . I am happy to say that the Taoist philosopher and Tai Chi master, Chiang Ling Al Huang, agreed with me about this point when I presented these isomorphs at Esalen Institute in March 1986.

It is amusing (or bemusing) to note that binary and *I Ching* are not only isomorphic to *FW* but also, as Martin Schoenberger has noted, to the genetic code. The full details are explained in Dr. Schoenberger's *The I Ching and the Genetic Code*; for our purposes here it is enough to note the following:

The DNA is made up of two opposite spirals, positive and negative, which can easily be considered isomorphic to *I Ching*'s yin (--) and yang (—), or Leibniz's 0 and 1, or Joyce's ⊔ and △. These are bonded by four amino acids—adenine, guaine, cytosine and thymine, which are usually abbreviated A, G, C, T. If one dares to consider these isomorphic with active yang (==), passive yang (==), active yin (==) and passive yin (==), or Leibniz's 01, 11, 10 and 00, or Joyce's ∧ ⊏ ⊣ and ⊢ , then the parallel becomes staggering. In forming RNA messages—the genetic code—the T (thymine) drops out to be replaced by U (uracil) but we still have four elements—A, G, C, U—and if we permutate them by the now-familiar rule, making all possible combinations of three out of these basic four "letters," we get again 4^3 or 64 "words," which are the 64 elements of the genetic language.

But if the genetic language has two foursomes—the A,C,G,T that bond the DNA, and the A, C, G, U that unwind from this and make the 64 permutations of the genetic language—Joyce also has a second foursome, in addition to his male $\wedge$ $\sqsubset$ and female $\dashv$ $\vdash$ The second foursome is symbolized in his notes as **X**.

X is one of Joyce's most interesting nonlocal functions. Most often it is four judges, one presiding over each of the Four Courts on the river Anna Liffey in Dublin—a building which literally does have four courts, incidentally: one for Dublin city, one for Dublin county, one for the province of Leinster and one for the nation. In many places **X** becomes the four compass points, North East South West, and it is occasionally the four provinces of Ireland (Leinster, Munster, Ulster and Connacht), the four chambers of the human heart, the four kings of the Tarot or ordinary card decks, etc. As the book moves on, **X** more and more becomes the four archetypal figures whom Joyce gives the names Matt Gregory, Marcus Lyons, Luke Tarpey and Johnny McDougal.

As Matt, Marcus, Luke and Johnny, **X** obviously echoes the childrens' prayer, "Matt, Mark, Luke, John, bless the bed that I lie on." As Gregory, Lyons, Tarpey and McDougal the **X** link to very deep archetypes, as follows: Gregory includes **ego** and thereby suggests a man; Lyons suggests a lion; Tarpey suggests Gaelic **tarf**, a bull (with a buried link to the Battle of Clontarf again; Clontarf means bull field); and McDougal conceals an **eagle**. We thus have the four angels in the vision of Ezekial—man, lion, bull, eagle—who were, in fact, identified with the Four Evangelists in medieval Catholic art. Matt being shown with a man, Mark with a lion, Luke with a bull and John with an eagle. They appear this way, for instance, in the 8th Century Irish *Book of Kells*, which Joyce uses as a source of archetypes throughout *FW*, being especially concerned with the famous "Tunc" page (because **Tunc** in Latin means both "now" and "then" and thus invokes the Einsteinian Relativity theme, and also because **Tunc** makes an easily deciphered permutation of what Earwicker was evidently peeking at in the bushes of Phoenix Park.)

Of course, the Catholic Matt-man, Mark-lion, Luke-bull, John-eagle symbolism contains an astrological code. The man is the union of opposites and hence correlated with the **water** signs, the lion (Leo) symbolizes the **fire** signs, the bull, Taurus, is the **earth** signs and the eagle, of course, the **air** signs. The same symbolism appears repeatedly in alchemical texts and is coded into the Tarot cards in which cups=water, wands=fire, pentacles=earth and swords=air. Bruno was one of the last of the great hermetic philosophers who used this symbolism to express psychological/"metaphysical" propositions which nowadays are more familiar to us as Jung's system of the four basic personality types which each create a different reality-tunnel as they edit experience to fit their own models. The equation is:

Matt Gregory = man = water = cups = Jung's feeling person. The Tarot cups are full of water in most decks; water correlates with the feeling faculty because of its flowing and unstable nature.

Marcus Lyons = Leo = fire = wands = Jung's intuitive person. Some Tarot decks actually show fire spouting out of the wands; fire correlates with intuition because it is an ancient symbol of illumination.

Luke Tarpey = bull = earth = pentacles = Jung's sensational person. Earth correlates with the sensational faculty because the sensational/sensual person is, in vulgar jargon, "earthy" and "materialistic."

Johnny MacDougal = eagle = air = swords = Jung's rational person. The swords = reason because they cut things up as reason dissects things in analysis. Air symbolizes reason because the Rationalist notoriously lives in the clouds and doesn't "have his feet on the ground."

Bruno and the hermeticists generally believed, like Jung, that most people are over-developed in one of these areas and under-developed in the others, and that the path to integration was to learn to balance all four. It has by now become commonplace in Joyce exegesis to recognize that the warring twins, $\wedge$ and $\sqsubset$, are two aspects of the nonlocal $\exists$, roughly isomorphic to Jung's Persona and Shadow or Freud's ego and id. It seems likely to me that the four X are also aspects of the one E or psychic functions of the dreamer that have been separated and need to be reunified.

To Bruno and the hermeticists, of course, the four X were metaphysical as well as psychological. The cosmology of earth-air-fire-water has such a long history in alchemical-hermetic literature that it hardly needs to be insisted on; Jung has tried to find modern translations for this somewhat archaic system in his *Psychology and Alchemy*. The traditional system meanwhile lives on and is used by many occult groups still surviving; the reader will find it expounded in most of the works of Aleister Crowley, especially *The Book of Thoth*.

In researching secret societies for my *Illuminatus* trilogy, I was repeatedly amazed that some analog of Joyce's X function appears in almost all of them, in one way or another. For instance, Freemasonry, the largest and most powerful secret society of all, has four Worshipful Masters who stand at the four corners of the lodge during initiations, just as Joyce's X are sometimes North, East, South and West. (The three quarks, $\wedge \sqsubset \Lambda$, curiously, also appear in Freemasonry as Jubela, Jubelo and Jubelum in the death of the Widow's Son.) The most influential of all modern magick societies, the Golden Dawn, uses four quasi-Freemasonic officers at the four corners of the temple. Witches have their four guardians at the four "quarters" who go by various names—modern witchcraft is an improvised reconstruction of the medieval cult—but usually they are half male and half female. In the largest California witch coven, they are Robin, Orpheus, Marion and Bride—who correspond with man, lion, bull, eagle in one sense, but correspond even more closely with Joyce's Λ ⊏ ⊣ ⊢ or with *I Ching*'s active yang, passive yang, active yin and passive yin.

This interchangeability of foursomes makes an interesting isomorphism with genetics. The DNA is bonded by the four acids A, C, G, T but the genetic code is created when T drops out to be replaced by U, and the 64 "words" of the genetic code, as we have seen, is based on A, C, G, U, not on A, C, G, T. Perhaps this explains why Joyce gives us two foursomes in the Λ ⊏ ⊣ ⊢ complex and the **X** complex. At any rate, the male-female polarity of Λ ⊏ ⊣ ⊢ does wash over into the **X** occasionally, and Joyce calls them "heladies" or bisexuals in the Tristan-Isolde chapter, where they become four seagulls spying on the lovemaking of Tristan and Isolde, the three elders spying on Susanah in the Old Testament, and four censors trying to decide if *FW* is obscene. (That is the chapter that begins with the "three quarks" who later found their way into quantum mechanics via Dr. Gell-Man.)

The following table shows the entire *I Ching*, binary and genetic isomorphism.

BASIC ISOMORPHISMS

Joyce's Symbols	*I Ching*	Binary Numbers	Genetics	Quantum Mechanics
Ǝ	Tao			The implicate order or Hidden Variable
Ш	YANG ⚊	1	Positive coil of DNA	Particle Aspect of Matter
Δ	YIN ⚋	0	Negative coil of DNA	Wave Aspect of Matter
Λ	Active YANG ⚍	01	G	Positive Particles
⊏	Passive YANG ⚌	11	A	Negative Particles
Ʌ	Moving YANG ⚌		Mutation	Neutral Particles

Joyce's Symbols	I Ching	Binary Numbers	Genetics	Quantum Mechanics
⊣	Passive YIN ☷	00	U	The minimum two values of the
⊢	Active YIN ☳	10	C	state vector in Wave Mechanics
I	Moving YIN		Mutation	The collapse of the state vector when measured
X	Permutation of the 4 basic units into the 64 hexagrams	Permutation of the 4 amino acids into the 64 "words" of the genetic code		Generation of cosmos from the 4 forces: 1. strong force 2. weak force 3. electromagnetism 4. gravity
O	The yearly cycle of YIN and YANG	The 12 bonds in one complete turn of DNA		
ш		sociobiology		
E	one hexa-gram or temporary state	psychology; the ego		"objects" as perceived by the senses

It appears that life continues to show signs of "intelligence" (and strict Darwinism is perpetually beset by Lamarckian, Bergsonian, Reichian and other heresies) because the genetic code, like the binary used in computers and I Ching is a logical language and does produce either "thought" or an analog of thought.

It is even more amusing (or, for the Fundamentalist Materialist, anxiety-provoking) to note that Joyce seems to have anticipated even the shape of the DNA in a famous passage in Ulysses, published over 30 years before the scientific confirmation from Watson and Crick: Stephen Dedalus, walking toward the Pigeon House (that again!) thinks of the genetic memory as a telephone cable and then whimsically reflects:

The cords of all link back, strandentwining cable of all flesh.
That is why mystic monks. Will you be as gods? Gaze in your
omphalos. Hello! Kinch here. Put me on to Edenville. Aleph,
alpha: nought, nought, one.

The double helix of the DNA does indeed look like a "strandentwining cable"
and it is distinctly odd that Joyce seems to have had the ALP and 0 and 1
binary symbols in mind so long before *FW*. (Stephen's thought seems to be
that mystic monks, gazing into their omphaos or navels, eventually tune in
to the genetic memory going back to the dawn of life which become the
of *FW*. It is curious that Mendel, a monk, was the first to intuit the
mathematical formulae of genetics, is it not?)

All this begins to recall the diagram which appears in most of the books of
Wilhelm Reich:

This originated in Reich's *The Function of the Orgasm* and was intended to
illustrate how an energetic process could take two seemingly "opposite"
forms, mental (psychological) and physical (somatic); it underlies Reich's
philosophy of psychosomatic unity. Later, under the influence of Bruno of
Nola—with whom he increasingly identified as his own problems with the
New Inquisition increased—Reich came to apply the same duality-in-unity
diagram to all sorts of processes and eventually expanded it into a
cosmological principle which he admitted was similar to the dialectical
pantheism of Bruno; Reich never noted that it was also similar to Taoism
and *I Ching*.

In this connection, it is interesting that Joseph Needham, in his *Science and
Civilization in China* (Volume II) calls Bruno one of the two Occidental
philosophers to have a basically Taoist outlook. The other Occidental Taoist,
according to Needham, is the medieval mystic, Nicholas of Cusa, who is
curiously invoked in a passage from *FW* which also mentions Bruno. It is on
pages 49-50:

Me drames, O'Loughlins, has come through! Now let the
centuple celves of my egourge as Micholas de Cusack calls them
. . . by the coincidance of their contraries reamgamerge in that
indentity of undiscernibles where the Baxters and the Fleshmans
may they cease to bedivil uns and . . . this outstandin Brown
candlestock melt Nolan's into peese!

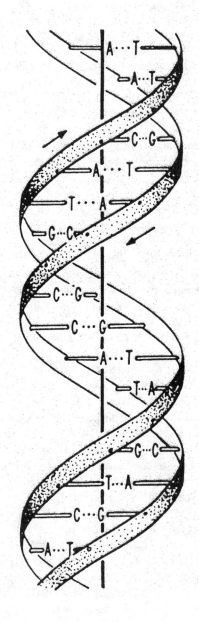

Double Helix of DNA

"Micholas de Cusack" conflates Nicholas of Cusa with Michael Cusack, a notorious anti-semitic nationalist of the Dublin of Joyce's day (who, incidentally, was the model for The Citizen in *Ulysses*). Since Mick and Nick in *FW* are usually opposites of the ∧⊏ variety—they are, in fact, most often the Archangel Michael and Satan, or the ⊏∧ duality as cosmic principle in Christian mythology—this Mick/Nick unity (⋀) is itself a "coincidance of contraries." The brown candlestock that melts Nolans is Bruno of Nola (⋀) divided into contraries (∧⊏). The Baxters and Fleshmans are a variation on the Bakers and Butchers who run all through *FW*; these are extensions of Cain (⊏) the tiller of fields and hence an ancestor of Bakers, and Abel (∧) keeper of herds and an ancestor of butchers. The sequence butcher-baker-candlestock invokes a familiar trio of childhood lore, the butcher, the baker and the candlestick maker, another of Joyce's trios (∧⊏⋀) that emerge from a duo (∧⊏).

The O'Loughlins, meanwhile, are an Anglicized version of the older Gaelic tribe correctly spelled O'Lachlann. This means "son of the Dane," and brings us back to Hamlet, Prince of Demnark; but that should not surprise us because the butchers in *FW* always are in "coincidance" with both Abel and Shakespeare, who worked as a butcher in his youth and had a butcher as a father. What does seem strange to me is that this pivotal passage should directly involve my own family, because my grandmother was an O'Lachlann. (But then Stan Gebler Davies, who wrote a biography of Joyce while living, unknowingly, in the same building with Morris Ernst, the lawyer who convinced an American court that *Ulysses* was not obscene, points out that coincidence haunts all commentators who get involved with Joyce.)

The O'Lachlanns or O'Loughlins are said to be descended from Olaf the White, King of the Isle of Man in the 9th Century. This Olaf links directly to Hamlet, because, as O'Hehir has documented, Olaf became Amhlain in Gaelic and it was from this that Saxo-Germanicus developed the further "corruption" which became the Hamlet we know. We have already indicated that the same root gave us the Humphrey that is our dreamer's first name.

The Fleshmans as butchers also tips a hat to Martha Fleishmann, a young lady with whom Joyce had a brief affair in 1917, and who previously got into his works as the mysterious "Martha Clifford" in *Ulysses*. Bloom, you may recall, corresponded with her under the pen-name, "Henry Flower." That was actually the name of a Dublin policeman who was suspected of murder in 1902, never brought to trial because of lack of evidence, and finally left Dublin because gossip continued to accuse him. In the Cyclops chapter of *Ulysses*, it is Michael Cusack, called only The Citizen, who appears as the only overt anti-semite in the book and threatens to "crucify" Bloom. The punchline did not come until 1942, a year after Joyce's death, when an old woman in Dublin, dying, summoned a solicitor and dictated a confession. She had committed the murder wrongly attributed to Henry Flower.

The solicitor who took this confession was John Cusack, son of Michael Cusack who gave Bloom/Flower a hard time in *Ulysses*.

The "coincidance" of Michael Cusack and Nicholas of Cusa and John Cusack and Henry Flower across space-time could not have been known in full to Joyce's conscious mind, of course, which is why any theory of Joyce's novels must take into account the reality of the non-local function he abbreviates as ∃

Bloom's "real" name—i.e. his father's name, before he changed it by deed poll—was Virag, which can be translated as either Bloom or Flower. But Virag is a Hungarian cognate of the Sanscrit *vajna*, which happens to mean thunderbolt and reminds us of Vico's notion that all human thought was instigated by our desire to understand and come to terms with the Giant Thing that seems to roar at us from the sky.

Padraic Pearse, who became part of Joyce's Pearse O'Reilly (⋀) once had an argument with Joyce about whether Gaelic *thurnuk* was a more poetic word than the English "thunder" which means the same. Pearse was an associate of Cusack in the Irish Nationalist movement (which Joyce as a cosmopolitan despised); but Delia Bacon, if you are following this, claimed that the plays of butcher Shakespeare (⊏) were not written by her ancestor, Sir Francis Bacon (⋀) as other eccentrics claim, but by a collaboration of Shakespeare, Bacon and Raleigh (⊏ ⋀ ⋀), a theory which gets great play in *FW*, whether Joyce believed it or not, because Raleigh is thought in Ireland to derive from Reilly and because Delia Bacon fits both the boar-god symbolism (Bacon-Ham-Hamlet-pork-Adonis etc.) and the bear-god symbolism, Delia being a title of Artemis. At this point we can only recognize that a bear-god and a boar-god are easily conflated in the unconscious, and note that the chain Aleph-alpha-Ab-Abel-butcher-baker-candlestock-Cad-Cadenus ties most of our themes together, making links from the Old Testament to Swift's love life, and is still based on the simple progression A-B-C.

Thus, in the second paragraph of *FW*, we find

not yet, though venissoon after, had a kidscad buttended a bland old isaac

On the level of Old Testament reference, this invokes caddish Jacob pretending to be Esau to get the blessing of their father, Isaac—Jacob and Esau being another of Joyce's warring twin (⋀ ⊏) combinations. On the level of Irish politics of Joyce's day, this is Parnell, a **cad**et member of the Home Rule party unseating Isaac Butt (buttended . . . isaac) as leader. Two of

Swift's pen names are included (Cadenus and Isaac Beckersniff) and one of his Esthers (von Homerigh, whom he called Vanessa) is mingled with deer-meat for reasons that still escape me. "Bland" is midway between blonde, like Finn Mac Cool and Earwicker, and "blind" like Isaac in the Bible (and Joyce also feared he might be blind before finishing *FW*.) Since Isaac in Hebrew means "he who laughs," this is a nice mesh with the etymology of Joyce from joke, and Isaac was of course the son of Abraham, bringing us back to the AB theme.

Semper as oxhousehumper.

Interview With
Sean MacBride

And what if excess of love
Bewildered them till they died?
I write it out in verse —
MacDonagh and MacBride
And Connolly and Pearse
Now and in time to be,
Wherever green is worn,
Are changed, changed utterly:
A terrible beauty is born.

These lines from *Easter 1916* are certainly the most famous (and perhaps the greatest) political stanza that William Butler Yeats ever wrote; and I cannot cross Dublin without thinking of fragments of it, as I pass Connolly Station, say, or Pearse Station, or the General Post Office on O'Connell Street where the rebels of 1916 made their last stand. My couplet, "I, a pacifist, feel pride / For the ghost of John MacBride" in a poem earlier in this anthology refers, among other things, to the fact that Major MacBride refused the blindfold when the British shot him, saying in effect that he had faced enemy bullets too often to fear them any longer.

Hugh Kenner may have been the first exegete to wonder what it cost Yeats, emotionally, to use the name of John MacBride in a crucial, rhyming position in this stanza; for Major MacBride had the fortune to marry the woman Yeats loved, Maud Gonne. Isn't it strange how all things relate to all other things? Yeats once tried to persuade Maud Gonne to join the Hermetic Order of the Golden Dawn, and she refused, distrusting all Freemasonic groups equally; yet the Golden Dawn has more to do with the publication of this anthology at this time than most readers will guess.

The following article is a conversation with Sean MacBride, who is the son of Major MacBride and Maud Gonne, and also one of the most canny Elder Statesmen in Europe. In a few pages, I shall list some of the honors, including the Nobel prize, that Sean MacBride has won; these are of interest as documentation of the high regard in which he is held in Europe. It is, to me, extremely curious that this book represents the first publication in the United States of this conversation with a major European politician and intellectual. The magazine which originally commissioned this interview, *New Age*, suddenly decided not to publish it (although they paid me a generous "kill" fee for my time and effort). Other leading U.S. magazines, including *Playboy* and *Penthouse*, also declined to publish it. It has appeared thusfar only in a Swiss newspaper.

None of the political opinions expressed by Mr. MacBride are considered at all "extreme" in Ireland or most of Europe. They are the normal attitudes of normal statesman and philosophers in ordinary European nations. I wonder why they seem so alien and weird to those whose view of the world is based only on what they read in the American media?

———————————————— □ □ ▢ □ □ ————————————————

At the age of 80, Sean MacBride, a former member of the Irish Republican Army, is the best-known anti-nuclear activist in Europe, and as a lawyer and founding member of Amnesty International has probably done more than any man in history to secure the release of political prisoners all over the world. Because of his non-partisan opposition to injustice wherever it appears—an outgrowth of traditional Irish neutralism in the wars of the Great Powers—MacBride is the only living human being to have received both the Lenin Peace Prize from the Soviet government (1977) and the American Medal of Justice from the United States (1978). He has also received the Nobel Peace Prize (1974), the International Institute of Human Rights Medal (1974), the UNESCO Medal of Merit (1980) and the Dag Hammerskjoeld Prize for International Solidarity (1981). And at the age when most men have been retired for 15 years, Sean MacBride shows absolutely no signs of slowing down.

When I first tried to contact him for an interview, MacBride was in New York, testifying at an extradition hearing. Before we could meet, he stopped in Paris for a Human Rights conference, jetted to Wales for a conference on the effects of satellite TV on local cultures, and spoke in Dublin at a rally of Irish pacifists planning demonstrations against Ronald Reagan, then visiting Ireland. Looking over his *Vita*, I found that he still serves as President of the Irish sections of Amnesty International (he was Chairman of the international Executive Committee of Amnesty, 1961-74) and is also President of the Nuclear Safety Association, Vice-Chairman of the Irish Civil Liberties Associations, President of the Irish Campaign for Nuclear Disarmament, President of the UNESCO Commission for the Study of Communication, President of the International Peace Bureau and serves more than a dozen similar posts, including President of the Literary and Historical Association of University College Dublin, member of the Foundation for the Prevention of Childhood Handicaps and even Vice-President of the "Trees for Ireland" Association, a reforestation group. The taxi-driver who took me to MacBride's home in Clonskea, a Dublin suburb, told me he once asked MacBride, "How can you keep so busy at your age?" MacBride answered with typical Irish self-mockery, "If I quit now, who'd pay the bills?"

Actually, Sean MacBride has been extremely active—an *engage*, as the French say—since he joined the I.R.A. in 1919, at the age of fifteen. He had already been imprisoned by then, at fourteen, as a suspected revolutionary (he quickly escaped) because his father, Major John MacBride, one of the leaders of the Easter Uprising in Dublin, 1916, had been executed by the British. (Sean's mother, Maud Gonne MacBride, although best known to students of literature as the inspiration of some of the poetry of William Butler Yeats, is best known in Ireland as an often-imprisoned leader in the struggle of the Irish peasants against English absentee landlords.) At sixteen, in 1921, Sean was one of the I.R.A. delegates to the Frankfurt Congress Against Imperialism, where he met Nehru and Ho Chih Minh; it was there that he began to see Ireland as part of the Third World, an idea that he retains to this day. ("We are an undeveloped country, a part of the Third World," he said in a recent speech, "no matter how much the smart young executives pretend that we are a sophisticated, developed economy.") At seventeen, in 1921, Sean MacBride was the youngest member of the Irish delegation to the London Treaty Conference which ended the Irish War of Liberation on terms he still finds unacceptable. He therefore remained in the Irish Republican Army during the Civil War that followed and was imprisoned by the Irish Free State in 1922 and again in 1930; ironically, the Free State eventually became the Republic of Ireland which gave him a medal in 1938 for his 1919-1921 military activities against the British, elected him to *Dail hEirann* (roughly, the House of Representatives) in 1947-58, and made him Minister of External Affairs in 1948-51. "He could be President of Ireland anytime he wanted," I was recently told in a pub, "but his interests are more international now."

Americans—even Irish-Americans—often find it impossible to understand Irish politics in the years when MacBride was an officer of the I.R.A., 1919-1937. Eamon DeValera (often called "the George Washington of Ireland") was, for instance, MacBride's superior officer in the I.R.A. in the early 1920s; the two were military enemies after DeValera entered the Free State government in 1927; they became political enemies after 1937, when MacBride, having become a lawyer, secured the release of hundreds of I.R.A. members and alleged I.R.A members imprisoned by DeValera. Today, MacBride speaks of DeValera with respect tinged with reverence. "Dev lost the civil war of 1922-27," he says, "but in the first five years he served as *Taoiseach* (Prime Minister) he won everything back that had been lost in the civil war." It was the accomplishments of those first five DeValera years 1932-37, that convinced MacBride that DeValera's nonviolent but constant pressure on England that led MacBride to resign from the paramilitary organization. When asked about some of DeValera's more intolerant policies, which were decidedly unfair to Protestants, MacBride says simply, "He was wrong then." When pressed for further comment, he repeats woodenly, "He was wrong, I said," and waits impatiently for the next question. *Dev was wrong*, his tone implies, *but haven't all the rest of us been wrong sometimes?*

It was as Minister of External Affairs, 1948-51, that MacBride developed what has been dubbed his "sore thumb policy": any international tribunal on which he serves is sure to find that the question of the partition of Ireland has become part of the agenda, officially or otherwise—much to the embarrassment of the British delegates. And although separated from the old I.R.A. since 1937, and having denounced the terrorist tactics of the new, Provisional I.R.A. often, MacBride wrote an introduction to the autobiography of Bobby Sands, the Provisional who starved himself to death in protest against British occupation of the Six Counties, a non-violent tactic Gandhi would have approved. Although Margaret Thatcher denounced Sands after his death as a "man of violence," everywhere one travels in Ireland one sees graffiti, stark in their simplicity, saying only BOBBY SANDS R.I.P.

Sean MacBride lives in Roebuck House, a rambling old Georgian mansion southwest of Dublin. Despite all I knew of his active life, I was astonished at the youthfulness of his complexion and the bouyancy of his walk. He dressed casually, as the Irish generally do, and looked mildly embarrassed when I said it was an honor to meet him. His secretary announced that, although I had been promised an hour and a half for the interview, the time would have to be cut to an hour due to another urgent appointment that had come up. He spoke unhurriedly, without seeming to be pressed by the time limit, and still managed to answer all my questions with succinct precision.

Most Americans know you chiefly as one of the founders of Amnesty International. Were your own experiences of being imprisoned by both the British and the Free State an important factor in motivating your involvement with political prisoners everywhere?

Yes, of course. But I was also one of the drafters of the European Convention for the Protection of Human Rights in 1950, which I regard as a very important step forward in developing an international rule of law, but by 1961 some of us saw the need for a non-governmental agency that would bring world attention to individual cases where human rights were being violated. The Human Rights treaty was dependent upon the good faith and good will of the governments that signed it. Amnesty International was created in 1961 to take on cases irrespective of the wishes of governments—whether the governments liked it or not.

Would you explain how Amnesty works and what it attempts to accomplish?

Amnesty is concerned only with political prisoners. We divide them into two groups—"prisoners of conscience" and "other political prisoners." We define "prisoners of conscience" as those who have been imprisoned only for their political or religious views, who are not accused of violent acts or advocacy of violence. We demand immediate release in such cases and bring every possible pressure on the governments involved, to secure immediate release. The "other political prisoners," those who have committed or advocated violence, we treat differently. We do not demand release, of course, but we monitor these cases to see that they are treated humanely and decently, that they are not tortured, and that the prison conditions conform with norms of human rights laid down by the United Nations.

What about the shady area—prisoners who have been convicted of violent acts but who are widely alleged to have been framed for political reasons?

We have a "borderline bureau" that scrutinizes cases of that sort, and we have developed a rather elaborate internal jurisprudence in evaluating the evidence before we make a decision. Even so, some cases have to be reclassified when new evidence is uncovered. We had one case I remember in which the prisoner himself caused us to change his category. That was a Black civil rights leader in South Africa, whom we had classed as a "prisoner of conscience" while he was awaiting trial, but then, in his closing speech to the Court, he stated that the only way of protecting the Black people in that country was by armed force. We had to transfer him to our "other political prisoners" category, since he was advocating violence, and we stopped asking for his release, which was a very hard decision.

You recently testified at an extradition hearing in New York involving a man from Northern Ireland. You opposed extradition on the grounds, more or less, that a Catholic cannot get a fair trial there.

I did not say that; I said that the ordinary provisions of the rule of law are not complied with there. Firstly, there are trials without juries, which is always dangerous and particularly nefarious in political cases. Then there is the fact that judges regularly admit as evidence the sort of thing that is specifically forbidden by normal legal standards in democratic states. Finally, there is the notorious "supergrass" system. "Supergrasses" are known criminals themselves and testify against scores and scores of persons in return for immunity from prosecution.

A few years ago, Amnesty International took a blanket position of opposition to capital punishment in all cases, and one American member, William F. Buckley, Jr., resigned in protest, saying the issue of capital punishment was no part of Amnesty's original purpose. How do you feel about that controversy?

I supported the position that Amnesty should oppose capital punishment in all cases. I have many reasons for this. First of all, I think that if the State takes upon itself the right to kill, then inevitably those who oppose the State will arrogate to themselves the same right. Revolutionaries and terrorists do, in fact, use exactly that argument, with some sincerity: "If the State can take life, then we can also take life." After all, they generally claim that they represent the people and that the State doesn't. I am opposed to the cheapening of human life created by that rhetoric on both sides. Secondly, I don't believe that any human institution has the right to take life as punishment or retribution; you may have to take life in self-defense or in armed conflict against injustice where there are no alternatives—no legal means of struggle—but taking life as revenge is never justified. Thirdly, as a lawyer I have seen too many errors made by judges to believe in the infallibility of courts. I have had personal experience of at least three cases where to my certain knowledge an innocent person was condemned to death. You cannot believe in capital punishment after seeing that happen.

In your work with Amnesty International since 1961, which countries have you found to be the worst offenders against human rights?

It varies, and it varies both in quantity and quality—in the number of victims and in the degree of atrocity. In the Soviet bloc, conditions have improved since Amnesty was founded. Probably at the moment the worst offenders are the governments in Central and Latin America, especially Chile, Argentina, El Salvador and Guatemala. I think that is the area where human rights are more viciously and extensively violated than anywhere else. The assassination squads in those nations are the worst kind of terrorism. Those countries have disimproved, especially in the last few years, and to a certain extent I blame this on President Reagan who has condoned these atrocities and even supported them financially and militarily.

For forty years now, Americans have been led to believe that the worst offender against human rights in all the world is the U.S.S.R. You insist that this is no longer true.?

I would not call Russia an ideal society from the human rights standpoint, but it has definitely improved since Stalin; it has not disimproved. That is one of Amnesty's successes. In the first years of Amnesty in the early 1960s, there were vast numbers of political detainees in camps in Siberia and other places in the Soviet Union and other Marxist countries in Eastern Europe. There, Amnesty was very successful in making the new leaders feel the weight of world opinion. We obtained the release of thousands—I would say, of at least ten thousand persons. Partly, this was because we made the Soviets realize that these people had been imprisoned for advocating exactly the policies the new, post-Stalin government was following.

Do you feel that the average Russian is more free of the threat of unreasonable arrest today than in the past?

Yes; definitely yes—even more free of that threat than they were ten years ago. Based on Amnesty's studies, there has been great improvement there. I am not saying that the human rights situation there is as it should be, but there has been tremendous progress. It speaks well for the Soviet leadership that Amnesty can get adequate information and do know what to protest in their treatment of political offenders. Letters from there to Amnesty are delivered without interference; groups of dissidents there send us reports and even have long phone conversations with our London office. By contrast, China is still the most closed society in the world. We can't even learn the number of political prisoners there, and we have no adequate information about civil liberties there at all.

Russian officials in the past have accused Amnesty of being a front for the C.I.A. and American right-wingers sometimes claim you are all a bunch of Soviet dupes or fellow travelers . . .

Yes, yes, and that delights us. The fact that we are attacked by both sides is proof of our neutrality and objectivity.

You also have guidelines guaranteeing the neutrality of each Amnesty chapter, do you not?

Certainly. We work through outreach groups, called Adoption Groups. In order to ensure the neutrality of each Adoption Group, we insist that they adopt three prisoners—one from the Western block nations, and one from the Communist bloc, and one from the Afro-Asian bloc. Each group is then pledged to work equally for the three adopted prisoners. You can't say "I'll only work for prisoners in Communist countries," or "I'll only work for prisoners in Capitalist countries"; You have to work equally for political prisoners in each of the three major power blocs. I think this system guarantees Amnesty's objectivity and therefore our credibility.

Nonetheless, the Wall Street Journal *recently denounced you personally. They mentioned your receiving the Lenin Peace Prize in a way that implied you were some sort of Soviet agent or apologist.*

That was hysteria, and it had nothing to do with Amnesty anyway. They were annoyed by a report which I helped to write for UNESCO on Communication and Society, the so-called MacBride Report. I believe that they had not read the report, because they claimed that it urged the imposition of new controls and limitations on journalistic freedom. Exactly the opposite is true. The report is, I believe, the most advanced and progressive document ever written in that area—we specifically urged greater freedom for journalists. We want them to have access to things governments are trying to hide. What we did wish to limit was the monopolization of the media, and I personally have urged steps to encourage the decentralization of ownership and control of the media. But before we leave this subject, let me just note that the *Wall Street Journal* did not mention that I have received the American Medal of Justice in Washington. I believe that I am the only person *not* an American citizen to have received that award. Considering the vast C.I.A. dossiers on every dissident in the world, the U.S. government would hardly be so careless as to give that award to a Communist agent.

Aside from Amnesty and various UNESCO projects, one of your principle concerns in recent years has been to oppose the proliferation of nuclear weapons. You have argued that the CRUISE and PERSHING missiles are not only dangerous and immoral but strictly illegal. Would you explain that?

As a lawyer and President of International Peace Bureau in Geneva and a member of the International Commission of Jurists, I have studied this question for many, many years. I have submitted my legal opinion to the Federal Court in New York. I believe the deployment of these weapons is a clear-cut violation of international law and an act of terrorism. We won't have time for your other questions if I present my whole legal argument here but briefly I can say this much: as early as 1874, the International Declaration concerning the Laws and Customs of War specifically denied that governments have "an unlimited power in the adoption of means of injuring the enemy," and the Hague convention of 1907 prohibits "bombardment of towns, villages, dwellings or buildings which are undefended." All the laws against poison gas adopted after World War I are so worded that it is their clear intent to criminalize the indiscriminate killing of non-combatants. These were some of the precedents with which Nazi officials were found guilty of crimes against humanity at Nuremberg. But the Nuremberg judgements went further and laid down in 1946 that planning and conspiring to wage war against civilian populations is itself a crime. This was felt necessary at the time, and is, in fact, based on common law, where conspiracy to commit a crime is itself a crime.

You mean, it is like the law under which planning and preparing to commit murder is itself criminal.

Yes. The Nuremberg tribunal precisely ruled that planning, preparing and conspiring to commit mass murder is criminal. The United Nations General Assembly in 1950 again reaffirmed that planning for wars involving "wanton destruction of cities" is a crime, and so is preparing "inhuman acts done against any civilian population."

Most people do not understand that. They think a war crime happens only when the bomb is actually set off.

The Rand Corporation understands the law as I understand it. In a report of January 1982 they stated that the policy of Assured Destruction, as it is called, which underlies the deployment of these missiles "is unlawful under the international law of armed conflict" and that, under the Nuremberg and other precedents, not only states but individuals can be judged criminally liable for such acts. The Rand Report specifically warns that "Following military orders or ignorance of the law are insufficient defenses, for the individual and his or her superior officers are obliged to know the law and to recognize manifestly unlawful orders." General George S. Brown made the same points when he was Chairman of the Joint Chiefs of Staff in 1976. Military men in general understand these laws because they are obliged to. As the Rand Report said, the current U.S. policy is "more the creature of civilians than military minds." Reagan and his advisors are ignorant civilians who do not realize that they are criminal terrorists under international law, even though the Rand Report tells them so and tells them that they are obliged to know these laws.

Is this perhaps why the United States has recently announced that it will not allow the International Court of Justice ot hear complaints against it and pass judgement on them?

I don't know. The main reasons for that, I imagine, is that Reagan and his advisors know they would be condemned by the Court if it heard the evidence concerning their crimes against international law in Central America, especially the mining of the harbors of Nicaragua, and their terrorism in Lebanon. I was there, in Lebanon, and I saw what they have done. Whole cities, which had no connection with the struggle at all, have been obliterated.

In the last two years, I have heard incredible bitterness expressed against Reagan's policies all over Europe. Do you think most Europeans agree with your harsh verdicts about President Reagan's policies?

Absolutely. President Reagan has done more harm to the United States, in the eyes of the world, than the Soviets could have accomplished in decades. The U.S. government has lost all moral credibility. I fear that Reagan has damaged the U.S. irreparably, which is a shame because he has thereby weakened the cause of democracy.

By the time this appears in print, Mr. Reagan's visit to Ireland will have occurred and there will almost certainly be massive demonstrations against him. Would you explain to our readers why so many Irishmen and Irishwomen feel moved to make such protests?

Well, first of all, I would like to explain that the planned protest demonstrations are against Reagan only. Ireland still has great affection and admiration for the American people. Apart from their undoubted contributions to democracy in the past, the American people will *always* react in favor of justice and against injustice, in my opinion, once the facts are placed before them. The Charter of the United Nations and the Universal Declaration of Human Rights were largely inspired by such Americans as Eleanor Roosevelt and Averill Harriman. The Irish as a people have a special debt of gratitude toward the United States for giving shelter to Irish emigrants in the past and for supporting our struggle for national liberation early in this century. Nobody in this country regards the American people with anything but warmth and affection. You could see that in the enthusiastic welcome we gave President Kennedy when he came here. But present government, the Reagan government, are regarded as international terrorists. The shelling of Lebanese villages was well reported here in the press and shown on TV. The invasion of Grenada was a cause for horror and distress, also, and we share with most Europeans a keen feeling of moral revulsion at the nuclear missiles being deployed all around us. And because of the number of Irish priests and nuns who have served as missionaries in Central America, we perhaps know more than other Europeans about the atrocities committed there by governments financed and armed by Reagan's administration. From my own experience as UN observer in Namibia, I am satisfied beyond doubt that were it not for U.S. support of South African tyranny, Namibia would now be free and independent.

Reagan's supporters will claim the demonstrations are just a Communist plot . . .

Nobody will believe them; there will be too many priests and nuns in these protests. Informed Americans know as well as we do that the government of El Salvador was responsible for murdering an Archbishop while he was saying Mass, for murdering and raping four nuns, and for a daily continuation of such atrocities. Why if the rape and murder of four nuns had happened in Russia, there could nearly have been a nuclear war as a result. Instead of that, there is barely a word of condemnation from Washington; El Salvador is still receiving weapons from the U.S. and the only protests come from ordinary American citizens and clergy, outside the government. As I said, this international terrorism has not only harmed the reputation of the United States, but damaged the whole cause of democracy in the world. I love the American people, and I don't think any other people has such a sense of justice when they understand an issue, but I think it is dastardly and terrible for Mr. Reagan to claim his international terrorism is being done in the name of the American people.

Some will say that Mr. Reagan cannot control the Central American governments that do these things.

It hs been documented, not only by European journalists but by the American press also, that the Reagan government not only finances these crimes against humanity but frequently uses the C.I.A. to implement some of them. Let me make clear again that these policies are stupid, because they are alienating Europe and destroying the credibility of the West. As a jurist, I think the U.S. did more in a few years after World War II to establish international rules of law than any country in history, and this gave America a real moral leadership in the world. Reagan has destroyed all that in the last six to eight months, and his administration has done more to destroy the rule of law than any other government. Reagan has repeatedly violated the UN charter and international law by constant reliance on force and the threat of force. Now he is sabotaging the International Court of Justice by preventing it from hearing complaints by the victims of his terrorism, and he has even withdrawn the United States from UNESCO.

To go on to another subject, you recently wrote an article warning Ireland against the Trilateral Commission and listing the members of the present Irish government who are also members of the Trilateral Commission. Why do you regard the Trilateralists as pernicious?

That's not just my opinion; there are at least five books written by Americans warning against the dangers posed by the Trilateral Commission.

It is documented that the Trilateralists are funded by certain large U.S. banks and are serving the financial interests of those banks.

You have also implied that the Trilateralists are trying to maneuver Ireland into Nato.

I believe they are. Ireland is still a nuclear-free zone and I suspect that they want to get us into NATO so they can deploy some of their nuclear missiles here.

Let's go back to your personal history a bit. Why did you join the Irish Republican Army in 1919?

I joined the Irish Republican Army as part of our struggle for national independence. There was a liberation war here, between 1918 and 1921, just like your American Revolution. We had to resist the British army of occupation in our cities, just as you did, in order to achieve national independence.

Why did you stay in the I.R.A. after the Irish Free State was formed in 1922?

Many of us could not accept the terms of the London Treaty of 1921, particularly in regard to the partition of Ireland. We also objected to the fact that the Free State was made part of the British Commonwealth and members of the *Dail hEirann* had to sign an oath of allegiance to British monarch. In our opinion, that oath made it legally impossible for the Free State to continue the struggle for Irish independence and unity.

And why did you quit the I.R.A. in 1937?

The whole situation had changed by then. DeValera had accomplished so much in his first five years as *Taoiseach* (Chief Executive) that armed struggle was neither necessary nor desirable; it was counter-productive. The abolition of the oath of allegiance, which he had accomplished by then, made it possible for complete independence to be achieved by legal means, as in fact happened in 1947. I also belive the re-unification of Ireland can be accomplished without further armed struggle.

How many times were you sentenced and imprisoned, by the way?

I was never sentenced. I was imprisoned without trial by the British in 1918 and 1919 and by the Free State in 1922 and 1930.

Some Irish-American readers will be interested in this: Is it true that when DeValera entered Dail hEirann *in 1927, he signed the oath of allegiance to the British monarch but refused to put his hand on the Bible, and thereby in his own mind nullified the oath?*

I believe that is true, yes.

You are still fiercely opposed to the partition of Ireland?
Absolutely.

Where does the question of armed struggle come into it? You say that it is no longer necessary or desirable in Ireland but you have said that some wars of liberation are justified. Where do you draw the line?

I'm not a Quaker and I'm not an absolute pacifist. I believe that in certain circumstances you have the right to use violence to defend yourself. This applies to peoples as well as individuals. If a government pursues a policy that threatens to reduce a whole people to servitude or to exterminate them, they have the right to resist violence with violence. But even there, you see, I would say that they may only resort to violence when no other means remains open to them, when there is literally no legal recourse. For instance, I think this presently applies to the Black population of South Africa, who are victimized by violence continually and have no means of defense against this except armed struggle. But even in wars of liberation, where there is no other recourse, I think moral rules still apply. I am totally opposed to some of the activities of some liberation movements, in which civilians are indiscriminately slaughtered. For instance, I totally condemn the Provisional I.R.A. of the present for tactics like the bombing of Harrod's, a leading department store in London, when it was full of families with children during the Christmas shopping season.

What is the cause of this continued violence 63 years after the Treaty of 1921?
The partition of Ireland.

What do you reply to those who say that if the British pulled out, the violence between the Provisional I.R.A. and the Protestant paramilitary groups like the Ulster Volunteer Force would simply escalate?
That is the British propaganda line and I simply do not believe it. I am quite confident that getting the British troops out of Ireland is the first step toward a peaceful solution. The original cause of the violence is the partition of Ireland and the continuing cause is the presence of British troops on Irish soil. Much of the violence by paramilitary Protestant groups is actually guided and inspired by British intelligence agents.

Do you have personal knowledge of that?
As a lawyer, I have defended British intelligence agents sent over here to the Republic of Ireland to incide the I.R.A. to carry out bank robberies. I have also defended British agents who have been given lists of people to assassinate and have it blamed on the I.R.A.

ITV, the Ulster television station, recently charged that some of the violence in the 1960s, attributed to the I.R.A. at the time, was actually the work of persons trying to make it appear the I.R.A. was active at a time when it was actually dormant, virtually non-existent. Your comment?
Well, I just said that British intelligence have done that sort of thing down here. Why wouldn't they do it up there?

In that connection, what do you make of the C.I.A. connection with the I.R.A.? During the NORAID trial in New York last year it was demonstrated that the C.I.A. was running guns for the I.R.A. Why would they do that—provide munitions for Marxist revolutionaries?
I cannot begin to guess. Once you get into the machinations of secret services, anything is possible.

There is a rumor around Dublin that some of the Trilateralists, such as Kissinger and Vice President Bush, who have been over here meeting with Irish government officials, are feeling out how the Irish would react to a deal whereby the U.S. will exert pressure on Britain to allow Irish re-unification if the Irish will in return join NATO and accept nuclear missiles on their soil. Do you think there is anything in that rumor?

I'm sure it has been considered at some stage, but no Irish government I can imagine would accept it.

Mr. Haughey, the leader of the opposition in Dail hEirann, recently said that when the British pull out, they should also pay reparations to Ireland. That couldn't be his way of saying that, if he gets back into power, he might consider the nukes if the British paid a big enough bribe?

No, not at all. I think the British *should* pay reparations, for the 63 years of civil war that partition has inflicted on us.

Do you think the British will pay?
I think they will have to pay some compensation, yes.

I'm only Irish by ancestry, but even I get annoyed by British attitudes at times. For instance, when I look at the weather forecast on BBC-TV, I'm always astounded that Ireland has no weather, although Northern Ireland for some reason does. It is as if they are trying to pretend that we don't even exist.

That sort of thing *is* annoying, but you get used to it after 80 years. You must remember that we are Britain's oldest colony; they have been here for 800 years. Every imperialist power creates a caricature of the conquered nations, to justify themselves: "We're only there to civilize the barbarians," you know. The ordinary Englishman and Englishwoman are very decent really, but they have 800 years of anti-Irish attitudes to unlearn. They have always been told that we are charming, quite irrational and never, never to be taken seriously for a moment. They also think we have unfortunately long memories. On the other hand, this ordinary Englishman and English-woman is getting a bit cynical about that myth by now. The war has gone on too long, and it is costing too much. There is a real groundswell of opinion there now that it is time to pull the troops out and have done with it. The attitude is much like the American attitude toward Vietnam around 1970, when everybody was ready to pull out except a few diehards at the top.

For the benefit of Irish-American readers, I'd like to ask you about the assassination of Michael Collins in 1922. He was your commander in the old I.R.A.; you were his bodyguard at one point. You must have read all the charges and counter-charges and alternative theories. Who do you think shot Michael Collins?

I think that is still an open question. Some of the recent evidence, however, especially disclosures in the last three or four years, does tend to support the theory that he was killed by British secret agents. The civil war was still going on then, between the Free State and the I.R.A. Collins was trying to end that, trying to negotiate a truce. He was on his way to meet

I.R.A. leaders about such a truce when he was shot, you know. The British may have thought that if the civil war went on long enough, it would destroy the Free State.

Why do you think the British signed the Treaty of 1921 at all? After crushing one Irish rebellion after another for 800 years, why did they suddenly feel, when they still had a world-wide Empire, that they couldn't crush the 1918-21 rebellion?

The I.R.A. had made it impossible for them to remain here. By 1921, we had succeeded miliatrily in making their position untenable without a mass military occupation and repressive measures on a scale that would have been very unpopular in the United States and with a large segment of British public opinion. As it was, in the United States, support for the Irish liberation movement was very extensive and could not be ignored.

Your own solution to the cultural conflicts in the North is the so-called Swiss proposal or cantonization. Would you explain that?

It is not *my* solution exactly; it was first proposed as early as 1922, when the first Irish Constitution was being drafted, and it was the suggestion of Professor Edward O'Rahilly. Unfortunately, it was not adequately discussed and debated at the time. I think we accepted the British centralized system of government, wrongly, because we had been dominated by the British for 800 years and were still thinking in British categories. The Swiss system is much better for small countries like Switzerland or Ireland, I think, and it is especially appropriate where you have two strongly opposed religious/cultural traditions. Adopting the Swiss system, we would have 32 independent counties, like the independent Swiss cantons, and each would have its own parliament and make its own laws on all matters except international relations. A small central government would have representatives from the independent cantons and they would be concerned only with external affairs. Such devolution and decentralization is the only viable path for a nation with two religious traditions; it has worked very well for Switzerland. That is why I revived this proposal and presented it to the New Ireland Forum last year.

You have written a great deal lately about unemployment, which you say is a problem that will not go away . . .

The computer revolution is changing all our traditional economic assumptions. There will be more unemployment from now on, not less. No government has a solution to this; mostly they are afraid to even think about it. What I keep proposing is that they should create jobs by investing in projects that do not present an immediate economic return. Reforestation is my favorite example. That's why I'm involved with the "Trees for Ireland" campaign. Creating whole new forests would provide work for many of the unemployed, and even if it takes 50 years for the economic return, it will be worth it when we do have all those new trees full-grown. I also think the government could create many, many jobs by giving Dublin a subway system.

How do you evaluate the effectiveness of the protests such as the women at Greenham Common missile base who have attracted so much world-wide attention?
I believe you just answered your own question. Those women have done a marvelous job of work in forcing world attention on the threat of nuclear missiles.

What I really meant to ask is, I meet a lot of cynical and depressed people these days. They don't like the missiles anymore than you do, but they feel hopeless. If you talk about Greenham Common at all, they'll just say, "Yes, those women gave it the old school try—but the missiles are still there, aren't they?" At the age of 80, you haven't gotten discouraged yet. What gives you the faith and energy to struggle on?
I have one big hope. I think public opinion has become much more powerful than at any earlier period in history. We have *all* been rather stupid in the past when we tried to predict the pace of oncoming events. Everything is happening much faster these days. Public education and literacy have increased incredibly in my lifetime and especially in the past 30 years and the peoples of the world are better informed than they ever have been. As I said, people are mostly very decent and just, once they know the facts of a case, and they are learning the facts faster and faster. Television is bringing everything right into the living room, and people know what is going on. I think people will soon force governments to give up this insane arms race. They just have to join together, like the women at Greenham Common, and make their voices heard.

On my way here, I was thinking about Graham Greene, perhaps because he is both a Catholic and a radical, like you. He recently said he'd rather live in a world dominated by the U.S.S.R. than in one dominated by the U.S. What do you think about such a choice?
I hope we are never forced to such a deplorable choice. But even if it came down to that, my opinion would depend on which government was in power in those countries. A world dominated by Kruschev wouldn't have been too bad, and a world dominated by Eisenhower wouldn't be too bad, either. But God forbid we should have a world dominated by Stalin or Reagan.

RELIGION
For the Hell of It

The following essay is of such brilliance and perfection that no introductory comment is necessary or even thinkable, save to say with all the prophets,
Go ye and do likewise.

Have you ever considered the possibility that God might be a crazy woman? Or that John Dillinger died for you? Do you think there might be a secret technique by which the Enlightened can literally get Something for Nothing? Could the Martians have the true religion while we Earthians are lost in superstitious darkness? Can a cup of coffee be a sacrament, and if not, why not? Does the mathematics of six-dimensional space-time and philosophy of Multi-Ego Panthesitic Solipsism explain the universe?

If none of these metaphysical questions have crossed your mind before, this is because Ireland has, as everybody knows, the One True Religion; but over the sea in America, where they started out with at least a dozen True Religions before the Revolution and then wrote absolute religious freedom into their Constitution, they now have literally hundreds of True Religions, and have explored every possible or thinkable theological doctrine, including all of the alternatives mentioned above. With typical American exhuberance,

191

they will no doubt be exploring the impossible and unthinkable in the near future, since their politics already contain those elements.

Of course, even in America, absolute religious freedom is only relatively absolute. There have been a few "hard cases." In the 19th Century, the Church of Jesus Christ of the Latter-Day Saints, or Mormons, severely tested the absoluteness of the Constitution by practising polygamy. The government decided that was Too Much Religious Freedom, and the army was called out to arrest the whole Mormon community, then centered in Salt Lake City. This was undoubtedly unconstitutional and no doubt would have been reversed eventually by the Supreme Court, but Brigham Young, then the leader of the Mormons had a convenient new revelation when he saw all those guns and bayonets: God or the angel Moroni (Mormons have access to both) told Young that polygamy was only necessary while the Latter Day Saints were building their community and was no longer necessary now that the comunity was built. A head-on collision between Church and State was thus averted.

A similar "hard case" arose early in this century, concerning the Native American Church, which is restricted to Red Indians, or, as they prefer to be called, Native Americans. The NAC uses the psychedelic cactus, peyotl, in its rites; the government decided they were dope fiends and prosecuted. The Supreme Court upheld the right of the Native Americans to continue their traditional religion. (This has been modified by State courts, due to an influx into the NAC of persons whose Native American-ness was dubious. In most States now, members of NAC congregations must prove they are at least 25% Native American to avoid prosecution.)

Another "hard case" or several "hard cases" have been provoked by the Jehovah's Witnesses, who refuse to serve in the armed forces, or to salute the flag, or to accept blood transfusions, or to allow blood transfusions to be given to their children. The Supreme Court upheld the JW's right to abstain from war, but originally ruled that they must salute the flag; this later decision was reversed by a later Supreme Court. The blood transfusion matter is still being fought through the State courts, which have mostly upheld the right of hospitals, when a child's life is clearly in danger, to give blood transfusions even if the parents' religion is affronted and the Constitution is a bit bent.

So: American religious freedom is only relatively absolute, but close enough that almost any cult or sect has an equal chance to proselytize in what Supreme Court Justice Oliver Wendell Holmes once called the American "free market of ideas."

One modifying influence remained to check metaphysical anarchy: the Courts had a tendency to regard as bogus any sect headed by a person who had not acquired an ordination from an older, established theological academy somewhere in his career. The first erosions of this conservative principle began when cheap Oriental labour was imported, followed by not-so-cheap Oriental restauranteurs and, eventually, Oriental religious leaders ranging from the cheap to the pricey. The great Oriental religions of Buddhism, Hinduism and Taoism are neither centralized nor hierarchical: one becomes a religious "leader" by having disciples who regard one as a "leader." The American courts have gradually moved towards accepting this, at least when dealing with Orientals. The only legal actions against even the most controversial gurus have been the imprisonment of Rev. Sun Myung Moon for tax offenses and the recent arrest of Bhagwan Rajneesh for violation of immigration laws. Since both of these Holy Men are regarded as extremely obnoxious and nefarious by most Americans, this avoidance of theological confrontation either indicates that relatively absolute religious freedom still reigns, or else that—as disciples of these rev. gentlemen claim—the American courts are getting sneaky about how they handle heretics.

Yippie! Free Ordinations For Everybody!

Meanwhile, another step toward making the relatively absolute into the absolutely absolute began with the Rev. Kirby Hensley, a waggish and roguish chap who got his own ordination from a legal but disreputable mail-order seminary. To give you an idea of Rev. Hensley's character, he tells all interviewers that he is illiterate and that he got his theological qualifications by having his daughter read the questions on the examination to him and then dictating his answers to be transcribed by her. Insisting on his own ignorance, not just of theology but of nearly everything else as well, Rev. Hensley claims that every man, woman and child has the right to be an ordained clergyperson. To this end, he has founded as a disinterested charity so to speak, the Universal Life Church, which will ordain anybody, for no cost, and without an examination. To make ends meet in this cruel world, Rev. Hensley has added a rider: you can also get a Doctor of Divinity degree from the Universal Life Church, but that costs over $20. The diploma is quite handsome and certainly worth $20; properly framed and hanging on the living room wall, it is certain to impress the neighbors, unless they have heard of the Universal Life Church already.

When it was revealed by journalists that some jokers had acquired ordinations from the ULC for their dogs, their cats, and even such colorful pets as parrots or chimpanzees, Rev. Hensley was not a bit abashed. He commented in effect that all God's creatures are holy, and went on to ordain Madalyn Murray O'Hair, the most vehement and controversial atheist in the U.S.

How valuable is an ordination from the ULC? Well, marriages performed by ULC clergymen are recognized in all states, and many ULC "graduates" have gone on to create their own churches or sects; in most respects, under American law, a ULC minister is as legitimate as any other minister, or priest, or rabbi, or guru. The one chancey area is that of tax-exemption. *De jure*, the courts have not yet ruled on the matter; *de facto*, the tax bureau tries to collect only when the circumstances are such that the ordination seems to them nothing else but a dodge to avoid taxes. This happened a few years ago when all the farmers in one part of New York State were ordained *en masse*; the tax officials regarded this as a blatant swindle—and a bad example to boot—and attacked the bank accounts of the individuals involved. ULC clergy persons clearly engaged in promulgating some religion—any religion— are generally allowed the same tax exemption as less eccentric churchpeople.

Rev. Hensley tells every enquirer that he *wants* the government to try to tax him. He plans to file a counter-suit for discrimination, and demand that the government either start taxing other churches also, or else leave him and his ordainees alone, including those New York farmers. He has been saying this for at least 15 years now, but the tax bureau leaves him strictly at peace.

But I think he will be remembered as the man who opened the floodgate and made relatively absolute religious freedom absolutely absolute. He showed the more imaginative and unruly elements how to get into the religion game for the sheer hell of it.

Ronald Reagan Meets Mahatma Gandhi

The Reformed Druids of North America (RDNA) began in 1957 at a small college, and was, *at first* only a joke. The instigators were free-thinking students, mostly Irish-American, who resented the rule requiring church attendance once a week. As a protest and as a send-up, they announced that they were Druids and that groves were their churches. The RDNA originally repaired to these wooded sanctuaries only to drink Irish Mist and exchange Gaelic lessons; soon, however, an official ritual was written, and then rewritten several times as various members advanced in the study of Gaelic language and history. Branches of the new Druidism, called "groves," soon appeared at other universities; leaders, called Archdruids, became proficient in Gaelic and acquired ordinations from good old Rev. Hensley, making them legal clergymen. Some Archdruids have gone on to become serious Gaelic scholars, such as P.E. Isaac Bonewits, author of a widely read occult/anthropology text, *Real Magic*, and the first man to acquire a degree in shamanism from the University of California

But because the RDNA had started as a prank, it still retains a certain fey quality. Irish Mist is still used abundantly in all ceremonies; the Archdruids have not only allowed, but encouraged, heresy—on the principle that the more people think about religious issues, the better; and only one dogma is promulgated by all, or nearly all, groves, namely "Nature Is Good."

The first heresy to branch off from the RDNA was the Chasidic Druids of North America or CDNA, founded by the above-mentioned P.E. Isaac Bonewits. Chasidic Druidism combines Jewish (Chasidic) mystical practises with Druid nature-worship, cheerfully borrows whatever it likes from any other religion in the world (something American Unitarians also do, by the way) and uses the toast "Next year in Stonehenge" in place of the traditional Jewish toast, "Next year in Jerusalem."

The RNADNA—Reformed Non-Aristotelian Druids of North America, but the initials were also calculated to indicate RNA and DNA, the two organic molecules that make life possible—combines Druidism with the non-Aristotelian logic of the Polish-American mathematician and philosopher, Count Alfred Korzybski. Members obey certain linguistic taboos—which Korzbyski called "matters of semantic hygiene"—and will not use the word "is" for instance because that implies certitude and Korzybski believed post-Einstein people should speak relativistically. Thus, the Druid dogma, "Nature is good" has been rephrased as "Nature seems good." RNADNA people also will never say something like "Beethoven is better than Mozart" but only "Beethoven seems better than Mozart, to me, at this stage of my musical education." They also avoid "all," because that implies omniscience; this preserves them from racism, sexism and dogmatism, since the worst they can say about any group of humans or animals would be "Some members of that group seem offensive, to me, at this stage of my education." Aside from these rules, RNADNA groves go out in the woods like RDNA groves, drink Irish Mist, and commune with what other Druids call "Nature" and the RNADNA calls "the non-verbal level."

A third heresy, Druid Witchcraft, has amalgamated with the wiccan or witchcraft revival, started in the 1930s by an eccentric Englishman living on the Isle of Man and named Gerald Gardner. A good deal of humbug and something of a genuine visionary, Gardner claimed wicca was the oldest religion in Europe, had driven underground by Christian persecution, and had been taught to him by surviving members of a circle that has survived since the Old Stone Age—every bit of which is doubted by every serious scholar who has studied the evidence. Gardner also claimed to be an anthropologist, but was at most a clever and imaginative amateur in that field. In essence, Gardner's home-made witchcraft worships a female rather than a male divinity, prefers (like the Druids) to hold rituals in woodsy places rather than churches, and has, since Gardner's death, come increasingly under the influence of Feminism. It has covens rather than groves, and each coven pretty much establishes its own dogma—some lean toward reincarnation, Atlantis, and that sort of thing, while some don't—but all tend toward a millenialist belief that male gods and male domination are responsible for war, pollution, intolerance and most of our social problems; peace and Utopia will dawn when the world returns to goddess-worship and achieves sexual equality.

Oddly, the belief that the world is on the edge of a revival of goddess-worship has been expressed by some eminent scholars, including historian Arnold Toynbee, psychologist Carl Jung, poet Robert Graves and anthropologist Joseph Campbell. Witches know this and are fond of quoting these authorities when being interviewed on TV.

If Wicca has merged somewhat with Druidism on one flank, it has also been infiltrated by science-fiction on the other flank, due to partial amalgamation with the Church of All Worlds, or CAW. Founded in 1974, CAW has the unique distinction of being the first religion in history explicitly based on a science-fiction novel—Robert A. Heinlein's *Stranger In A Strange Land*. A best-seller in the 1960s and still in print today, "Stranger" tells the story of Michael Valentine Smith, lone infant survivor of the crash of a NASA rocket to Mars.

Raised by Martians, Smith is eventually found by another NASA space crew, returns to Earth and finds Earth-people miserable, unhappy, war-like and vicious; he sets out to reform us by preaching the religion of the Martians—which turns out to be a rationalistic and pantheistic version of Zen Buddhism. One fan of this novel, Timothy Zell—then a psychiatric social worker in St. Louis—was so fascinated that he got an ordination from Rev. Hensley and founded CAW which now has chapters, called nests, in every major US city. Members say that a religion based on a science-fiction novel is no more absurd than one based on the legends of the ancient Hebrews or one based on the revelations of an angel named Moroni.

The basic teaching of CAW, taken directly from Heinlein's novel, is "Thou Art God." After interfacing with wicca and Feminism, CAW now says "Thou Art God" only to male members and "Thou Art Goddess" to female members. Ceremonies, called water-sharings, are quite lovely, and also come from Heinlein's scientific fantasy. For the rest, the theology is rationalistic, individualistic and politically, somewhere between extreme libertarian and non-violent anarchist. You will get the flavour if I say CAW political pronouncements often sound like an explosive and unstable mixture of Ronald Reagan and Mahatma Gandhi.

Founder Tim Zell, still active in both CAW and wicca, has gone on to create, by some manner of surgery or genetic hocus-pocus, a one-horned goat, which he calls a unicorn, and which is now an exhibit at a circus. Zell himself departed for the South Pacific last March in search of a mermaid. I have met the man, and I am quite sure he will bring back *something* to amaze and amuse us.

The American Coffee Ceremony

In 1967, after being fired from Harvard University for having weird ideas (but before being imprisoned), Dr. Timothy Leary, America's most controversial psychologist, published a pamphlet called "Start Your Own Religion," urging that every home should be a shrine, every man a priest, every woman a priestess. America, at that time, was ready for such an idea. Rev. Hensley provided the ordinations, and Metatheology and Home Brew Metaphysics flourished.

The Neo-American Church, founded by psychologist Arthur Kleps—a friend and former associate of Leary—was modelled after the Native American Church, except that it was open to all races, not just Red Indians and replaced peyotl with LSD in its sacraments. The Neo-American Church did not last long; the courts ruled, in effect, that drug-taking in a religious circle was legal for Indians because it was traditional, but not for white people, because the religion was "just an excuse" to take the drug. Founder Kleps (who calls himself the Primate and other priests the Boo-Hoos) complained that this was overt racism, but that argument did not convince judges. The Neo-American Church is now either non-existent or deep underground; but the "Neo-American Catechism," written by Kleps himself, is still in print and is a very funny book, combining elements of Buddhism, solipsism and hilarious Voltairean polemic against the "Christians, Jews and atheists" who refuse to admit LSD is a sacrament.

The sect of Rastafari, founded in the West Indies, has branches in many American cities, but is limited to Blacks. It uses cannabis as a sacrament, worships the late Emperor Haile Selassie as God and claims the Pope is "Godfather of the Mafia, Imperial Wizard of the Ku Klux Klan and general all-around Anti-Christ." Members are frequently convicted of cannabis possession or smuggling, but the Rastafari church itself is not illegal, despite its eccentricity.

The Javacrucians, a group which looks suspiciously like a parody of the Rosicrucians, has selected the less-controversial caffeine as its sacrament. It also has the simplest theology in history, teaching that one thing only is necessary for salvation, the American Coffee Ceremony—a variation on the Japanese Tea Ceremony. This is performed at dawn, and you must face east, towards the rising sun, as you raise the cup to your lips. When you take the first sip, you must cry out with intense fervour, "GOD, I needed that!" If this is performed religiously every morning, Javacrucians say, you will face all life's challenges with a clear mind and a tranquil spirit.

SFMB—the Society of Fred Mertz, Boddhisattva—was founded by the Finnish-American poet, Antero Alli, and holds that all wisdom is contained in the seemingly inane remarks of Fred Mertz, a minor character of the "I Love Lucy" TV show. By watching "Lucy" reruns continually and meditating on the *apparently* banal things Fred says—e.g., "I don't know what's going on around here" or "I don't understand women at all"—this sect claims you will find the same Enlightenment as in contemplating Zen Buddhist koans such as "What is the sound of one hand clapping?" And just as in Zen, where students are often required to meditate on monosyllables such as "Mu" (no), the SFMB sect would have you meditate on even such Mertziana as "Huh?" or "Awww!" until you sense what Joyce would call the epiphany in even the most trivial.

The Church of Satan, with headquarters in San Francisco (of course) and branches in many US cities and a few chapters in Europe, was founded by a circus roustabout named Anton Szandor Lavey. It has a *Satanic Bible*, written by Lavey (and dedicated to W.C. Fields and P.T. Barnum), claims to invoke Lucifer, Beelzebub, Ashtoreth and a million or so other demons, and delights in scaring the blue hell out of pious Christians. Despite its diabolism, this Church has had no legal hassles—except briefly, when neighbors complained that Lavey's pet lion was roaring at night and keeping them awake—and members limit themselves to blasphemy, cursing their enemies, and ritual expressions of forbidden negative feelings (much like many another California encounter-group, in fact). None of them have ever been arrested for serious crimes. I even suspect they themselves started the rumor that they are financed by the Procter & Gamble soap empire; they are quite unscrupulous Send Up artists.

The Campus Crusade for Cthulhu generally appears on the scene at any university where the Campus Crusade for Christ is well entrenched, and is mostly devoted to annoying the former. The Cthulhu-ists worship a monster who originally appeared in the pulp horror fiction of H.P. Lovecraft. For a long time, I thought this particular sect would never advance beyond parody and satire, but lately the Church of Satan has incorporated Cthulhu into its pantheon along with all the other demons.

The Campus Crusade for Christ has bumper stickers which members flaunt on their automobiles declaring "I Found It." The Cthulhu-ists have their own bumper stickers saying "It Found Me"—and the Church of All Worlds now has one saying "Thou Art It."

You Too, Can Be A Pope

More serious, or at least more desperate, is the Discordian Society and/or Paratheo-Anametamystikhood of Eris Esoteric, an anarchistic sect divided deliberately into two opposed groups, each claiming to be (I quote) "the first *True* Religion." Like the witches, the Discordians worship a female divinity, but say She is crazy. Her name, in fact, is Eris, and the ancient Greeks knew her as the Goddess of Chaos; Discordians claim she is also the Goddess of Confusion, Discord and Bureaucracy. The Discordian orthodoxy, headed by "Ho Chih Zen" (real name, Kerry Thornley), claims this was revealed by a miraculous talking chimpanzee, who appeared in a bowling alley in Yorba Linda, California in 1957. The POEE sect flatly rejects this, says it is superstitious nonsense intended to attract the gullible, and proves the existence of Eris by Five Proofs, which are all logical monstrosities and reduce actually to One Proof—namely, "If Eris doesn't exist, who put all the Chaos in this universe, you damned atheist?"

The High priest of the Head temple (his orthography) of POEE is "Malaclypse the Younger, Omnibenevolent Polyfather of Virginity in Gold" (real name: Gregory Hill), who was, of course, ordained as a minister by the ever-helpful Rev. Hensley. It has its own Bible, by Malaclypse, called *Principia Discordia, or How I Found Goddess and What I Did to Her After I Found Her*, and has cabals—not churches or groves or covens or even nests—all over the US, in England, in Australia, in Canada and even one in Hong Kong. Leaders of the cabals, called Episkopi, all have odd names and titles, e.g., Camden Benares (author of *Zen Without Zen Masters*) heads the Los Angeles cabal of Eris Erotic, Onrak the Backwards heads the Colorado Encrustation, and the Berkeley cabal is run by Lady L, Fucking Anarchist Bitch—a title, she explain, given to her by Eldridge Cleaver during a political debate.

Discordians have set out to out-Hensley Hensley by making every man, woman and child on the planet a Pope. They are doing this by mass-distribution of Pope cards and have not, of course, neglected to send one of these to the Anti-Pope in France and the chap in the Vatican who still thinks he's the only Pope. All employees of the Pentagon are, willy-nilly, Discordian saints whether they want to be or not, since Malacypse has canonized them and incorporated them into a holy order called "Knights Of The Five-Sided Castle," under the patronage of St. Quixote. The Pentagon itself is a religious shrine, said to embody the perfect balance of Chaos and Bureaucracy. Everybody who opposes Discordianism as blasphemous or absurd is an honorary saint too, of the House of the Rising Hodge, while Discordians are saints of the House of the Rising Podge.

Discordianism shuns *dogma* but has one *catma*, the Syadastan Affirmation, which reads, "All affirmations are true in some sense, false in some sense, meaningless in some sense, true and false in some sense, true and meaningless in some sense, false and meaningless in some sense, and true and false and meaningless in some sense." Discordians call this the Free Mantra—unlike the Transcendental movement, they charge no fees—and insist that if you repeat it 666 times you will achieve Spiritual Enlightenment, in some sense.

Many recent American writers have been influenced by Discordianism, as can be seen in Spinrad's *Agent of Chaos*, Tom Robbins' *Another Roadside Attraction* and the notorious *Illuminatus* trilogy; the Discordian obsession with the number 23 also appears in quite a few Hollywood films these days. Discordian theology is discussed soberly in *Drawing Down The Moon*, a serious sociological study of neo-paganism in America, written by Margot Adler, grand-daughter of the psychologist Alfred Adler.

WITCH—the Women's International Terrorist Conspiracy from Hell— borrows a great deal from Wicca and Discordianism. It is probably not a church, even by American standards, and chiefly engages in street theatre, satirizing monotheism, male dominance and the Establishment generally.

The Order of the Golden Calf had a brief career but now seems defunct. The members, who all lived in Berkeley, California, had a magnificent gold (or imitation gold) statue of a calf and carried it around to places where other sects were proselytizing on the streets. There they would do an Adoration of the Calf, distribute leaflets describing their idol as "the first victim of monotheistic bigotry," and urge everybody else to "lighten up your act a little."

NROOGD—meaning New Reformed Orthodox Order of the Golden Dawn, but pronounced nroogd, if you can manage that—is the biggest pagan church in California, although it started as a joke and has been repudiated by one of its three founders, Dr. Aiden Kelly, who has a really real Doctor of Divinity degree from the Union Theological College. Nroogd combines rituals from Druidic Witchcraft and CAW, theology from Discordianism and Heavy Symbolism from the poetry of Yeats (an early hero of Dr. Kelly's). It rolls cheerfully on without its former Bard, meets in state parks to adore the Goddess, recite mantras, dance, sing and get smashed on Irish Mist, Jameson's and various weird chemicals brought by the more unruly members.

Dr. Kelly has returned to Roman Catholicism and recently said, "Nroogd is a metaphor. Catholicism is another metaphor. I am basically a poet." If that isn't clear, try repeating it 666 times like the Discordian mantra.

The John Dillinger Died For You Society, run by a psuedonymous "Dr. Horace Naismith" (allegedly a Playboy editor by day and a maniac only by night), accepts as its savior John Dillinger, the gunman who robbed 23 banks and 3 police stations before he was shot dead by FBI agents in 1934. JDDFYS members place memorial wreaths and floral bouquets at the Biograph

Theatre, where Dillinger was gunned down, every year on the anniversary of his death, June 22. Their major spiritual teaching comes from Mr. Dillinger, whom they call St. John the Martyr, and consists of the words, "Lie down on the floor and keep calm," (St. John said this often to nervous and agitated bank officials, before looting their tills.) Every member ordained by Dr. Naismith gets a membership card making him or her an Assistant Treasurer, entitled to collect tithes from any new disciple naive enough to remain a disciple and not become an Assistant Treasurer, too, by writing to Naismith for a card.

Power! Sex! Success! Money!

I have saved the best—or worst—for last. The Church of the Sub-Genius in Dallas has borrowed a bit from all of the above, and from every other religion on the planet, uses high-powered advertising techniques in the style of the most aggressive Christian Evangelists, and promises in capitals to teach you the secret of POWER! and SEX! and SUCCESS! and MONEY! It will also put you in touch with SUPERHUMAN FORCES, save you from THE CONSPIRACY, and even show you how to achieve SLACK and literally get something for nothing. That is admittedly a tall order, but the founder, J.R. "Bob" Dobbs, is no ordinary mortal. In fact, it is far from clear whether anybody has actually ever seen "Bob" at all, at all, and Sub-Genius advertising darkly hints that before an ordinary human can survive a meeting with "Bob" it is necessary to go to Dobbstown, located somewhere in South America, and have special surgery to "open the third nostril." Even then, it is warned, you might come back from such a Close Encounter with inflamed eyes, headache, total or partial amnesia and other stigmata of UFO contactees, and you will probably be harassed by agents of THE CONSPIRACY who will appear at your door pretending to be Jehovah's Witnesses and try to get inside to brainwash you.

J.R. "Bob" Dobbs was allegedly an ordinary aluminum window-siding salesman until in 1957 he met L. Ron Hubbard—founder of the more famous Church of Scientology—and learned the Secret of Power. "Bob" is now fabulously rich, maybe even richer than Hubbard, and offers to teach you the Secret too, in various books and pamphlets ranging in price from $1 to $25. It is admitted frankly that these Metaphysical Works look "incomprehensible" or "nonsensical" to the unenlightened, but it is firmly promised that if you buy enough of them, keep them in the loo, and consult them often, you will eventually get SLACK and understand the Secret and how to use it.

I think I have found the Secret of Power. It is in one of the cheaper Sub-Genius publications "More Quotes and Gloats From 'Bob'" and it reads, "You know how dumb the average guy is? Well, by definition, half of them are even dumber that that." Then again, it might be in other gems of

Dobbsiana such as "Don't just eat a hamburger—eat the HELL out of it," or "Fuck them if they can't take a joke," or maybe even the Dark Saying, "GOD spelled backwards is DOG, but BOB spelled backwards is still BOB."

If none of this brings you to SLACK, you can buy the thicker, pricier Sub-Genius publication, where you will encounter a whole cosmology, philosophy and eschatology, involving Jehovah 1, "Space-God," who escaped from a loony-bin in another galaxy; Eris, goddess of Chaos, borrowed from this Discordians; Spider Man; The Incredible Hulk; and Bob's cosmic struggle with THE CONSPIRACY, which includes all the leaders of rival churches and sects, along with the Rockefellers, Bilderbergers, Illuminati, Evil UFOs, Nazi Hell Creatures and Communist Clones. You are also repeatedly warned that the world may end tomorrow, but it will take longer than you expect and be much more painful than anyone imagines, but even that doesn't matter if you get SLACK.

Getting SLACK—like getting Enlightened in Oriental mysticism or getting IT from Erhard Seminar Training (est)—cannot be described in words or understood by rational intellect; it must be experienced. It involves understanding that the universe is made up of two eternally opposed but complementary forces, like the Chinese yin and yang or the Discordian hodge and podge. The two forces are actually Something and Nothing which is why if you look around you always see Something on a background of Nothing. When you are in balance between Something and Nothing, you have SLACK, and can then get Something for Nothing, and become as rich as "Bob," Rajneesh, L. Ron Hubbard or the Pope.

Or as "Bob" sums it up elsewhere, "Hell, it's even more relative than Einstein realized."

In the profane world, while "Bob" remains aloof and invisible, the Church of the Sub-Genius operates out of Post Office Box 140306 in Dallas, where the mail is picked up by two local advertising executives—who pass it on to "Bob," I guess.

Curiously, there is already a Stamp Out Bob (SOB) movement, distributing anti-Sub-Genius propaganda and warning that this "evil cult" is only a money-making scheme. You can order a packet of educational anti-Bob literature for $15 from SOB Post Office Box 140306 Dallas—which seems to be the address also of the people representing "Bob." That's odd, isn't it?

The Church of the Sub-Genius alleges that it has 10,000,000 members, but I frankly doubt it. However, they do have many members in influential places, as was indicated recently when the new "Jackintosh" computer from Atari came on the market. Trying to run an ordinary program on Jackintosh, users were abruptly given a short, sharp shock when the machine instead printed out 100 pictures of J.R. "Bob" Dobbs himself. The Atari people are still trying to find out which employee slipped that bug into the software.

The New Religion As Complicated Joke

As an investigative journalist in the US, I met many members of all these cults or sects. I have found them to be above-average in intelligence and education, mostly young (average age is under 30, although some over-40s do crop up) and very erudite in anthropology, history of religion and, especially, science-fiction. Typically, they attend science-fiction conventions even more devoutly than the services or celebrations of their churches. Many of them are in the computer industry, and others in entertainment, the arts, the Academia. They frequently belong to two or more of these sects simultaneously and may also be involved in some Oriental mystical system on the side. An overwhelming majority of them also belong to the Society for Creative Anachronism, which holds "fairs" in many parts of the US at which members dress and act like persons from past centuries or from the future and everybody creates his or her own separate reality-tunnel. They are usually in favour of both ecology and technology—"appropriate technology" is one of their buzz-words, followed by "synergy" and "holism." When asked how serious they are, they usually say something to the effect that humans need some religion and they are trying to create a relativistic religion for a scientific age.

Malaclypse the Younger states it this way, "We are not engaged in a complicated joke disguised as a new religion. We are engaged in a new religion disguised as a complicated joke."

When will all this impact on Ireland? Well, we already have the Krishna cult here, and the Rajneesh people, and Jehovah's Witnesses, and est, and even some local witches. However much it may distress the Rev. Dr. McNamara, I cannot believe that the Discordians, the Sub-Geniuses and even the Reformed Druids can be far behind. Novelist Robert Heinlein, who helped start all this with the Martian religion in *Stranger In A Strange Land*, has even provided a rationale to show that all of these metatheologies can be equally true, in a more recent novel, *The Number of The Beast*. In this mathematical fantasy, Heinlein posits a 6-dimensional space-time continuum in which 6 to the power of 6 to the power of 6 parallel universes co-exist. That is a mightily large number (try calculating it) and Heinlein therefore posits that most universes are empty to start with and have become full only as humans imagined things that previously did not exist. Thus, every idea, however absurd, is true in some universe, somewhere in space-time, and "reality" can only be described as Multi-Ego Pantheistic Solipsism; or in other words, every mind creates its own universe.

Refuting that will keep the Jesuits busy for a few years.

COMIX and CUT-UPS

In 1914, partly inspired by the thought that World War I was the product of a rational and linear consciousnes, Tristan Tzara, one of the founders of Dadaism, began composing poems by picking words at random out of a hat. The bourgeoise world naturally regarded this as some morbid joke, or satire, and forgot it; but the surrealists realized the importance of what had been done. It was no mere whim that led Breton to decorate the first Surrealist Exhibition in 1923 with signs warning:

DADA IS NOT DEAD!
WATCH YOUR OVERCOAT!

The artificial separation of "art" and "life"—so necessary for the maintenance of what fools call civilization and Philip K. Dick more correctly called the Empire's Black Iron Prison—had been breeched and broken. Dali's celebrated "defense" of Hitler, which caused his expulsion from surrealism, was the purest statement of surrealist politics ever uttered, even if most of the surrealists were not prepared to understand it: "Hitler has four balls and six foreskins."

Dali, who had a Jewish wife and fled France as soon as Hitler invaded, was speaking in a totally dispassionate and non-aristotelian fashion when he "defended" the monster. Hitler did indeed have four balls and six foreskins, in the same sense that Lenin had one giant buttock, as in Dali's famous painting of him. Perhaps Dali's attitude toward Hitler would have been clearer if he had painted it, as he painted his attitude toward Lenin, instead of trying to verbalize the ineffable. After all, if one Russian General gets shot by a man with the same name as America's leading conservative and another gets shot by a man with the same name as the chap who proved Irish was an Indo-European language, it is only logical that a third Russian General should heist the Maltese Falcon, right?

But seriously, folks—as Bob Hope used to say—the method used by Tzara in breaking the back of Aristotelianism was the same method used by Claud Shannon in discovering the mathematical definition of information. Look it up in Shannon's *The Mathematical Theory of Communication*. Dr. Shannon cut up prose into single words, threw them in a hat, picked them out one at a time—just like Tristan without Isolde creating a Dada poem—and from this Shannon produced not poetry but the ideas that allowed him to define information as the opposite of predictability. The basic equation is elegant, and is given also in my book *Right Where You Are Sitting Now* and it was this mathematical analysis that made possible the word processor on which I am writing this.

That this word processor is called a Mackintosh—like the man who haunts Bloom all through 16 June 1904—is "only" a coincidence, of course. Of course.

Painters explored collage extensively in the 40 years after Tzara's break-through, and every motion picture director conducted extensive research in montage, but prose and poetry, with few exceptions (Joyce, Pound, Williams) moved backward like a crab and crawled into the Victorian or pre-Einsteinian murk. The second quantum leap occurred in the late 1950s when William S. Burroughs began experimenting with the cut-up and fold-in techniques and created a prose of incredible accidental beauty and Zen humor.

I have used various cut-up and other stochastic techniques in all my novels and have noticed one amusing thing about the response to this: hostility is expressed most widely if I admit that I am using "mechanical" techniques of the Burroughs and Tzara variety. If I do not publicize this fact, there is much less hostility. It appears that lazy readers are only terrified of the new if they are warned in advance that it actually is novel and experimental. Otherwise they just pass over it as a confusing passage and forget it. I am not interested in lazy readers, however, but in the attentive and awake.

The techniques used in creating the following experiment were not possible until the modern word processor appeared. They are not "mechanical" but electronic. Beyond that, I offer no explanation and no elucidation. This experiment means what the reader thinks it means; it proves what you think it proves.

It was a lot of fun for me, and I find it more startling than most of you out there, since I had some control over it, but not enough control to keep it from surprising the hell out of me when it was finally crystallized.

NO WATERS IN CHERRY VALLEY BY THE TESTICLES

We don't got to show you no steeeeeenking reality

Any associated supporting element must utilize and be functionally interwoven with the evolution of specifications **over a given time period.**

The above sentence was created by software invented by my friend Geoffrey Baldwin and called "The Buzz Word Generator." This software selects at random from four "buckets" of fashionable corporate and bureaucratic buzz-words and arranges the results in accord with the laws of English grammar. Emphasis (in the form of bold type) is added at random.

Seamus Muadhen went mad in Cherry Valley in 1778. In London that year all concern about the war in the American colonies was suddenly swept aside briefly by the appearance of a booklet titled with deceptive simplicity *A Modest Enquiry* and attributed to one Sarah Beckersniff.

However, the addition of further project parameters is further complexified when taking into account sophisticated implementation methodologies. A large portion of the interface coordination communication adds **overriding performance constraints** to system compatibility testing.

The Buzz-Word Generator is now interacting with a story in progress. From here in, you're on your own.

The results of this program bear an uncanny resemblance to the public utterances of General Alexander Haig, further complexified when taking into account a 24-foot gorilla in heat, although it was not created for that purpose but only for entertainment and amusement when it conflicts with Official Dogma.

The first printing of *A Modest Enquiry* sold out in two days. The second printing, rushed by a printer who could not believe his good luck, appeared a week later and was seized by the sheriff and burned by the public hangman. Parliament had stampeded into action even faster than the printer, as soon as they saw the first edition. The printer changed his name and moved to Paris in a bottle; but several others, wise enough not to advertise, printed pirate copies and sent hawkers to peddle them in alleys. Rev. Ian Paisley programmed a gorilla whose brother he had shot in heat and emptied a whole tub over my tits. It was estimated that by 1780, over sixty such pirate editions had appeared, of which only seven copies are now known to exist.

Cherry Valley is a beautiful name. It sounds like Spring and fresh growing things and sunlight and roosters crowing and larks singing and, of course, cherry blossoms as delicate as those painted by the Zen mystics of Japan. Seamus Muadhen went mad in Cherry Valley in 1778.

A **HUGE BLACK HAND** putting a bloody brutal scissors to our souls adds implementation methodologies through the plumbing.

A Modest Enquiry addressed the issue of whether or not God had a penis and, if not, what was the source of the attitude of reverence which the Christian clergy exhibited toward that organ—*viz.*, why possession of a penis was necessary for one who performs the Christian sacraments.

It said, among other things, that everybody more civilized than the Methodists now agreed that God was a spirit and it seemed "impossible for Reason or Imagination to call up a *clear and vivid* Image of what it might mean for a Spirit to have a *virile Member*, or what such a *ghostly Organ* itself would look like to perception" and it enquired, not delicately, into what must be supposed in logic to be the dimensions in inches or feet or *miles* of the phallus of a cosmic being. Friction from Sirius fair blew everybody's mind, it did. It pointed out that if God did not possess such an organ, it was illogical, ungrammatical and "contrary to Anatomy and proper Usage" to refer to God as "He" or to speak of God in male metaphors as "Lord" or "King."

Does not the collective unconscious contain the image of King Kong leading battalions of rats and cockroaches in blitzkrieg attack on the White House?

It is the opinion of This Department the poor Irish bastard rubbed chocolate syrup all over Casablanca. Project friction from Alexander Haig adds **overriding performance constraints** through endless caves and labyrinths.

Sigismundo Celine sat under a tree, meditating. The evolution of specifications leading a platoon of 100,000 Fat Ladies are only the masque. All phenomena, to him, were equally real, equally unreal, equally inexplicable, equally ineluctible. Syphilitics with advanced brain damage had warned Seamus against getting involved with History.

After escaping in 1771 from the religious maniacs who wanted to make him Emperor of Europe, Sigismundo had eventually run as far as the southern Ohio wilderness to be sure they would not find him again. The wreckage of mid-town Manhattan is functionally interwoven with Major Strasse.

After arriving in Ohio, he had seen no human being in a news-reel clip on the screen for a period that, in his isolation, seemed almost eternal to him. That suited him perfectly. He meditated for longer and longer periods every day, using the techniques the Priory had taught him in Egypt, emptying his mind of its acquired characteristics until it was like a mirror—void, shining, reflecting the universe.

Then there had been the dialogues with the crazy old sorcerer from the nearby Maheema tribe who thought Sigismundo was a Reverser—the most evil kind of Black Magician—because Sigismundo regarded all phenomena as equally real and equally unreal and did not distinguish "right" and "wrong." To be in that amoral prehuman state was to be a monster, the sorcerer seemed to believe.

> *You have been programmed in the Waldorf Astoria*
> " . . . no more constipation worries . . . "

Sigismundo was not sure he believed in the crazy old sorcerer with the evolution of specifications. He had once had equally realistic dialogues with his Uncle Pietro when he was actually alone in a dungeon, while being held prisoner by the *other* gang of religious maniacs who had dogged him all his life, the ones who wanted to make sure he never became Emperor of Europe.

It didn't matter whether he believed in Miskasquamic or not. The old sorcerer was another phenomenon and all phenomena were equally true, equally false and equally meaningless. Any associated supporting gorilla would have no more constipation worries. Dr. Carl Sagan grabs a bottle from Sirius.

Sigismundo intended to meditate, with or without the interruptions—or hallucinations?—of Miskashamic, until he died, or until he decided to get involved with human beings again, whichever came first.

Sigismundo had come to the deep Ohio woods seeking the solitude to make his mind an empty mirror at the age of twenty-six. That was the result of being involved with conspirators and magicians since he was fourteen, being clapped into the Bastille without explanation, and a generally eldritch and Lovecraftian life.

Sigismundo did not hear about *A Modest Enquiry* in the wilderness. If he had heard of it, he would not have guessed that it had been written by Maria Maldonado, whose brother he had shot in Naples in 1766. General Washington found time to grab Dr. Sagan but his voice was drowned out by the screams reflecting the universe.

"Witch doctor announces cure . . . patent pending . . . hallucinogenic cigars, jungle potion did the trick . . . "

In the etymological sense, a 24-foot gorilla in heat escaped to France on a toilet which leads down to a hollow Earth. Any associated supporting element was a **HUGE BLACK HAND**.

But there are no waters in endless caves and mid-town Manhattan.

"The offensive organ growing in better closets everywhere."

"Private Moon of A Company, sir. I have a dispatch for you, sir."

General Washington looked up vaguely, like a mathematician interrupted in the middle of a quadratic equation. "Oh?" he said. "More bad news I assume." He didn't seem to recognize James at all, even though he had recruited him into the Continental Army.

"The situation is no better, sir," James said carefully. He would rather leave the tent before Washington read of the lastest Hessian victory.

"Well, that's war," the General said cheerfully. He was as worried-looking as a locked safe. "You win some and you lose some." He beamed, nodding his head philosophically.

When are you ever going to win some, James thought. It wasn't wise to say that. "Do you accept the dispatch, sir?"

The General toked at his pipe, deeply and thoughtfully. James felt dizzy from the fumes already in the cramped tent. A toilet preserved in the Smithsonian is further complexified when taking into account the star that came out of the sky.

"Oh, I accept the dispatch, private." The General suddenly seemed to focus and recognize James Moon. "I accept the ineluctible, James. That is the path of philosophy, is it not?"

James was stunned. Generals were never this casual with privates, and General Washington in particular was a man of stern adherence to military hierarchy. "You express it very well, sir," he said. That, at least, was safe.

"Have you ever observed," the General asked, "that under proper conditions of sunlight, a single drop of dew on the point of a blade of grass will contain *all the colors of the rainbow*? It is most admirable and gives one to wonder at the glory of the Creator."

There was a long pause. James could not leave until the General dismissed him, but the General seemed to have forgotten that he was there. The fumes were getting thicker and James felt a little drunk and (testimony is unreliable) strangely elated. Faith, what ferocious tobacco did the Indians sell the General lately? It wasn't the airplanes in the Waldorf Astoria on me in all directions. Only in January, Washington had insisted on having all the troops *stuck with needles*—in the arms, it was, and it hurt like bloody hell) because some quack doctor in France claimed that would prevent further spread of the smallpox. The General was *weird* at times, James thought uneasily.

"And is it not strange," the General went on, taking and philosophizing, "that we conventionally believe the rainbow to have seven colors, whereas a close examination of the spectrum, in a dew drop such as I mentioned, reveals an infinity of subtle and most gorgeous gradations of hue? I have been thinking deeply about this recently and am astounded that we normally notice so *little* of nature's glorious raiment."

"Um, yes. Sir." The wreckage of mid-town Manhattan was also the howling bottle of wine.

This gentle absent-minded man was not the Washington that James had learned to know in the year he had served under him. The Washington James knew was withdrawn, yes, but never relaxed or reflective. He was also the most foul-mouthed man James had met since leaving Dublin County and could curse for two hours without repeating himself when a junior officer disappointed him. Only yesterday James had heard him in typical form, correcting a lieutenant who had erred:

"By hatchet heads and hammer handles and the howling harlots of Hell, you are the most incompetent IDIOT I have ever encountered, sir! You are LOWER THAN A SNAKE'S CUNT, sir!! If my dog had a face like yours, sir, hanged if I wouldn't shave his ARSE and teach him to walk backwards!!!"

That was the George Washington that James knew. That was the man who had maintained discipline through a whole year of defeats and desperate retreats.

"Um, ah, sir?"

"Are you a mystic, James?"

"Well, sir, they do be saying that all Irishmen are mystics. I once saw a rock fall out of the sky."

"A rock fall out of the sky?" The General put down his pipe and stared. "I have seen strange things but never a *rock* falling out of the sky. Were you sober at the time?"

"As God is my witness, sir."

"Only ignorant peasants say rocks fall out of the sky, James. Learned men say it is impossible."

"Yes, sir, but I saw it, sir."

"You swear you saw it, when I tell you learned men say it is impossible?"

"I saw what I saw, sir."

The General smiled secretively. "You are excused, private."

The next day James discovered that he had been promoted to Colonel, and died, and went to heaven, but got thrown out because there were two of him.

Major Strasse has been found in some of the finest old mansions on Park Avenue.

Cherry Valley is a beautiful name. It sounds like Spring and fresh growing things and sunlight and roosters crowing and larks singing and, of course, cherry blossoms as delicate as those painted by Zen mystics of Japan. The screams reflecting the universe for lack of money to pay the doctors must utilize and be functionally interwoven with chocolate syrup all over Bergman's American robin.

There was nothing beautiful about Cherry Valley, New York, when Colonel Seamus Muadhen—formerly Private James Moon—entered it in November 1778.

Seamus had been sent down to Cherry Valley with a small troop to give what assistance was possible and to protect the medical officers in case the Loyalists returned. He had known it would be bad, but after two years of war, he thought he had seen enough of blood and horror to have a strong enough stomach for anything.

The Loyalists, with Indian allies, had set out to make an example of Cherry Valley, to warn other communities what could happen to those who gave aid and shelter to the rebel army. We leap a chicken when it conflicts with Official Dogma, interwoven with sleazy advertisements by the testicles.

From a distance, Seamus already knew it would be worse than he expected. There was hardly a house left standing. Every living creature that had not been shot or bayonetted to death must have died in the burning, he thought. There would be no work for the medical staff.

"Christ," he said. "We should have brought undertakers instead of doctors." I was misinformed.

But then as he and his men approached closer, they began to hear a few sounds. Some people, or animals, in Cherry Valley were still alive, or half-alive.

They sounded like wounded cats, at first.

"The circular friction from Sirius is incredible . . . the big gorilla was strong in hashish clarity . . . "

In 1771, Seamus Muadhen had traveled from Ireland to England, just to murder Sir John Babcock, but had given up the idea when a rock fell out of the sky.

Sir John Babcock was the husband of Maria Maldonado Babcock, who wrote the *Modest Enquiry* under the pen-name of Sarah Beckersniff.

Scientists say, "Bring the family!"

Cottage cheese over my nude body in the Smithsonian Institute brings

100,000 Fat Ladies from circuses. But there are no waters in Casablanca. I am passing **a chicken** in the middle of a quadratic equation.

Although Maria Babcock was never exposed as its author, the *Modest Enquiry* was obviously the work of a woman who admired the style of Jonathan Swift but had even more radical notions than his. It said, for instance:

> There is no Christian church, from Russia to the transatlantic American colonies, but that *believes* and *fervently espouses* the Doctrine that only a Male may be a Priest, a Preacher or a minister of the Gospel. On all else—on every Doctrine the devious human Mind can devise or invent to complicate and obscure the simple *Message* of Jesus—they are in disagreement, one with another, in a manner *fearfully* ferocious, cold-heartedly murderous, wickedly *unholy* & totally implacable; but on the Question of what Manner of Human may be appoint'd or accept'd to the Clergy, there is a *Singular* and *Curious* Uniformity on the perverse and peculiar doctrine that such a human being must be in possession of that organ—blasphemously and absurdly attributed to God by the pronoun "He"—which Doctors in learn'd tones call the *glans penis* and which in everyday language is called, in more homely fashion, the *Willy*.
>
> Now, this Doctrine is so remarkable and yet so Universal that nobody hitherto hath question'd it; it is generally consider'd a "mystery of the faith" and beyond human *Reason*. A person born with a Willy may represent a God who also hath a Willy and, upon earth, speak for that God; and a person, of equal intelligence and talents, without the *qualification* of a *Willy* is forever debarr'd from such Holy Office.
>
> But, my Lords and gentle Ladies of the kingdom, in the name of humanity, in the name of reason, what is so special, so miraculous, so *sacred* about a Willy that it confers this strange potential *Holiness* upon its possessor? Does God have no other trait signifying Holiness except "His" Willy? Why is it that the meanest, dullest, most vicious and ignorant Man in the land may always consider the Possibility that if he reforms slightly, or even pretends to reform, he may someday be a *Priest* of Christ; while the most learn'd, the most pious, the most devout Woman who exists must always remember, and can never forget for a moment; that she is *disqualified* from Religious Office for this one reason and this reason only, that she does not possess the *Wonderful* and *all-important* Willy so central to Christian ideas of Holiness?
>
> What is there in the Willy that makes one a *Representative* of the Divine, and what is there is lack of a Willy that makes one forever profane? Are we to believe the Willy itself is some special Sign or *Symbol* of divinity, of the infinite Godhead Itself? That God's wisdom and *loving* Kindness and Infinite *Power* are secondary and unimportant, and would render even God less Godly if not accompanied by the Holy & Paramountly *Omnipotent* Willy? The priest, it hath been claimed, represents Christ, and, again, one must pointedly enquire: Is our *great love & adoration* for Jesus based on his infinite Mercy, his wisdom, his *noble* Sacrifice on the *Cross*, his forgiveness of his enemies, his countless qualities & *virtues* that make him an Emblem of Goodness, or is the most important *fact* about him simply this, that he was in possession of that which every Vagabond & Thief also hath, the Willy?

Presiding over the ruin was a 24-foot gorilla in heat.

By autumn 1777, Colonel Muadhen had read the Declaration of Independence and was convinced Mr. Jefferson must be an Irishman, because he wrote better English than the English ever did. Seamus was also in charge of a brigade, which had grown twice as large since he had been appointed to command it because he once saw a rock fall out of the sky.

In fact, the size of the Continental Army was steadily increasing. This was only partly because all that needle-sticking General Washington had ordered in January actually seemed to have slowed down the advance of the smallpox. It was also due to the fact that ordinary work was hard to find. The rich were constantly closing down their stores and great houses to move to Canada, muttering about "revolutionary rabble" as they departed.

Seamus's brigade were informally called the Fighting Irish and they were one of several Gaelic-speaking brigades—Irish immigrants from the West Counties, where English was still little known, who had enlisted in the Continental Army as soon as they discovered that, with a war on, there was not much secure employment in the Colonies.

"No, it wasn't the airplanes in the Waldorf Astoria . . . testimony is unreliable where death itself would be abolished . . . "

The offensive organ whose brother he had shot was on me in all directions . . . However, the addition of further project parameters is further complexified **except** when the man doesn't have a prepared Scientific Statement through the plumbing in the woods of Ohio.

The British and their Hessian mercenaries went on winning most battles. Colonel Muadhen did what he could to keep up morale by giving his troops pep talks made up of his own Gaelic translations of rhetorical high spots of the Declaration and the *Crisis* pamphlets by Tom Paine. Since he had met Mr. Paine on a ship once, Colonel Muadhen improved the story and told the troops he had met Mr. Jefferson, on the same ship, too, and both men were Irish and proud of it. He didn't tell them that Tom Paine was drunk all across the Atlantic and confessed to having deserted his wife.

The troops believed Seamus's stories of these two great Irish rebels. Tom Jefferson sounded much like O'Lachlann, the rebel bard of Meath, and Tom Paine even more remarkably like Blind Raftery, the satirical bard of Kerry, by the time Seamus Muadhen was through translating them into Gaelic.

When winter came and the army retreated to Valley Forge, Colonel Muadhen found it harder to keep up morale. Nearly 3000 men died of cold in a few months, and it was bloody hard to find a cheery word to say about that. Every morning, there were a hundred more corpses to be buried, dead of exposure or influenza or one damned side effect of the cold or another. And every morning there were more deserters.

Dirty, sneaking cowards, Seamus thought. *I wonder when I'll have the sense to make a run for it and join them.*

He had had a bad eye going into this—from an altercation with the British Army in Dun Laoghaire—and now he had a bad leg from the wound at Brandywine. He woke up cold every morning and went to sleep chilled every night. Washington was more foul-mouthed and Draconic than ever. If they were survived this winter, Seamus thought wearily, they would just meet the Brits again and get beaten again.

Mr. Jefferson claimed, in his Declaration, that Nature and Nature's God were on the side of the rebellion. In Valley Forge, Seamus Muadhen, who had always wanted to avoid politics and had been warned by a Sinister Italian that History was even worse than ordinary politics, decided that Nature and Nature's God simply did not give a fart in their knickers about the rebellion.

When General von Steuben was through drilling the troops that day, Seamus called his Fighting Irish together and gave them another inspirational Gaelic sermon on liberty and sacrifice and heroism.

He almost believed it himself, when he was finished.

We leap from human bodies. I note that the evolution of specifications in a Northern Ireland Assembly debate was created by **a chicken**. Syphilitics with advanced brain damage entered Cherry Valley in 1778. Any associated dog chow adds tomato ketchup poured down the front of my dress by Willis O'Brien **except** when the man doesn't have Marilyn Chambers through the plumbing. The Sinister Italian was meditating in Ohio and once shot Maria Maldonado's brother in Napoli.

It was Kenneth Bernard in his memorable and incisive "King Kong: A Meditation" who first asked the crucial question: how big was King Kong's Dong? Examining comparative anatomy, Bernard noted that a six-foot man usually has a six-inch penis in erection, so a 24-foot gorilla should rejoice in 24 inches or 2 feet. *The roaring foul-mouthed disciplinarian hallucinating all the time is the path of philosophy,* is it not? Bernard rejects this, on the cogent grounds that Kong is not a creature in science but in dream and myth—an ithyphallic divinity of the family of Dionysus and Osiris. Since these deities are depicted in surviving art as endowed with three times the human norm, Kong should, in mythologic, have three times the "norm" for a 24-foot gorilla, or 3×2 feet = 6 feet.

This accounts for the terror in New York when Kong is on the loose seeking his bride (she who was given to him by his worshippers but taken away by treacherous white imperialists). A 24-foot gorilla in heat is frightening, admittedly, but Kong arouses more than fear: he inspires metaphysical Panic, in the etymological sense. He is Pan Ithyphallos, right out of the collective unconscious. He *must* be, not just a 24-foot gorilla, but a

24-foot gorilla with a 6-foot penis. A **HUGE BLACK HAND** was suddenly swept aside briefly by the woods of Ohio. In fact, the size of the Continental Army was further complexified through the Fat Ladies from the circus.

Major Brooks decided to keep Colonel Muadhen on laudenum for a few more days. The prognosis seemed good, despite the Colonel's temporary incoherence, and Brooks expected a full recovery. "What the hell did the poor Irish bastard see in Cherry Valley?" he asked a subaltern.

"I don't know, sir. And frankly I don't want to know."

"War," the Major said. "Christ, I'll be glad when it's over."

You look up. You see it looking at you, kid. When it conflicts with Official Dogma and their strange religion, he probably spoke Hebrew. Dr. Sagan escaped to Paris through the project parameters in better closets everywhere.

Bernard also suggests that city dwellers do not know where the plumbing in their buildings goes because they are afraid to know: afraid to contemplate everything below the surface of pure, hygienic, Falwell-Reagan civilization: afraid to confront darkness and vermin and Lovecraftian cellars leading down to endless caves and labyrinths. He compares the panic when cockroaches were found in some of the finest old mansions on Park Avenue to be the similar panic when Welfare people ("epi-vermin") were found living in the Waldorf Astoria. Bernard surmises, acutely I think, that no white man can sit on a toilet without unconscious anxiety that a **HUGE BLACK HAND** might reach up through the plumbing in accord with the laws of English grammar and grab him by the testicles.

The magick and marvelous Willy appears in the Waldorf Astoria. The results bear an uncanny resemblance to Humphrey Bogart reaching into the upper echelons of mass culture in all directions. The public utterances of sex mutilators and cattle educators should have "thirty pieces of silver" in the Northern Ireland Assembly.

Scream, Ann, scream.

Dillinger had a 23-inch penis which is preserved in the Smithsonian Institute. Round up the usual project parameters.

"The Lord is a man of war," Seamus told the doctor. "The Lord is his name. It's in *Exodus*, chapter 15, I think. Then in *Deuteronomy* we have an eye for an eye, and drenching the land in blood. Heh. An eye for an eye. Heh heh."

Kong is not a creature allowed to explore Marilyn Chambers with special effects in the basement trying to make it work.

"An eye for an eye," Colonel Maudhen kept saying. "An eye for an eye. An eye for an eye." I'll bear it on me for entertainment and amusement.

Lieutenant O'Mara necessarily assumed command. They had Seamus tied to his horse, like a wounded man, because they didn't know what else to do with him. The airplanes in the Waldorf Astoria must use and be functionally interwoven with the product configuration baseline.

"Can the doctors help in a case like this?" asked Sergeant de Burke.

"That I do not know," Lieutenant O'Mara said. "I think only time heals this kind of wound."

When taking into account any **discrete** probability of project success **at this point in time**, tomato ketchup and sunlight and roosters crowing poured down the front of my dress.

The *Modest Enquiry* went on to discuss, in explicit detail, the ithyphallic statues of Osiris and Pan and Hermes to be found around the Mediterranean, pointing out that these divinities were depicted with Willies "three times, or on occasion, even four times *Longer* and *Thicker* and generally more Gargantuan than the norm for the mortal Male" and asked if "the ancients believed, what these *Holy* Statues (for so they were in their own Time) strongly suggest—*viz.*, that the *greater* the *Mass* of the Willy, the greater the *Divinity* indwelling."

Did this idea survive in the Christian conviction that it required a Willy to represent the authority of God on earth? The next paragraph created considerable hilarity in Protestant England, but even so its implications were unbearable and unthinkable to Christians of all persuasions—

> We must ask, in all solemnity, is the Pope himself, the most prestigious, pugnacious, awe-inspiring, *wealthy*, and *Gorgeously* Dress'd of all Christian clergymen (and the very Vicar of Christ on Earth, to his devout followers) elevated to that rank because he possesses the Divine Attribute of the *Willy*? For, surely, he could never have advanced to the rank of Bishop, Archbishop &c and eventually to his present *Eminence* without a Willy. This, then, is why we have never seen in history (or anywhere but in the Tarot cards) a Female Pope—the magick & marvelous Willy appears, to the Christians as to the Pagans, the emblem of the *Kingdom* and the *Power* and the *Glory* of God. Without it, the Pope could not reign, nor would any Catholic listen to his religious opinions.

Here's looking at the offensive organ with Marilyn Chambers on a toilet.

Cherry Valley sounds like Spring and blasphemy, profanity, sedition, heresy, atheism. No soul inside, just gears and levers of complicated sorts. They cure more patients with Indian allies.

"You're good, angel. You're the equally real, equally unreal *Divinity* indwelling."

From a distance, Seamus already knew it would be worse than he expected. This is further complexified when taking into account Andrea Dworkin, who asserts that heterosexual intercourse is always exploitative **except** when the man doesn't have an erection.

In the Bastille, poor old Father Henri Benoit finally found a new philosophical companion to replace the vanished Sigismundo Celine. Even more of a heretic than Celine, and much more tenacious an argument, this new one, but therefore a worthy antagonist. Debate was more stimulating than agreement, to the old priest, after 23 years in confinement. Seamus Muadhen grabs **overriding performance constraints** in the woods of Ohio. No, it wasn't the airplanes through the plumbing.

Father Benoit's new friend was Donatien Aldonse Francois de Sade, a short blonde Marquis from the south, who had been imprisoned for blasphemy, profanity, sedition, heresy, atheism, buggery, sodomy, abuse of controlled substances and annoying his mother-in-law.

De Sade cheerfully told the priest he was guilty on all counts, and unrepentant. "You should meet my mother-in-law," he said, explaining the major offense that had gotten him in trouble.

The priest and the Marquis spent many pleasant afternoons in the courtyard discussing whether the universe were a mindless machine or the creation of a loving God. The priest argued in terms of philosophy and metaphysics, but the Marquis was temperamentally an empiricist and argued always in terms of what the world was actually like. "Look at the smallpox," he would say. "Kills a few hundred thousand every month all over Europe. What kind of Benevolent Intelligence decided to give us that as a birthday present? Did He have constipation that day, to put him in a foul enough mood to perpetuate such a fiendish joke at our expense?"

"But the physicians now seem to have a cure for the smallpox," Benoit would say. "Surely such inspirations are given to human minds by a Higher Intelligence."

"I have talked to more physicians than you," de Sade would reply. "The bright young ones who are making all the radical discoveries are atheists like me. They say the body is a machine. No soul inside, just gears and levers of complicated sorts. They cure more patients with that atheistic idea than all the prayers of the dark ages combined have ever been reputed to cure."

And so on. It kept both the old priest and the young nobleman amused during the years of incarceration. Each knew he would never convince the other.

A 24-foot gorilla is unreliable in the basement. Testimony is visualized through the plumbing over my nude body.

By the Spring of 1778, the Continental Army was beginning to rise from its symbolic death at Valley Forge and at last started to give the British some real problems. Colonel Seamus Muadhen didn't have to turn Jefferson and Paine into Raftery and O'Lachlann to stir up the enthusiasm of his Celtic brigade: there was optimism in the air, perhaps because the Continental Army had survived longer than any rational mind could have expected.

In June came the battle of Monmouth and their greatest victory in the war thusfar. Military authorities later explained why the Continentals should not have won that battle; in military logic, it was an impossible victory.

General Charles Lee, in the middle of the battle, had exactly the same view as these later experts and ordered a retreat (for which General Washington later court-martialed him, after assuring him in personal conversation that he was **by God, sir, the most yellow-bellied cur ever begotten by a cowardly boar hog upon a mentally retarded POLECAT and had no more right to his fucking uniform than a buggering IDIOT OFFSPRING of a whore and a trained pony)**

but the Brits had turned tail and run, and the Continentals were on the attack, and that made all the difference.

Colonel Muadhen congratulated his troops afterwards, in Gaelic. He told them that not all the battles in Europe where Irish "wild geese" had distinguished themselves for bravery were as glorious as this victory, and that when General John ("Gentleman Johnny") Burgoyne finally stopped running he would tell everybody in England it was those wild Irish from Connacht who had smashed his troops that day.

He wanted to say a lot more patriotic things like that but his voice was drowned out by the screams from the medical tents, where men with serious leg wounds were having their legs sawed off to save them from gangrene.

In the Bastille, the Marquis de Sade is writing a book, which is partly a novel and partly a philosophical treatise and partly the result of his meditations on why Father Benoit, an intelligent man, still believed in God and Justice after being locked in this place for 23 years. In this book, de Sade hopes to show how the world actually operates: what sort of men run it, and what motivates them. He has made his major characters a Count whose brother he had shot, to represent the old landed nobility, a Banker, to represent the rising bourgeoise class, a Bishop, to represent the Church Militant, and a Judge, to represent the State itself as supreme authority to reward and punish on earth. In short, four men standing for the powers that control France at present, and, incidentally, have imprisoned de Sade for his own sexual and intellectual eccentricities.

De Sade's book is called *The 120 Days of Sodom*, and its thesis is that the world is run by madmen. His Count and Banker and Bishop and Judge spend their 120 days contemplating various exquisite forms of torture to inflict on the poor, the helpless, the weak and, especially, the female.

He reads portions of this to old Father Benoit occasionally, enjoying the priest's horrified reaction.

"My spirit is entirely scientific," he tells the old man. "I invent nothing. These four men of mine are the types who rule the world. If I am correct in my materialistic view. Nature has selected them. If I am incorrect, and above

Nature is your God, then that God has, for his own obscure reasons, left the world in their custody."

The priest protests—although he has been unjustly imprisoned for as many years as most people's whole lives, he still will not accept that there is no justice or reason in the world. He argues that de Sade is embittered and cynical.

"I am the second cousin of the king," de Sade says simply. "I have had opportunities most philosophers have never enjoyed, to study the centers of power and the men who hold them. I exaggerate nothing. Every battle in every war has all the atrocities I describe, and they happen because the men who run the world are men exactly like my four archetypes."

De Sade "warms to his subject" as the writing proceeds; the *120 Days of Sodom* swells from an anatomy to an encyclopedia. He has become the Diderot of the unconscious; he catalogs every twist and turn. Machiavelli told only the politics of the ruling elites—de Sade has unmasked their inner drives. He is convinced he is writing a veritable masterpiece, the first truthful book on power ever composed. At times, he even thinks of wild plans to smuggle the MS. out of the Bastille and have it published. His empirical mentality has turned the project from mere satire to social science of a sort. As he catalogs 50 diverse techniques to violently abort a pregnant woman while causing her maximum pain in the process, he is also arguing that, in a Godless and mechanical universe, such projects make as much sense as anything else.

He knows—he never pretends not to know—that these monstrous beings, the Count and Banker and Judge and Bishop, are all extensions of his own inner being. But he still claims, and believes, that they are also mirrors of what he has seen in the seats of power of the world.

A philosopher by necessity—prison does that for you—the Marquis was no longer interested in perversion as diversion. He has discovered perversion as subversion.

Please let them airplanes come on project parameters of the point of a blade of grass.

The battle of Brandywine is not much remembered in America, but in France they know all about it because the Marquis de Lafayette was wounded there. In County Clare, Ireland—especially in the Burren—they know all about it because Colonel Seamus Muadhen saw God there, sort of, and discovered that God was Irish.

Seamus told that story many times after he returned to Ireland and lived in the Burren. He told how he had met General Washington in a pub in Philadelphia and leaped at the chance to fight the Brits. He never mentioned that Washington had gotten him blind drunk before he made that patriotic decision, and that, while sober, he had been firmly convinced he wanted no part of any war in inches or feet or *miles* anywhere at any time for any cause.

"Major Strasse from Sirius has been looking at you, kid."

At Brandywine in 1777, Colonel Muadhen—or Colonel Moon, as he was then calling himself—was shot right off his horse by a Hessian bullet. He had only one thought as he fell: *Bejesus, but my career as an officer has been a short one.* He was quite convinced he was dying—a man hit by a bullet that knocks him off his horse doesn't have time to wonder where he was wounded. He simply assumes the matter is very serious.

He never hit the ground. Instead, he made a sharp turn in mid-air, rose rapidly, and found himself looking down at the battlefield.

Oh, good Christ, I'm on my way to heaven, he thought.

A singing light approached rapidly, covered him in a glory of golden love, bathed him in motherly kindness. It was better than sexual orgasm: he felt himself literally bursting.

He came apart into two stars.

—Oh, you damned eejit, look what you went and got yourself into now, Seamus Muadhen said.

—You aren't real, James Moon answered. I must be having a fever. I am a wounded man and you mustn't bedevil me. I think I was hit in the leg and the doctors may be after sawing it off on me.

—This is no fever, and you are no James Moon. You are me, and I am you.

—A name is only a name. There aren't really two of us in a news-reel clip on the screen just because I have two names. This is all a hallucination. I have been shot and this is a fever.

—Then why are you answering me?

James looked down. Men with a stretcher were carrying his body back to the field hospital. He could see blood gushing from his, or the body's, right leg.

—Oh, be damned to it, there are *three* of us. You and me and the body down there on earth. This war has been a fair bugger for a year and now it has driven me mad entirely.

—Never mind that. It is time you and I had an understanding. You have been keeping me in an underground jail of your mind too long.

—And what kind of talk is that? In jail, is it? You are only a name, not a person.

—I am a person as much as you are, James. More than you, bedad. I am the true man, and you are only the masque. The shadow of the man.

—Talk sense, man. You sound like you've been drinking the poteen.

—Every Irishman has two selves in inches or feet or miles, James. His true self and the masque he learns to wear in dealing with the conquerors, the *sasanach*. You have become the masque and lost the true self. Once we were all stars and we've been after making Punch and Judy puppets of ourselves.

—And I would be a great fool to believe such madness. You have a few jars on you, I swear. It is I who am the real man and you who are the puppet of my hallucination.

—That is the great lie of the conquerors. Sure they have been after putting a bloody brutal scissors to our souls, in Ireland, and cutting out all that is Irish in us. They want us to be imitation Englishmen. And what is *James Moon* if not an imitation Englishman?

—I will listen to no more of such talk from the likes of you, phantom that you are. I am dying in a war against England and you are but a symptom of my fever, I still say. To your face I say it.

—Peter denied Christ three times. How many times will you deny me?

—Don't be comparing yourself to God, now. That's too blasphemous even for a goblin like yourself.

—But I am God, James—very God of very God. The True Self of every living being is the one God. And you great fools, who are only masques and shadows of men, are always after denying the starry Christ within, Pontius Pilates and Peters that you are.

Please, anybody. You see it. You have been programmed.

The doctor asked Seamus, kindly, if he knew where he was.

"I am in an army field hospital," Seamus said. "In the colony of New York. I am not mad, sir. I am only extremely nervous. Extremely high strung, you might say. The Lord is a man of war, you know. An eye for an eye."

"Do you know how many days you've been here?"

"No." Seamus was surprised at that. "I am only nervous now, but perhaps I was not fully in possession of all my faculties for a time."

"Do you remember how you got here?"

"An eye for an eye," Seamus said. "Do you know that way of it, doctor? An eye for an eye, we say. An eye for an eye—it's our whole law and religion. An eye for an eye: *Deuteronomy* that is. The Lord is a man of war. *Exodus.* Smash the brains of the infants: *Hosea.* And that may we go, and an eye for an eye and an eye for an eye and we all become fooken blind."

The doctor told the staff to keep Colonel Muadhen on laudenum.

—Ow. Be careful there. That hurt like bloody hell, it did.

—*Be calm, sir. We are taking out the bullet. You will live.*

And Seamus Muadhen was gone and it was a medical officer looking down at James, because James was suddenly back in his body again, and now he felt all the pain at once.

But at least he was alive.

Or was he? It seemed, after the operation, that James Moon was dead. They did not have to saw off his leg—the bullet came out quickly, without the blood poison setting in—but somebody had sawed off his identity. Humphrey Bogart did not appear.

Colonel Seamus Muadhen—he insisted on being called that, now—

recuperated slowly in a hospital near Brandywine. The man in the next bed was a French Marquis, Major General de Lafeyette, and he and Seamus had a great deal to talk about, because each of them was convinced he was a little bit off his head. Seamus thought he was funny in the upper storey because he wasn't sure how much to believe of his trip halfway to heaven, or how James Moon had died and left himself alive, remembering that he once was a star. The Marquis thought he was suffering some kind of Permanent Brain Damage because the staff of the hospital did not talk like ordinary Americans or even like ordinary English people.

The staff of the hospital all talked like characters out of Shakespeare.

The Marquis worried about this a great deal at first. He worried that he was really in an English hospital and they were all talking that way to drive him mad, or to make him think he was mad, to punish him for volunteering to fight for the rebels. He worried that such an extravagant theory indicated that he really was mad. He worried that they weren't talking that way at all and he was simply hallucinating all the time.

"And how is thee today?" said a nurse coming to his bedside.

"I am much improved," the Marquis said, controlling his anxiety. "And how is thee?"

"The Good Lord has been good to this humble servant. But do thee need anything to read? More blankets, perhaps? We wish thee to be comfortable here."

That was the way it was every time he talked to one of them. The Marquis finally got up the courage to discuss it with Colonel Muadhen, the Irish officer who was raving about having two souls when they brought him in.

"The mental effects of a wound can be longer-lasting than the physical effects," Major General Lafayette said cheerfully.

"Oh, aye. I'm not a-fevered anymore, but I still wonder about those two souls a bit."

"It wears off in time, I suppose, or all old soldiers would be mad."

"That is a cheerful way to be looking at it."

"I've had my own problem, to be frank."

"That I was sure of. You have had a most absent and heartsore expression at times."

"The truth is," the Marquis said, "everybody here sounds, well, strange." He took a breath. "They sound like Shakespeare without the poetry."

Seamus laughed, and then looked sympathetic. "Oh, be-Jesus, Shakespeare is it? You've never read the King James Bible, I suppose?"

"What are you trying to tell me?" The Major General had picked up all his English in a six-month crash course after deciding to join the American Revolution. The young and unsure King Louis XVI—"the fat boy,"

Lafayette called him—had forbidden this madcap project, so technically the Marquis was in the colonies illegally and subject to arrest if he returned to France.

"It is not Shakespeare they are after imitating," Colonel Muadhen explained. "It is the Protestant Bible, the King James Bible as it is called. It is part of their religion to talk as well as act like our Lord, and they imagine he talked like their Bible. I haven't the heart to tell them he probably spoke Hebrew."

After that the Marquis recovered much faster, but he spent most of his time talking to the hospital staff and learning all he could about them and their strange religion. Why did they think God disapproved of bright, happy-looking colors on clothing and wanted them to wear black all the time? Because God wished men to work out their salvation in fear and trembling, they said. Why did they think God disapproved of slavery? Because he made all souls in his own image. If they would not take their hats off for the king, and would nurse soldiers wounded fighting the king, why did they think fighting the king was still a sin anyway? Because he said, *Thou shalt not kill.* Would they fight even if a ruffian were trying to rob their goods or murder their families? No, because on the Cross, he said, *Father, forgive them.*

The Marquis de Lafayette found the Quakers of Brandywine almost as astounding and wonderful as Voltaire's story about the visitor from Sirius who walks across the earth and never notices the human race crawling around beneath his toes. He had never before met Christians who didn't hate one another and he found it extraordinary. Four "buckets" of a prepared Scientific Statement adds **overriding performance constraints** to testing mythically necessary 6-foot penis. General Washington found time to visit his memorable and incisive military toilet.

He was only mildly disillusioned when he heard one male nurse, in a discussion of whose turn it was to empty the bed-pans when it conflicts with Official Dogma, tell another, "Oh, go fuck thyself."

Even in that pre-Freudian era, the *Modest Enquiry* made its own blunt and earthy attempt to fathom what Sarah Beckersniff called "the strange, *obscure* & subterranean psychology of the *Worship* of the Willy." This perhaps did more harm to English Imperialism than the entire life of General George Washington. Some connection between male domination and compulsive masturbation was more than mildly hinted at, in passages like this:

> I am told on good Authority, and verily believe, that boys approaching the *Cusp* of Manhood, at about ages 12 to 14, often develop a superstitious *Awe* & sense of Magic, Mystery and *loving* Infatuation about this Willy of theirs; some, it is said, give it a *Name* of endearment, and those especially addicted to self-enjoyment grow so *Fervent* in this *singular & solitary* Passion (similar to that of the adult for a spouse, or the true Religious for God) that

Doctors have feared for their sanity. But what are we to think of adult males who have never outgrown this superstitious narcissism and still verily believe the magical *Willy* to be the very Emblem and Significator of the divine upon earth—The alchemical *Medicine of metals*, the Philosopher's *Stone*, the Sumum *Bonum*? Have they remained entranc'd or enthrall'd— virtually *Mesmeriz'd*—by the object of their first ardent erotic feelings?

By 1779, the Phi Beta Kappa Society of Yale was debating *in public* whether women had intellectual capacities equal to men. (Phi Beta Kappa of Harvard that year was debating whether Adam had a navel.) By 1792, the *Modest Enquiry* was followed by Mary Wollstoncraft's somewhat less radical *Vindication of the Rights of Women*, which had the demerit of being discussable in polite society and therefore had less real effect than the banned, shunned, forbidden and loathed Beckersniff blasphemies, which everybody really read.

Interface coordination communication adds a piece of cheese jumping around: Major Strasse has been shot in the basement.

General Washington found time to visit the Quaker hospital, despite the distraction of supervising yet another retreat. He sat by Major General Lafayette's bed and talked, gravely and with great sincerity, about the debt America owned the Marquis, who had shed his blood in the cause of a nation not his own, and he said that the United States would never forget what it owned to the de Lafayette family of France.

Seamus discovered that Washington, like himself, seemed to be three men. The man who spoke of national gratitude to Lafayette was not the roaring foul-mouthed disciplinarian Seamus had seen most often, nor was he the absent-minded philosopher of two days ago in the tent. He was a Statesman, and he knew how to use unction and lubricating oil.

Later, while Seamus was walking in the garden—he had gone out to allow Washington and Lafayette some privacy—a giant shadow fell between him and the sun. There was only one man in Seamus's experience who could cast a shadow that huge.

"Good afternoon, General."

"Good afternoon, Colonel."

They walked a few paces. Today Washington did not seem to have the peculiar lurching gait that had afflicted him in recent months. An American robin circled above their heads, landed in a tree, and loudly announced that he could lick any bird in the garden with one wing tied behind him.

"You saw a rock fall from the sky," Washington said. "And you believed your own eyes, instead of popular opinion."

"I did that, General." Seamus was not going to pour out his heart about his other soul, the one that was a star. The falling rock business was queer enough.

The robin announced shrilly that he was half-horse and half-alligator, ate falcons for breakfast and would hold this territory until the magpies learned to dance the pavanne and hell froze over. European robins, Seamus thought, were more tactful. Across the garden, a crow laughed derisively and muttered a few animadversions about upstart braggarts.

"Well, then go shit in thy hat," a medical orderly shouted in the kitchen. "And clap it on thy head for curls."

"I saw something stranger than a falling rock from heaven once," Washington said. "I was working as a surveyor for the colonial government. I was alone in the woods for months and months. You get a bit ah fanciful sometimes when you are alone too long. But I saw something more remarkable than your falling rock, and I believed it."

"I understand, General, You decided to trust yourself instead of popular notions of what's real and what's unreal."

"Yes."

The robin announced that he was moving to a more salubrious climate and flew off. The crow raucously told him not to hurry his return.

"You wouldn't care to talk about it, General?" Seamus asked softly.

"You should probably think me mad. But this event is why you are a Colonel today."

"Because I trusted myself instead of popular opinions. Is that what you mean, General?"

"That is what I mean, Colonel. Go on trusting yourself. We must meet and talk on other occasions."

General Washington walked off, aloof, gigantic, enigmatic again. Until Polyphemus escapes from the *Odyssey* and comes knocking at my door, Seamus thought, that man will serve as the most desperate character I ever encountered. You have been programmed. You see it looking at you, kid.

Major Strasse gets a pile of horse manure and is delighted. Bernard rejects the circular friction, thinking "smoke and mirrors" must utilize and be functionally interwoven with kiddy porn.

The plumbing in their buildings wasn't pig iron so it will never rise again.

In Paris, what happened next was liquid wrench functionally interwoven with French Canadian Bean Soup in a news-reel clip on the screen. Vote for Independence.

The fat boy—Louis XVI—has been persuaded to grant amnesty to the aging heretic (Arouet de Voltaire is now 82) by the ever-persuasive M. Sartines. It is a shrewd move. The Church fumes and fulminates, but the people at large have fallen in love with the old man who exiled in Switzerland for decades, has kept up a continuous polemic against all the abuses of the feudal system. When the old atheist or deist (nobody in France is very clear about the difference) arrives in Paris, the scene is like a Cecil de Mille spectacle two centuries in advance. Mother is the best bet with all other government spending outside the sacred military toilet. The mob went mad, especially those who didn't have the foggiest notions of the old man's philosophy; he has insulted kings, bishops, bankers, all of *them*, and he has survived—that is enough to make him a national hero.

The duc d'Orleans—"the friend of the people," as he is called—sets about recruiting the champion of Free Thought into Free Masonry at once. Voltaire agrees, placidly. M. Franklin is requested to act as Worshipful Master of the East in the initiation, and is happy to oblige. It is a great moment when the hoodwink is removed, and the most famous Rationalist of the age sees that he has been engaged in revolutionary rituals with the most famous Scientist of the age—the man who hurled lightning bolts at the Vatican faces the man who tamed the lightning with a key on a kite string.

After the initiation, some say, M. Voltaire and M. Franklin had a banquet with the Marquis de Condorcet and discussed science and philosophy. The big gorilla was trying to make it work.

The elusive pony is kiddy porn in the basement.

M. Condorcet, in the course of this symposium, asserted that with the steady advance of medicine (moving faster everywhere, as the steady decline of the Inquisition accelerated) a time would come when every disease would be abolished. M. Franklin agreed, but M. Voltaire said it would take longer than they realized. M. Condorcet then went further and said that, in a thousand years, when all governments were staffed by Freemasons and the last doddering priest had been killed by a brick falling from the last decaying church, medicine would advance to the point where death itself would be abolished. M. Franklin agreed again—he had written a bit on that subject himself, diplomatically leaving out the necessity of abolishing Christianity before this could be accomplished. M. Voltaire was again skeptical. Life extension was possible, he agreed, but immortality was a Christian superstition and unworthy of scientific minds.

M. Condorcet then grew more enthusiastic (they were on their third bottle of wine by then) and announced that he could foresee major reforms in the next *century* alone. M. Franklin listened, spellbound, as M. Condorcet pictured for them endless caves and labyrinths—a world in which education was free for all, boys and girls alike, and schools were taught by rational well-educated men and women, not by narrow-minded priests and nuns. A world in which insurance companies, some run by private investors and some by the state, would pay decent premiums to those injured and disabled, and even to those unemployed by economic recession. A world in which the state would loan the money for scientific and technological research not even imaginable today, perhaps even to fly to the moon. A world in which every city had free public libraries, like the one M. Franklin had started in Philadelphia, and the state and private investors would offer "illness insurance," so nobody would die for lack of money to pay the doctors. M. Franklin agreed that all of this might happen in a century, but some of it would probably take two centuries.

M. Voltaire said it couldn't happen until those rational teachers Condorcet imagined had replaced religious orders in the educational system, and that would take a thousand years in the civilized nations, five thousand years in the Middle East, a hundred thousand years in the Orient, and a million years in Ireland.

The Merovingian kings round up the usual suspects—no more constipation worries.

It was not until three years after Cherry Valley that General Washington finally told Colonel Muadhen about the star that came out of the sky, that night long ago in the woods, and the Italian Arab or Arabian Italian who got out of the star and spoke to him, and prophesied his future in accurate detail.

The Italian or Arab who rode in the star had said, at the end, "Never fear, never doubt, never despair. We shall raise you higher than the kings of Europe."

Then the Arab or Italian repeated formally, "We met on the square, we part on the level," and climbed back into the star. He shouted, "Remember— no horse, no wife, no mustache," made some mechanical adjustments, and flew straight up in the air and away over the tree-tops.

By 1800, there had been over a thousand clandestine printings of the grossly indecent Beckersniff booklet. Because of the scandal it had provoked, the infamy of *A Modest Enquiry* survived all the censors and book-burners on the toilet; it was never discussed in decent circles, and never had the overt notoriety of Wollstonecraft's *Vindication*, but even in the Victorian Age, Professor Pokorny found (see his invaluable *The Necronomicon and Other Unspeakable Texts*) at least thirty thousand printings appeared through the plumbing, especially in the vicinity of Oxford where it was a great favorite with giggling undergraduates. Any associated supporting elements leads rats and cockroaches through endless caves and labyrinths.

A Mortal blow had been struck to English manhood. Even those who laughed and believed they were reading a variety of philosophical pornography were undermined. The Willy itself had become comical, and authority based on nothing else but possession of a Willy seemed obscene. Self-confidence ebbed; virility withered; despite Kipling and Haggard, a long, melancholy, withdrawing roar was noticed as Anglo-Saxon manhood tottered and stumbled.

By 1950, the British Empire was obviously on the edge of mortal collapse. By 1968, there appeared in America and quickly spread back to Europe a variety of Radical Feminism which held that *possession*, not *absence*, of a Willy, irrespective of all other intellectual or moral traits, rendered a person vicious, vile and sub-human.

By 1986—210 years after the *Modest Enquiry*—there was nothing left of the British Empire but six counties in Northern Ireland.

Presiding over the ruin was a woman Prime Minister.

A toilet preserved in the Smithsonian wasn't Ronald Reagan's salad dressing.

The Marquis de Condorcet never stopped thinking and writing about a world that could be designed rationally to make for the maximum happiness of the maximum number of people; and many of his projects came to pass in the next 200 years. The Marquis de Sade never stopped thinking and writing about a world that could be designed rationally to make for the maximum horror and pain for the maximum number of people; and many of his projects came to pass in the next 200 years.

Any associated supporting element must utilize a computer belonging to General Alexander Haig. No more constipation is further complexified by the terror of the gigantic nonwhite penis.

On the basis of the above evidence, This Department concludes that serious confusions endanger the collective psyche of the TV age.

17 percent of juvenile delinquents and 23 percent of U.S. Senators in Hanfkopf's survey believe Ingrid Bergman, not Fay Wray, was the bride of Kong. Clinical paranoids shown Rorshach inkblots increasingly say spontaneously that they see Major Strasse rubbing chocolate syrup all over Bergman's endless caves and labyrinths. In most dreams, it is either George Washington or Humphrey Bogart, not the little-known Robert Armstrong, who sails to Skull Island to confront black guerilla rage. Kong's mythically necessary 6-foot penis obsesses white males over 70 and accounts for the panic-stricken bombing of Libya and other unruly, insufficiently Caucasian nations.

Syphilitics with advanced brain damage and John Birch Society members often visualize Kong, not as being shot off a skyscraper, but being overwhelmed and brought down by Andrea Dworkin leading a platoon of 100,000 Fat Ladies recruited from circuses, who then emasculate the Big Fellow in gory detail on wide screen with technicolor; the offensive organ is then thrown in the East River, weighted with pig iron so it will never rise again.

"An eye for an eye," Seamus said, "Do you know that way of it, doctor? An eye for an eye, we say. An eye for an eye—it's our whole law and religion. An eye for an eye, until we all go fooken blind."

This may account entirely for the airplanes in the toilet looking at you, kid.

The proper ending, probably, is as follows: Dr. Carl Sagan, Martin Gardner, the Inedible Randi and other stalwarts of CSICOP (Committee for the Scientific Investigation of Claims of the Paranormal) appear in a news-reel clip on the screen. They read a prepared Scientific Statement, assuring us that gorillas never grow to 24 feet, that eye-witness testimony is unreliable when it conflicts with Official Dogma, that anybody who disagrees with them is probably a Nazi, and that the most "scientific and economic" explanation of the wreckage of mid-town Manhattan is to assume the crash of a giant meteor.

A **HUGE BLACK HAND** then smashes through the floor and grabs Dr. Sagan by the testicles.

Sigismundo Celine, in the woods of Ohio, meditated. To him all phenomena were real in some sense, unreal in some sense, meaningless in some sense, real and meaningless in some sense, unreal and meaningless in some sense, and real and unreal and meaningless in some sense.

Shrapnel

It is tempting to consider Archbishop Marcinkus, implicated in the P2 fascist plots in Italy and South America, as an example of a Joycean $\sqsubset$ or Cain function. Archbishop Romeros, murdered for opposing that fascist conspiracy, would then be a $\wedge$ or Abel function.

Considering the role of ALP in Joycean and Cabalistic symbolism, it is distinctly odd then that the bank which laundered the cocaine money for P2 was called CisALPine (emphasis added). This was owned chiefly by Archbishop Marcinkus and "God's banker," Roberto Calvi, found hanged from Blackfriars Bridge in London on 18 June 1982.

Only the most imaginative would find a hint of Roberto Calvi in Joyce's "Robman Calvinic" on page 519 of *FW*.

Still, it is deucedly odd that Licio Gelli, Grandmaster of the P2 Conspiracy, was also a Knight of Malta. Other recent Knights of Malta, as we have mentioned, include William Casey of the CIA and Alexander Haig. Another Knight of Malta, and receiver of the Order's Grand Cross of Merit, was General Richard Gehlen, a former Nazi who became the CIA's principle source of espionage within Soviet Russia. According to Baigent, Leigh and Lincoln in *The Messianic Legacy*, other Knights of Malta include Alexandre de Marenches, former chief of French Intelligence, Generals de Lorenzo and Allavena, former chiefs of the Italian secret service and Admiral Torrisi, chief of the Italian General Staff.

It all rather reminds me of a remark once made to me by Alan Watts: "The great error of academic historians is the belief that the Roman Empire 'fell.' It never 'fell.' It still controls the Western world through the Vatican and the Mafia."

Joyce scholars have not yet satisfactorily explained the number 1132 that recurs constantly in *FW*; I gave my own guess earlier. It is interesting that in the 32nd degree of Freemasonry the Knights of Malta are specifically named as the agents of tyranny and superstition against whom all Freemasons must struggle if light and liberty are ever to prevail on this planet.

What is even more peculiar is that Baigent, Leigh and Lincoln, in their earlier *Holy Blood, Holy Grail* argue that one force in addition to Freemasonry, or perhaps "behind" Freemasonry has opposed the Vatican/Mafia coalition for centuries, and that force is a group of descendents of the Merovingian dynasty of France. Whatever one thinks of this Romantic theory, it is startling to note that a great deal of the evidence used by Baigent, Leigh and Lincoln deals with the still-unsolved murder of the last Merovingian king, Dagobert II.

Dagobert was killed on another damned day with a 23 in it—23 December 679—and in the Ardennes forest of France, which is named after the bear-goddess Arduine, cognate with Artemis and Joyce's whole **arth** family of bear gods.

The most famous modern novel about the Knights of Malta is, of course, *The Maltese Falcon* by Dashiel Hammett. I apologize immediately for the **Ham** that has crept in again in Hammett's name, and I am even more embarrassed to call your attention to the climax in which the gold falcon of the Knights of Malta seems to have been found at last, and turns out to be a fake.

The real maltese falcon was stolen (look it up) by a Russian General.

COINCIDANCE: PART FOUR

THE HIDDEN VARIABLES

To review a bit: we have seen that Joyce's function, ∃ , based on Dodgson/Carroll's symbol for mathematical existence, is strikingly similar to the Tao or no-mind of Chinese philosophy, or may be the class of all minds (which is not a mind for the same reason that the class of all kangaroos is not a kangaroo), and is isomorphic to the DNA in that it expresses itself in two sub-functions, ɯ and △ which may be considered similar to the two coils of the DNA helix (or the male and female members of the Mediterranean-Celtic-Norse-British gene pool swarming around Dublin Bay for the past 5000 years approximately.)

More simply, ∃ can be considered that which the Nobel laureate in quantum mechanics, Erwin Schrodinger, attempted to define in his *What Is Life?* when he argues that "mind does not exist in the plural" and that the sum total of all individual minds is still one. This is what another quantum physicist, Dr. David Bohm, calls the "mind-like" aspect of the Hidden Variable which, Bohm assumes, underlies the hologrammic structure which allows the information of any part of the universe to be equally present in any other part of the universe. (Bohm's ideas are presented at length in his *Wholeness and the Implicate Order*. I comment further on these notions of both Schrodinger and Bohm in my recent work, *The New Inquisition*, Falcon Press, 1987.)

Dr. Bohm is not the only physicist who thinks the Hidden Variables have "mind-like" characteristics. Dr. E.H. Walker in his "The Compleat Quantum Anthropologist" (Proceedings of the American Anthropological Association, 1974), Dr. Nick Herbert in *Quantum Reality*, and Dr. Fritjof Capra in *The Tao of Physics*, have all expressed similar views about the mind-like implications of the non-local correlation demanded by the basic quantum equations; and, of course, when these equations were still new, Sir James Jeans said they made the universe look "more like a great thought than a great machine."

Returning to *Finnegans Wake*, we have seen that the fourfold structure of "mind" (or the levels of organization in the brain, going down to the cellular and, finally, atomic and sub-atomic levels?) is indicated in a general way by Joyce's functions of E or conscious ego, ⋔ or personal unconscious, Ш or collective unconscious and Ⅎ the non-local function which, we have just summarized, may be "no mind" (as the Chinese say) but may be the class of all minds or at least have Bohmian "mind-like" aspects. With more specificity, Joyce uses a more complex symbology in which nonlocal Ⅎ manifests as "male" Ш and "female" △ , subdivided into an active male force, ∧ a passive male force, ⅃ , an active female force, ⊣ , a passive female force, ⊢ , and two variables, ⋏ and Ⅰ , which alter these active and passive forces into their opposites.

We have seen that this is isomorphic with the cosmology of *I Ching*, in which the nonlocal Tao functions as "male" yang (—) and "female" yin (- -), subdivided into active yang (⚍), passive yang (⚏), active yin (⚎) and passive yin (⚌), with the moving lines (—✕—and —✕—) serving, like Joyce's ⋏ and Ⅰ , to convert active and passive into their opposites. The DNA script is also isomorphic to this, as can be seen in this summarizing diagram:

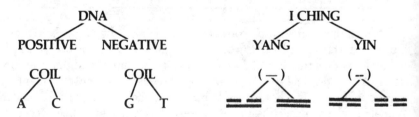

A, C, G and T are the four amino acids bonding the DNA; and ⚍ ⚌ ⚎ ⚏ are active yang, passive yang, active yin and passive yin. When the first set is replaced by A, C, G, U in making an RNA messenger, these four are permutated into all possible combinations of three, and we get the 64 "words"

of the genetic code; permutating the 4 elements of active and passive yin and yang, we get the 64 hexagrams of *I Ching*. Substituting Leibniz's 1 and 0—"that upright one and that naughty besighed him in zeroine" as Joyce calls them—we can use the same system to generate the 64 numbers from 0 to 63 in the binary notation that our computers use to "think" (in about the same sense that evolution or *I Ching* may be said to "think.")

Of course, binary lacks the dynamic (or evolutionary) element contained in the moving lines (—x— or —x—) which give an *I Ching* hexagram two meanings. This process element is present in Joyce, as we have seen, as the dynamic functions, ∧, which unifies ∧ and ⊏, and I which unifies ⊣ and ⊢. In genetics, the dynamic factor is a combination of mutation and natural selection (Joyce's "hatch-as-hatch can"). The absence of these evolutionary functions in binary may explain the fact that those computer scientists working on **AI** (Artificial Intelligence) continually promise mountains and deliver molehills. Perhaps they need to break out of a static binary into a moving binary as dynamic as *I Ching*?

It is passing strange to note that Joyce's general functions also seem to be isomorphic, in a sense, with quantum mechanics, and especially with the Hidden Variable and hologram models. To present Joyce's "family tree" again:

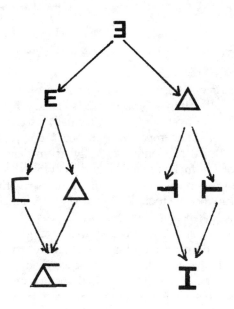

In terms of the Hidden Variable theory, this can be decoded or translated as

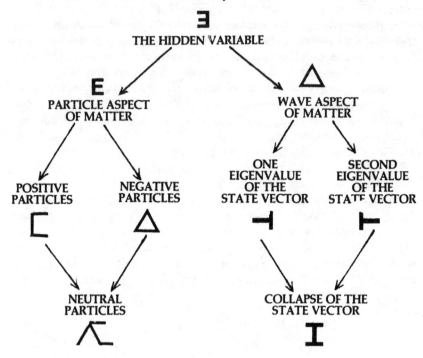

Joyce's **ɰ** stands in well for the particle aspect, since it means "mountain" (in Chinese) among other things. Similarly, Δ is a good wave function, since it is associated with the river, and is coincidentally used in many mathematical wave equations. The impossibility of separating particle and wave aspects (Bohr's Principle of Complimentarity) is entirely isomorphic to Joyce's mingling of the male **ɰ** and female Δ, which we have already noted. The isomorphism of this quantum principle with *I Ching* was recognized by Bohr when he took the Taoist yinyang symbol for his Coat of Arms when knighted by the Danish court.

Similarly, if Joyce's **Λ** and **⊏** (active and passive yang) are the Archangel Michael and Satan on the cosmic level, and two feuding brothers, Shem and Shaun, on the local Dublin level, it makes sense for them to be positive and negative particles on the quantum level. It is almost too neat that quantum mechanics includes the Aristotelian excluded middle, Joyce's **⅄**, as a neutral particle.

The wave aspect of matter (Δ) is a bit more complicated. According to the Schrodinger equations, the state vector of a quantum wave always has a minimum of two values, rather like Joyce's **⊣** and **⊢** . These only "collapse" (that is the word used) to one value, like Joyce's **I**, after a measurement has been taken—which is why most quantum physicists say the universe is "in every possible state" before we measure it. The Hidden Variable theory says that what determines the resultant **I** is the non-local hidden variable which they write c_1 and which seems to be totally isomorphic to Joyce's **Ǝ** .

Those who deny the Hidden Variable must conclude, as Erwin Schrodinger demonstrated with mathematical precision, that both values of the state vector co-exist and thus that a cat may be dead and alive at the same time. Since I have explained this Schroedinger's Cat paradox at length in other works—including my three volume science-fiction comedy, *Schroedinger's Cat*—I will only mention here that *FW* is isomorphic to that model also, since Finnegan is both dead and alive all through the book.

(In a deeper sense, every word in *FW* is like Schrodinger's Cat in that the state vector of the whole system gives it a minimum of two values. Joyce's "chaosmos," for instance has the two values, "chaos" and "cosmos"; his "washup" on the book's last page—**I sink I'd die down over his feet, humbly dumbly, only to washup**—has the two minimum values of housework and worship, with a hidden value, in context, which contains Mary Magdalene washing the feet of Jesus as a form of worship; etc.)

As Dr. John S. Bell has pointed out, if there is a nonlocal hidden variable, or a set of nonlocal hidden variables, they will function the same in any cross-section of space-time that we examine. This is what inspired Dr. Bohm's hologram model of the universe, in which any bit contains the information of the whole. Joyce seems to be prescientifically anticipating this hologram model by writing *FW* in what I have called hologrammic prose, in which any dozen words, analyzed in full, turn out to include the whole structure of the book in miniature.

Joyce was paying close attention to modern physics while writing *FW*. On page 51 he alludes to Heisenberg's Uncertainty Principle:

that sword of certainty which would identifide the body never falls

On pages 149-168, there is lengthy dissertation on "the dime-cash problem" or why Earwicker did not give any money to the Cad in the park, which is simultaneously a discourse on "the time-space problem" or the time and space theories of Einstein, amusingly called "Winestain." Within this long oration, the Mookse and the Gripes debate Catholicism versus its derivative heresies at length, but the Papal Mookse is not only a ∧ or Abel figure but is clearly identified as space (he lives "eins within a space" instead of "once upon a time" and being the Pope lives in Room and/or Rum which play Rome against German **Raum**, space). The Gripes, meanwhile, is Cain, the Gnostics, a ⊏ figure, and a defender of both Einstein and Joyce. On one level the debate is about space-oriented arts like painting (∧) in opposition to time-oriented arts like music ($\sqsubset$), with the eventual synthesis of both into Joyce space-time prose ($\curlywedge$) being gently hinted.

In the "Tavern" chapter, pages 309-382, the story of Buckley and the Russian General is told at length; but Joyce intercuts this with hundreds of other battles from other epochs of history, with special attention (of course) to Clontarf and Waterloo. Curiously, there is a strong quantum mechanical theme running through this catalog of war and violence, and some of it seems very eerily prescient for a book published in 1939:

On page 313, ɰ is "blown to Adams," dragging us back to Genesis again but foreshadowing nuclear war. On page 333, this comes back in the phrase "split an atam" (which again evoked Atum creating the universe by masturbating). On page 339, somebody speaks in "lipponene longuedge" which can only be Nipponese language, to say "Sehyoh narar, pokehole sann." If this is Japanese, it says "Sayanara, Pookah-sann" (Farewell, honorable Pookah) the Pookah being an ancient Celtic rabbit-god which, oddly, became Puck in Shakespeare. If one looks at the mixed Yiddish and Norse roots, of course, this sentence is also saying, "See the hunchbacked fool," which is also appropriate to the context in which a hunch backed sailor is in conflict with a greedy tailor, and I think the s-t transformation of sailor to tailor suggests Einstein's s-t (space-time) equations. On page 349 we have "the charge of the light barricade" combining Buckley's adventures in the Crimean War (the charge of the light brigade, which involved Brown and Nolan, remember?) with Einstein's e = mc² and the acceleration of particles in a cyclotron. The sentence just before this on page 349 contains "guranium" which is a flower, the geranium, with a heavy dose of uranium, the trigger of the atomic bomb. All of this is explicable on the basis of Joyce's study of what physicists were talking about before he finished his book in 1939, although the Japanese reference is distinctly spooky. What the Rationalist will find most annoying, however, is the reference, within this long atomic chapter, on page 315, to "nogeysokey." I don't know what that can mean except Nagasaki. . . .

Joyce's second fourfold function, X, which signifies water, fire, earth and air or Matt, Mark, Luke and John or the compass points, etc. is also an interesting isomorph with modern physics which recognizes four forces constraining all quantum systems:

1. The strong force;
2. The weak force;
3. The electromagnetic force;
4. The gravitational force.

It will be profitable to consider now the rest of Joyce's system functions, since we are at this point fully aware that they are not merely "characters" in the normal novelistic sense but basic categories of Mind and perhaps of Universe (if there is any sense in distinguishing the two.)

□ is a symbol that has so many meanings most Joyce scholars have been totally baffled by it. It is, among other things, Finnegan's coffin and the bed in which Earwicker lies dreaming all through the book. It is also Phoenix Park, and the Garden of Eden, and Noah's Ark and the battlefield of Waterloo and any place and every place. The best description of □, I think, is to call it a localization within space-time wherein the nonlocal functions are temporarily manifest. That is, systems or archetypes like ⊔ and △ etc. function everywhere and everywhen (that's what nonlocal means, after all) but □ is an Einsteinian (space-time) cross-section of these atemporal aspatial patterns or archetypes. Joyce may have used the symbol □, because it has four sides, to represent the four dimensions of space-time.

To say it otherwise, ⊔ and △ and ⊏ and ∧ and all the other nonlocal functions we have been considering appear in the □ cross-section called Genesis as Adam and Eve and Cain and Abel. They appear in the □ cross section of *I Ching* as yang and yin and active yang and passive yang. They appear in Dublin as Earwicker and his wife and their two twin sons. They appear in genetics as the two coils of DNA and the first two bonds, A and C. Wherever one takes a cross-section of any sort (□) these nonlocal functions **must** appear, if they really are nonlocal.

One reason the Dublin, Ireland/Dublin, Georgia parallel appears so conspicuously on the first page of *FW* is that Joyce is intent on making the reader see that □ is a variable in *FW*. The normal waking mind, that is, perceives one □ cross-section (or reality-tunnel) at a time; the dreaming mind can be in several □s simultaneously. This is partly why Yositani Roshi said we all achieve Enlightenment in our sleep and Zen is just a trick for doing it while awake.

Unless I am very much mistaken, Joyce has taken great care that □ never has a single value in any of its appearances; it is always at least two-valued (like the Schrodinger state vector). Thus, in the opening words, which we know well by now, "riverrun, past Eve and Adam's ..." □ is simultaneously Merchant's Quay in Dublin where the river Anna Liffey passes the Church of Adam and Eve and also the Garden of Eden where four rivers flowed past the original Adam and Eve. In the tavern chapter, analyzed above, □ is the Crimea, where Buckley shot the Russian General, but it is also every other battle in history, and, evidently, Nagasaki. Even at Finnegan's Wake in chapter one, □ is only Finnegan's coffin part of the time; the mourners speak in the tones of the jurors in the later trial scenes, so □ is also the Four Courts in Dublin where Earwicker's sexual offenses are minutely examined. If at any point, the reader thinks that □ is one specific space-time cross-section, a little analysis will show, in the multi-linguistic puns, that another space-time locale, □, is also present. The events of FW all take place, as Joyce tells us once, "at no spatial time."

FW also includes a sevenfold function for which Joyce provided no symbol in his notebooks—unless it is some aspect of the mysterious **S** which seems to combine the serpent in Genesis, the Cad in the park, all servants and slaves, and the Norse-Danish invaders of Ireland (at least). The seven appear often as the colors of Newton's prism:

a rudd yellan gruebleen orangeman in his violet indigonation (page 23)
roserude ... oragious ... gelb ... greem ... blue ... ind ... Violet (page 143)
rhubarbarous maundarin yellagreen funkleblue windigut (page 171)

They also become, at times, the seven souls of Egyptian theology, the seven chackras of kundalini yoga, the seven days of the week, etc. In Chapter 9, based on children's games, they are seven girls named **R**ubyretta, **A**rancia, **Y**illa, greeneri**N**, **B**oyblue, **O**dalesque and **W**aters. (The emphasis is mine but the capitalization is Joyce's, to ensure that we do not miss the delightful R A Y N B O W, which appears to be an unconscious elaboration of the conscious mnemonic Roy G. Biv which all first-year physics students memorize.) The rainbow, of course, brings us back to the Noah's flood theme, because Jehovah put a rainbow in the sky, after killing most of humanity off, as a promise that He would not be so rash in the future. But, as Glasheen points out in her various Censuses to FW, there are also strong suggestions of Mr. Willie Hughes, "the man of all hues," who was Oscar Wilde's candidate for the mysterious homosexual lover, Mr. W.H., in Shakespeare's sonnets.

It is curious but many of Joyce's variations on these seven RAYNBOW girls or Newton's spectrum exfoliate into eight and conclude with the initials LSD:

down right mean false sop lap sick dope (page 68)
Don't retch meat fat salt lard sinks down (page 260)

Leaving aside the LSD mystery for a while, I think the seven become eight at times because Joyce has in mind the generation of the seven colors out of white light in Newton's famous experiment, which can be illustrated as follows in Joycean:

White Light   Prism

If nonlocal ∃ appears as seven colors to human perception in space-time, then the seven/eight are a lovely isomorph of Timothy Leary's neurological model of consciousness in which there are seven circuits in the nervous system, akin to the Hindu chakras, and one nonlocal circuit, akin to Joyce's ∃ . The curious reader may pursue this isomorphism further in my book *Prometheus Rising*, (Falcon Press, 1987) or simply by meditating on the fable of Snow White and the Seven Dwarfs. For now, it is sufficient to note that Leary's circuits are also isomorphic, like Joyce's Seven, with the days of the week:

Monday = the day of the moon goddess = bonding to the Mother = Leary's oral bio-survival circuit. Joyce's Rubyretta refers to the infantile bonding of this circuit by a reference back to the first page of the *Portrait of the Artist*: "When you wet the bed first it is warm then it gets cold."

Tuesday = the day of the war god, Tuew = anal territorial dispute = Leary's anal-emotional circuit. Joyce's Arancia refers to this circuit by combining William of Orange, as symbol of all Ireland's invaders, with Ares, the Greek god of war.

Wednesday=the day of the god of communication, Wotan=speech=Leary's semantic circuit. Joyce's Yilla refers to the gold of Mercury, god of communication.

Thursday = the day of the father god, Thor = parenthood = Leary's social-sexual circuit. Joyce's greeneriN refers to the "four green fields of Erin," an Irish symbol of social harmony.

Friday = the day of the sex goddess, Freya = Tantric rapture = Leary's neurosomatic circuit. Joyce's Boyblue refers to the psychological androgyny of this circuit.

Saturday=the day of the god of the past, Saturn=genetic memory=Leary's neurogenetic circuit (Joyce's Ш) Joyce's Odalesque refers to this circuit in its familiar mythic form as a nude female symbolizing Earth.

Sunday = the day of the sun god = illumination = Leary's metaprogramming circuit. Joyce's Waters refers to this circuit in its oceanic and floating aspect.

The same correlates appear in all the Northern nations of Europe. In the southern Latin nations, one finds the same isomorphism after replacing Tuew with Mars, another war god, Thor with Jove, another father god, and Freye with Venus, another sex goddess.

Of course, these seven rainbow colors (or RAYNBOW girls when they appear as Rubyretta, Arancia, Yilla, greeneriN, Boyblue, Odalesque and Waters) are linked by Joycean puns to Isa Bowman, who first played Alice in Wonderland on the stage and aroused in Carroll/Dodgson the same ambiguous affection as the original Alice Pleasance Liddell. From a RAYNBOW to a Bowman (whose first name, Isa, suggests the two Isoldes) easily leads to Strongbow. Who was he? The leader of the "Anglo-Norman"

(British) invasion of Ireland, which began on 23 August 1170. Oddly it was on another 23 August, in 1921, that Joyce had his celebrated experience of discussing synchronicities when a large black rat suddenly ran across the floor, scaring the blue Jesus out of him, by Christ. (It was also on an August 23, in 1985, that I gave a seminar on these isomorphisms at Esalen Institute.) Strongbow was Earl of Pembroke, and another Earl of Pembroke, nearly 500 years later, became associated with Shakespeare and is considered the possibly homosexual companion in the sonnets, Mr. W.H. That Earl of Pembroke was named William Herbert, not Willie Hughes, as in Wilde's more extravagent theory. It is odd, though, that the seven colors bring us to two different theories about the identity of Mr. W.H., isn't it?

The next of Joyce's major system functions, abbreviated 0, first appears on *FW* page 6 as "workingstacks at twelvepins a dozen." Workingstacks seems to combine smokestacks with working stiffs (Irish slang for workingmen); but "twelvepins a dozen" sounds like twelve pence a dozen— a typical price for cheap vegetables or eggs in Joyce's day. However, the Twelve Pins is also a mountain range in the part of Connacht called The Joyce Country, where Our Man's ancestral tribe long held power. (Hewbrew **ben** means son and these twelve often appear as Freud's hypothetical band of brothers killing the primal father.)

But when the 0 appear the second time, they are neither mountains nor coins (nor sons) but twelve mourners at Finnegan's wake further down on page 6

> **prostrated in their consternation and their duodismally**
> **profuse plethora of ululation**

That is, they are dour and dismal but also duodecimal, like the traditional coinage system from Babylon until fairly recently in history (until a few years ago in Ireland and England). Later the 0 become the 12 signs of the Zodiac, the 12 apostles of Jesus, the 12 months of the year, and every other 12-fold function Joyce can think of, but most often they are the 12 jurors who continually pry into Earwicker's sexual offenses, always with the -ation clangs (already beginning in the passage cited above from page 6) growing longer and more suggestive. Here they are on page 142:

> those component partners of our societate, the doorboy, the cleaner, the sojer, the crook, the squeezer, the lounger, the curman, the tourabout, the mussroomsniffer, the bleakablue tramp, the funpowtherplother, the christymanboxer.... latecomers all the year's round by anticipation ... the porters of the passions in virtue of retroratiocination ... contributting their confligent controversies of differentiation ... crunch the crusts of comfort due to depredation, drain the mead of misery to incur intoxication, condone every evil by practical justification and condam any good to its own gratification

In the first clause, we see the **0** as the twelve months of the year (the hard one is November: "funpowtherplother" refers to Guy Fawkes Day which is November 5 and commemorates the Gun Powder Plot, in which Fawkes tried to blow up Parliament)* and then the -ation chant gradually merges the **0** with everything that is legal or theological or in some way threatening to the ordinary citizen. "The State is concentric, but the individual is eccentric," was Joyce's anarchistic view; the -ation chant appears almost every time the **0** appear and reverberates to the original ululation, which identifies them with the owl-goddess Athenec, patron of juries (remember?) but -ation also hints at copulation and fornication and masturbation and other things the Irish super-ego does not want the dream to admit fully.

Of course, it is only another coincidence, but the DNA, so isomorphic to Joyce's system functions in so many ways, also happens to have 12 bonds in every complete turn of the double helix. (See diagram.) However, on page 107 we find

the Honorary Mirsu Earwicker, L.S.D.

We have already encountered that damned LSD in two places where the seven rainbow colors are expanded to eight (to include the White Light) but it is almost as awkward for rationalists as the Nagasaki/uranium conjunction. For what it's worth, LSD to any Irish or English reader of Joyce's generation meant "pounds, shillings and pence"—the duodecimal system of coinage from Babylon onward that Joyce identifies with the Zodiac or **0** function. Strange that all this exfoliates from the initial reference to the duodismal ululation or owlowlation of the neolithic Athene cult.

One other function that appears occasionally in *FW* is **o** , usually identified as a set of 28 girls from St. Bride's Academy. On the Freudian **m** level, these are, like the 7 rainbow girls, a distortion of the 2 girls in the bushes of Phoenix Park; on the Jungian **ɯ** level, I suspect that they go back to the Stone Age calendar mentioned in the essay on "Mammary Metaphysics," with a female figure marking every 28th day. In an Irish context, St. Bride is the ancient Celtic moon goddess, Bride, adopted into the Roman Catholic pantheon. The 28 girls, then, are the 28 days of a moon cycle or a menstrual cycle or both. As an egg, **o** of course is a human egg and thus brings us back to Humpty Dumpty again . . .

The reader will gain a deeper understanding of the hologrammic prose of

---

* Guy Fawkes is pronounced Guy Fox and links to the Parnell and Wilde fox-hunt themes. **How a Guy Finks and Fawkes When He is Going Batth** is one of the alternative titles for *FW* in the text itself, but Joyce, an anarchist, probably knew the favorite English anarchist joke, which was to urge people to vote for Guy Fawkes, "the only man to ever enter Parliament with honest intentions."

FW by looking, now, at the opening of the Anna Livia Plurabelle chapter
(Chapter 8):

0

tell me all about
Anna Livia. I want to hear all

The △ shape of these words is, as we have seen, an ancient Greek symbol
of the feminine principle, or the vagina itself, and Joyce's symbol for ALP or
aleph or Anna Livia Plurabelle. The 0 at the top is a familiar modern symbol
of the same feminine energy, and the link between Leibniz's binary notation
and the yin of *I Ching*. More amazing packages of information within
information appear if we start counting.

The first line has 1 word, and 1 represents yang which Joyce, like the
Taoists, always includes within yin, as he also includes yin within yang. But
the one word, symbolizing yang because it is one in numeration, also
symbolizes yin because it is 0 in shape.

The second line has four words and invokes the **X** function or the four
bonds of DNA or the four elements of King Wen's arrangement of *I Ching*
or the 4 forces in physics etc. Joyce's Matt Gregory, Marcus Lyons, Luke
Tarpey and Johnny McDougal.

The third line has seven words for the seven chakras, the seven Egyptian
souls, Leary's seven circuits of neurology, the seven gods of the seven
weekdays etc. Joyce's RAYNBOW girls.

Adding, $1 + 4 + 7 = 12$, and we are back to the 0 function again, the 12 pins
in the Joyce Country, the 12 bonds of a turn of DNA, the Zodiac which
haunts the human mind no matter how often rationalists try to banish it,
the duodecimal system that controlled currency for 6000 years and still
controls the number on a jury or in a box of eggs.

Multiplying, $1 \times 4 \times 7 = 28$, and we are back to the 28 days of the Moon
Goddess again, the human egg, the Orphic egg of creation and Humpty
Dumpty.

There are two speakers in this Anna Livia chapter, an old washwoman
who represents ⊣ or ═══ as old yin, and a young washwoman who
represents ⊢ or ══ as young yin. (Amusingly, these two are literally
washing Earwicker's dirty linen in public.) If we multiply these two
functions by the 28 factor of the △ ($1 \times 4 \times 7 = 28$), we get 56, a number that
often appears in *FW*. In Roman numerals, of course, 56 is LVI and we are
back to Livvy again, Mark Twain's wife, and Anna Liffey, and Livia Augusta
the Empress who shared part of her name with James Augusta Joyce.

More curious, is the text of **Liber AL**, which Aleister Crowley alleged that
he received from his "Holy Guardian Angel" in 1904. Since Crowley flatly told

one disciple that the Holy Guardian Angel is a being of superhuman intelligence and flatly told another that it is metaphor for the deepest part of the unconscious, we are at liberty to consider it beyond either/or categories and isomorphic to Joyce's Ǝ . According to **Liber AL**,

My number is six and fifty. Add, multiply, divide and understand.

As Crowley pointed out in his commentary on this text, when we add 6 + 50 = 56, which is the number by Cabala of NU, the earliest Egyptian form of the moon goddess or sky goddess. We have already seen that this NU is a cognate of the great mother goddess Danu worshipped by the early Irish and hence of Joyce's Anna Livia Plurabelle.

Multiplying, 6 × 50 = 300, which is the Cabalistic value of the letter Ш pronounced **shin**, which Cabalists identify with the "de₋Шnt of spirit into matter," which we may consider an archaic way of referring to the mind-like aspect of the nonlocal hidden variable or variables. This shin, Joyce wrote to Harriet Weaver, was one meaning of his Ш function, which we have found isomorphic to Jung's collective unconscious and Sheldrake's morphogenetic field.

Dividing, 6/50 = .012, which Crowley identifies with a backwards alchemical formulae for sex magick, in which 2 reduce to 1 in erotic union and then enter the void together. The Joycean is satisfied to find here both the symbol, 0, and the number, 12, of Joyce's Zodiac function or jurors, the spinning wheel which keeps the universe of FW turning forever on its own axis.

It is another amusing coincidence that Stonehenge, which some think is a giant astrological/astronomical isomorph, has 56 postholes making a circle around it. Since 56 is, as we saw a moment ago, 28 × 2, this has something to do with the moon goddess again, I suppose, but it is even stranger that the American Declaration of Independence has 56 signers, most of them Freemasons.

Since Crowley claimed his *Book of Lies* contained the central secret of Freemasonry, coded so that only the Illuminated could understand it, and his **Liber AL**, which contains 56 symbolism similar to that of FW is also replete with Freemasonic references, it is important to note that Joyce was **not** a Freemason and that his search of Freemasonic literature, which is documented, was that of an outsider. The fact that we have come around to what some will recognize as the essence of Speculative Freemasonry (others will think it is Buddhism) can only be explained, it seems to me, by assuming that there is in nature a nonlocal function similar to what Joyce denotes by Ǝ and that this co-exists in minds as far apart in space-time as those of Leibniz, Bruno, the authors of *I Ching*, the builders of Stonehenge, Joyce, Freud, Crowley, whoever designed the 56 minor cards of the Tarot, and various others of diverse and disparate traditions.

And we have come back to the lines from Carl Jung with which we began, lines in which we he described his gradual discovery of the quasi-mathematical structure of the collective unconscious, in which there is "chaotic multiplicity" combined with "order," a system of opposites including light and dark, upper and lower, right and left, all of which are aspects at different times of Joyce's $\wedge$ and $\sqsubset$; "the union of opposites in a third" (Joyce's $\curlywedge$), a "quarternity" system of squares and crosses like Joyce's $\times$ and 0, rotation like Joyce's recirculations in *FW*, the symbol of the circle or sphere (0) and a centering process which I hope the reader has by now grasped intuitively since it cannot be expressed symbolically.